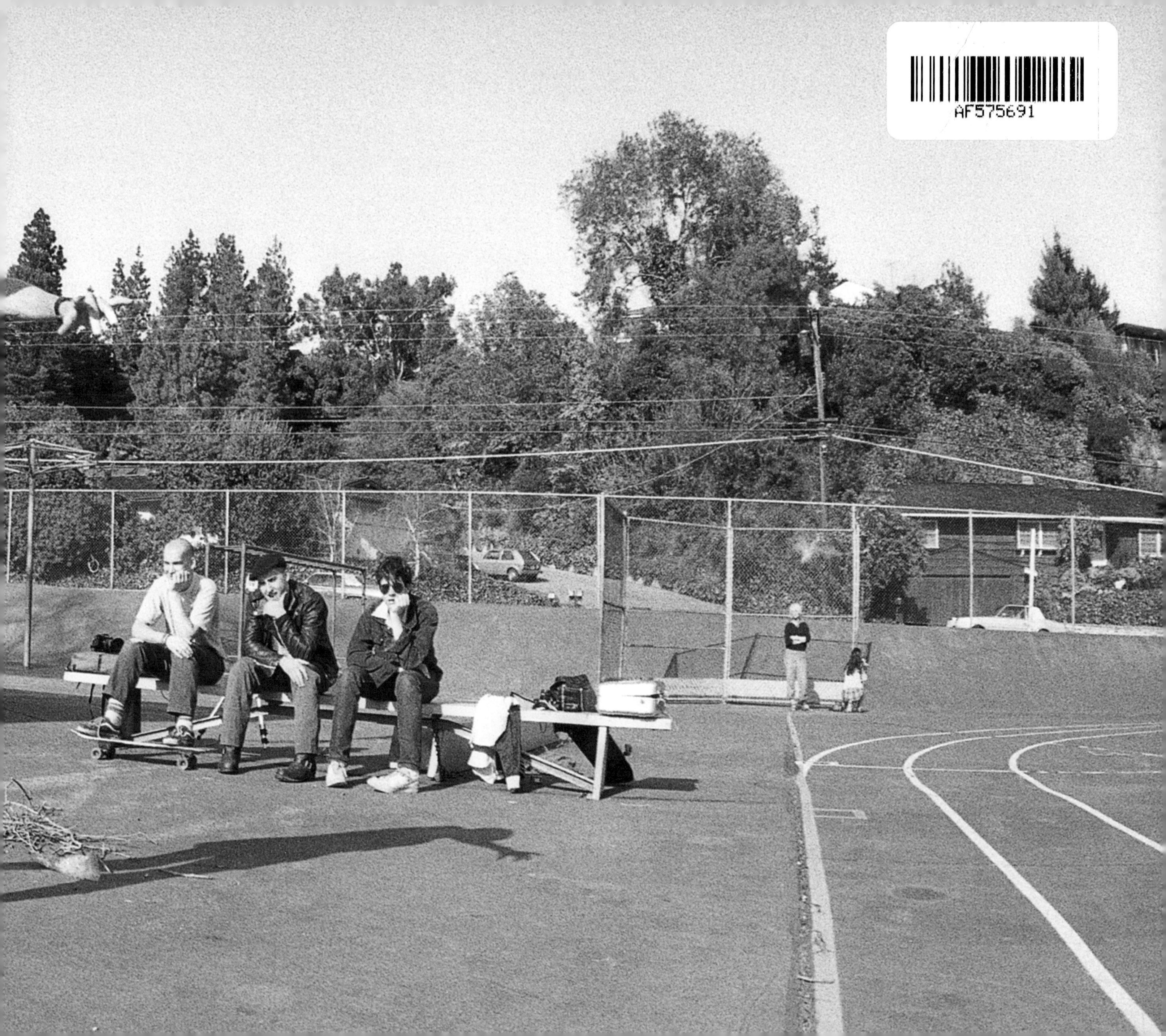
AF575691

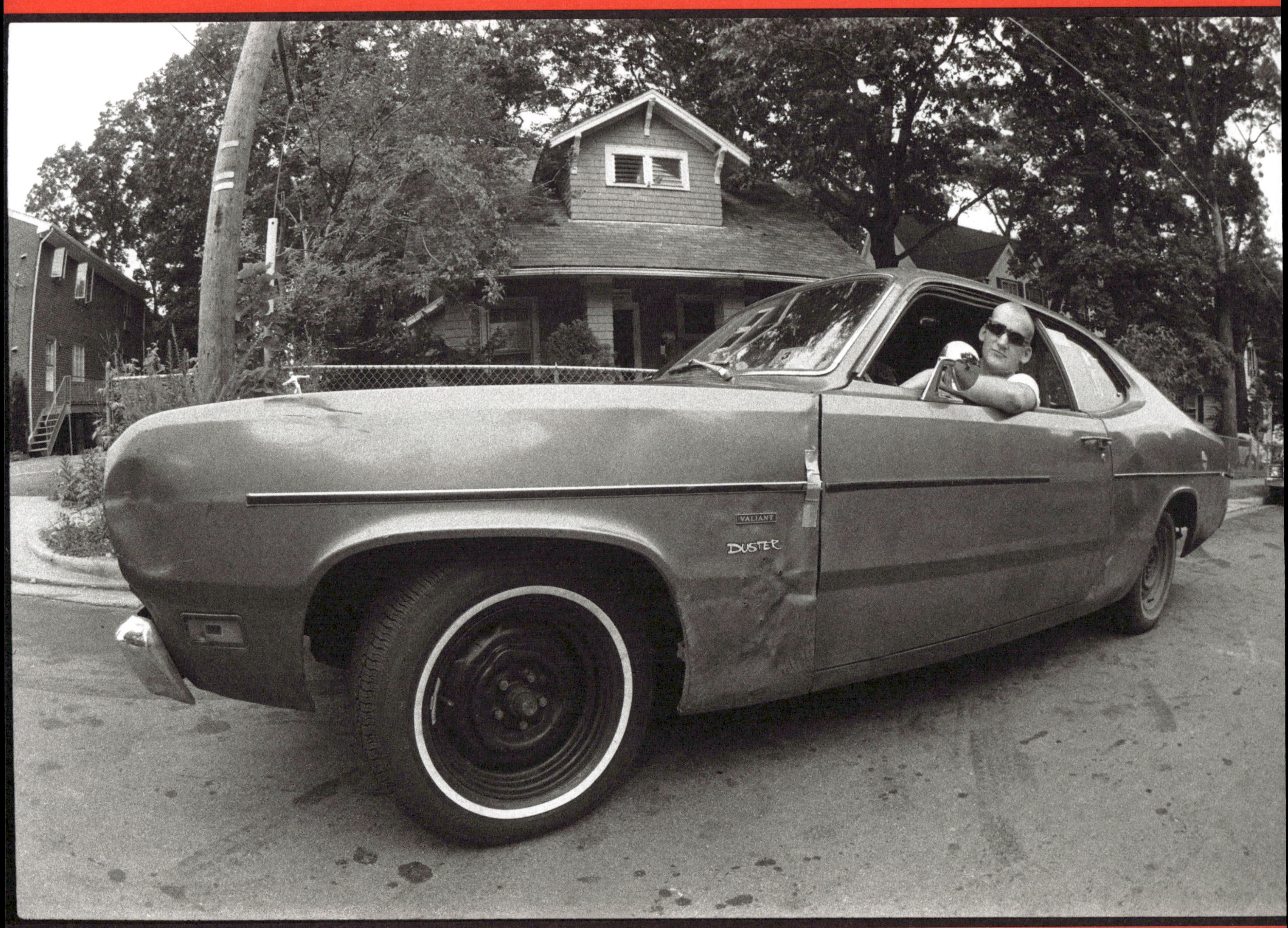
VALIANT
DUSTER

JUST A MINOR THREAT

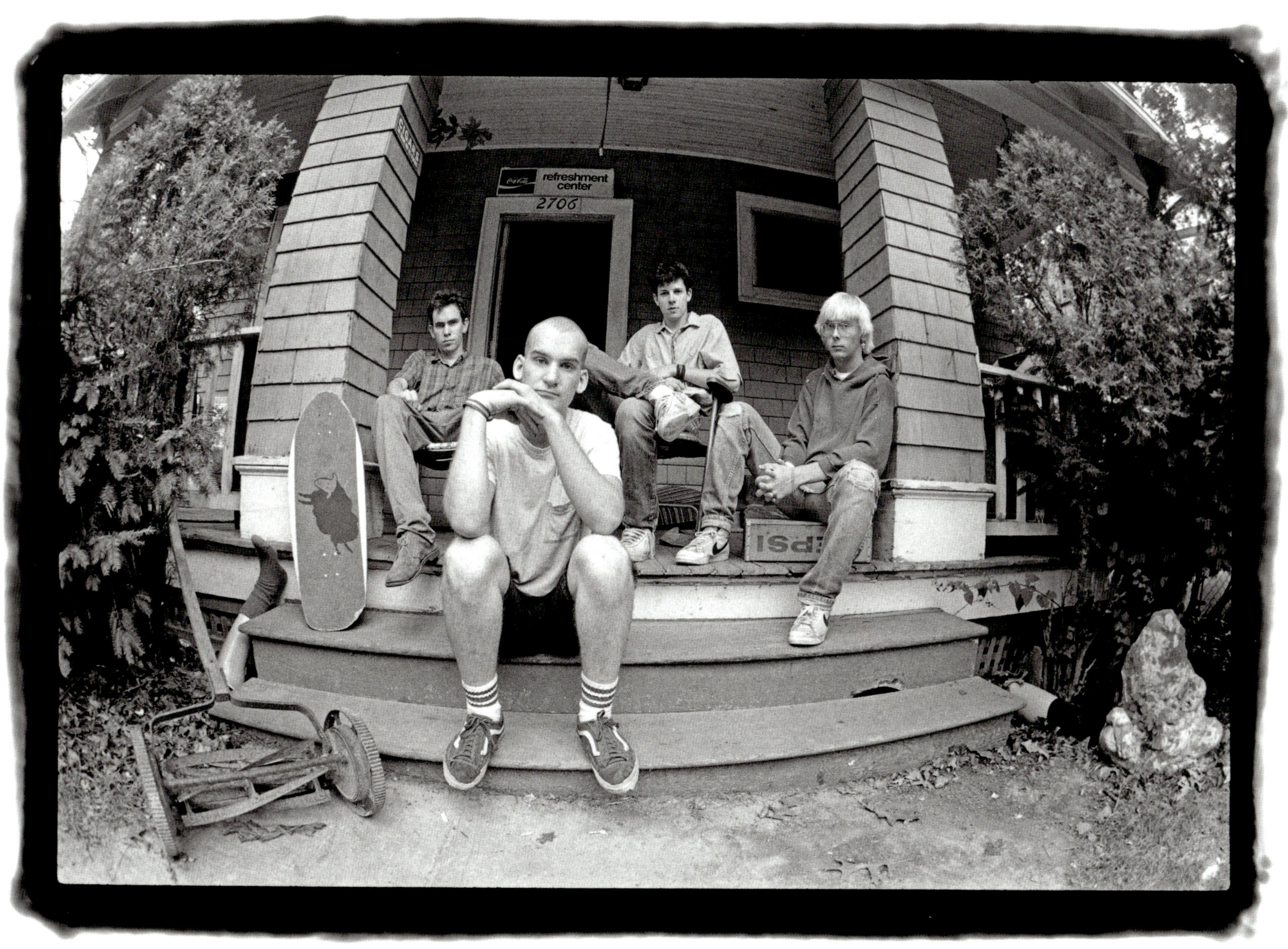

the Minor Threat photographs of glen E. friedman

JUST A MINOR THREAT

the Minor Threat photographs of glen E. friedman

FIRST EDITION

Published by Akashic Books
Copyright © 2023 Glen E. Friedman
ISBN: 978-1-63614-136-7
Library of Congress Control Number: 2023933958
Printed in China

All rights reserved.
No part of this book may be reproduced in any form
without written permission from the publisher.

All photographs by Glen E. Friedman
Essays by Guy Picciotto, Ian F. Svenonius, and Zack de la Rocha,
with additional words from Jello Biafra, Alec MacKaye, and Jamie Shanahan

This book was edited and designed by Glen E. Friedman, with Sohrab Habibion
Editorial assistance by Zack de la Rocha, Johnny Temple

Special thanks for technical photographic assistance to Astrida Valigorsky, Michael Vorrasi

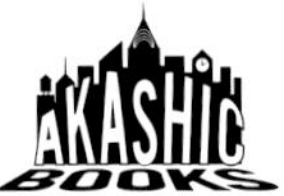

Akashic Books, Brooklyn, New York
Facebook, Instagram, Twitter: @AkashicBooks
info@akashicbooks.com, www.akashicbooks.com

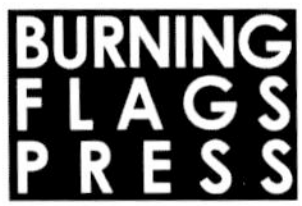

Burning Flags Press
PO Box 69, New York, NY 10003
www.BurningFlags.com

"What the fuck have you done?" by Guy Picciotto

Growing up in Washington, DC, I happened to go to the same high school as two members of Minor Threat—Brian Baker, who was in my grade, and Lyle Preslar, who was a year above us. I was also fairly close neighbors with Jeff Nelson, who I would see walking the quiet Chevy Chase streets on the way to his job at Dart Drug on Connecticut Avenue, his personalized punk gear always top-shelf outrageous for the time. As for Ian MacKaye, though we had both actually been at the same first punk show, the Cramps in February of 1979, my being only thirteen at the time rendered our three-year age gap a pretty large chasm. Still, by 1981 I had seen Minor Threat play from its second show on and was beginning the process of integrating my more solitary enthusiasm for punk rock into what was quickly becoming the larger DC hard-core scene. Though I would soon be hanging out most often with bands like S.O.A, Deadline, and the Faith, the scene was tight by necessity and we were all friends, so it wasn't super unusual that one day in early 1981 I got invited to tag along after school with Brian and Lyle as they made their way to Brian's mom's house near Ward Circle for Minor Threat practice. I got to sit in the corner of the basement as they worked their way through their early set, and most impactfully, I got to watch them write and arrange a new song, "Screaming at a Wall."

I myself was an aspiring guitar player, but the extent of my experiences to that point comprised a series of one-offs that were little more than amusing tantrums and not really anything approaching a real band. Basically, my understanding of what bands actually did was at about finger-paint level. That is why watching that practice was so revelatory to me. They weren't just clowning around and cracking each other up. They were *working*. They were making art. They were finessing that epic swinging midtempo breakdown in "Screaming at a Wall"; then they were matching a short drum pattern to back up a specific vocal line ("*You're . . . SAFE INSIDE!*") as a considered move; they were talking to each other about how to make it all work, not just zoning out in a wall of feedback and hoping for the best. The song was so fucking good and it was being put together methodically in real time in front of my face. I've never forgotten it. I left that practice thinking that I had seen craftsmanship that was well beyond me but also that maybe it was something that could be aspired to. Minor Threat were both setting an impossibly high bar but also outlining possible paths.

So, when I think of Minor Threat now, what lasts beyond memories of the communal, joyful turmoil of their gigs are the songs themselves. It is true that hardcore quickly became formulaic. In no way do I mean that as an insult, because as a genre it was still an explosive rupture from everything that came before it. But the result was that many of the greatest bands of that time were more sonic in signature—known as the bearer of a specific sound if not necessarily for specific songs. The thing about Minor Threat is that they wrote hits. Total fucking hits.

These were songs engineered as much as any Pete Seeger song for crowds of kids to sing along to at the top of their lungs. There was nothing better than being part of the massed human roil vocally punctuating the two syllables of "*FILLER!*" back at the band, unamplified but still drowning out a full PA and backline. Every Minor Threat show was *about* that exchange between singer, song, and crowd, and it worked because the songs were all crafted like diamonds—so melodically memorable and lyrically so tightly focused and provocative that every single song they cut is ingrained in my brain for life.

It had to do with the qualities that each of the members brought to bear. Their thing was their precision. There were many hardcore bands whose power was in their mutilated, chaotic approach, but for Minor Threat it was the violent clarity of their attack that distinguished them. Lyle didn't smear his chordings no matter how fast they got. He played and voiced all six strings in his barre chords cleanly and with power, and through his Les Paul and his Marshall he basically trademarked a sound. This exactitude was equally matched by the piston-like gallop of Jeff's drumming, which was such a huge part of how visually shocking it was to see them live. Watching Jeff work his snare and hi-hat was enough to make your head feel like it contained an agitated beehive—it was just that thrilling. In a town which boasted an unreal roster of genius hardcore drummers—each with their own posture and moves and flair—Jeff still stood out for his utterly maniacal intensity. Jeff was also the band's resident graphic designer, and it cannot be stressed enough how his unique sensibility informed every aspect of how the band's work was presented to the world. The iconic record sleeves he made for Minor Threat were a huge part of what cemented their legacy, each one a punk masterpiece. Finally, having Brian Baker as bassist was the ultimate secret weapon, as he was already known for being a child prodigy on guitar by all of us at school from well before punk rock even existed. To have that kind of skill level and musicality underpinning the rhythm inverted the usual "Sid can play bass" punk formula. Barring the Bad Brains, Minor Threat were that early era's most accomplished players, and when you added Ian's vision, charisma, and the revolutionarily tenor of his lyrical approach, you were dealing with something entirely new.

In Ian's songs there was no posturing, no vague "I'm pissed" material, rather each song matched the precision of the music with the specificity of the lyric—and each song outlined an ethic. Nothing is more routine in rock and roll than the avoidance of a stance or a perspective. Rock and roll thinks of itself as hedonistic or outrageous or "bad," but it never actually means much of anything. It is for this reason that for many rock critics, hardcore will always be unknowable as it doesn't share the same values as their established canon, worthy as some of it may be.

Minor Threat's deepest aggression was to mean something. These new values felt to me infinitely more illicit, more dangerous, and more demanding than anything the old rock and roll guard had put on the table. When I read Ian say in a fanzine interview that shaving one's head was an exercise in confronting your own vanity, I instantly realized the band was simply not interested in defining postures of "cool." They were interested in a completely different project—one of dealing with yourself and dealing with the world under new terms. And their songs outlined those terms. I shaved my head.

I think maybe it can be hard for people nowadays to really understand what it meant to cross cultural lines in that way in the 1970s and '80s. The conformity of the dominant monoculture was suffocating but also rigidly enforced. To be a punk at that time in the USA was to invite the disgust and derision of most adults, as well as full-on violence on the street. For a station wagon full of drunk forty-year-old men to squeal to a halt on McKinley Street, jump out, and beat your ass was certainly awful, but it wasn't particularly surprising. You were knowingly crossing a threshold and taking a risk, and in so doing you were learning precious lessons about what was really under the mask of the world when faced with difference.

When Minor Threat's first 7" came out, those compact, blistering songs became part of the armor you could use to buttress your will in what really felt like some kind of existential battlefield. That may sound over the top, but that is what the songs of Minor Threat and Black Flag and the Bad Brains felt like for punk kids of that era. Early Minor Threat songs like "Bottled Violence," "Stand Up," and "Seeing Red" were not fantasy exercises but were realistically descriptive of what we were navigating and instructive on how we might deal with it.

Still, it was when their next 7", *In My Eyes*, came out in late 1981 that the band reached what was for me their peak. The title song was a gauntlet thrown down not just to the scene in DC but to hardcore as it had come to exist nationwide—setting a new standard and drawing a line. Beyond the genius stepladder ascension of the verse chords, so much of its power had to do with Ian's voice, with its almost unbearable disappointment and anger, with its lyric that approaches the abusive in its systematic breakdown of all the bullshit we accept of ourselves and others. Every line dismantles a different hypocrisy or equivocation, including a tight formulation that still impresses me with its compact depth: "*You tell me you want to be different / You just change for the same.*" I know this idea of "change for the same" would be central to Ian's thinking going forward as he returned to it with a subsequent band, the great, short-lived Skewbald, and it really encapsulates a core puzzle: what is real progressive, radical change and what is just the seductive trappings of the straight world perceived as novelty? Other lines puncture sexual gamesmanship, cynicism, and nihilism with equal fury. Relentless in its savage takedowns, "In My Eyes" still to this day makes me feel both energized and accused, enlivened and ashamed—it's an unsettling combination that just doesn't exist in any other music, and it remains galvanizing.

When Ian asks just before the chorus in his most acid, outraged delivery, "*What the fuck have you done?*" your average teenage hardcore kid might well have asked of themselves (as I did), "I'm only fifteen years old—am I supposed to have done something already?" to which Minor Threat, by specific example, answered back unequivocally, "YES."

In that way the question shifts in the mind from "What the fuck have you done?" to "What *will* I do?" and in that moment the world's possibilities are cracked open like an egg. People may generically call some music empowering, but this was the real-deal empowerment—you heard Minor Threat and you were called out. It was time to stand up and be counted.

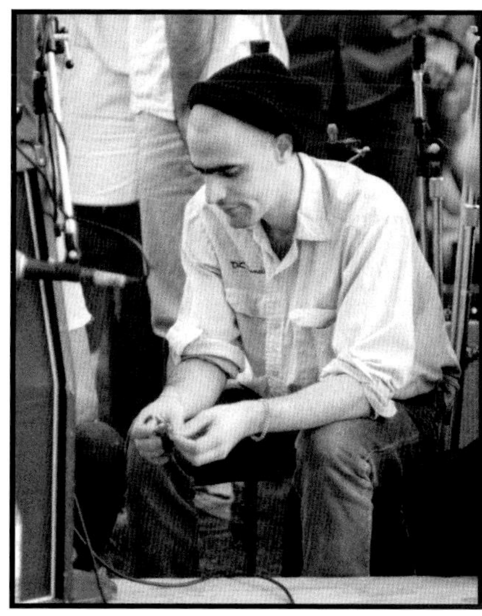

Guy, Fugazi early days, Dupont Circle.

On Minor Threat

by Ian F. Svenonius

Punk and hardcore were the music of neglect. They were spawned from lack of access, resources, and opportunity. Due to the paucity of their means and suppression by the industry, the punks made the most primitive music in the history of rock and roll. The players had few resources, little to no musical education, and no institutional encouragement. The music was akin to something created in a prison colony, composed not for fame or fortune but out of sheer frustration, for fun, and the need to communicate.

Tiresome rock and roll clichés permeated radio and MTV in the early '80s, as the flower children of the "Woodstock generation"—who had terrorized the world with their arrogance, exhibitionism, and garish style—tightened their grip on the reins of power.

Power was always an obsession for the hippies. Even in childhood they had been ambitious; in the '50s, as teenyboppers, they had insisted it wasn't "puppy love"; their love was real! They wanted to be treated as adults, as equals, and they wanted the sexual rights of adults. As coeds, they occupied the universities and clamored for "student power." By the late '60s, they had pushed their elders into early retirement and climbed into the executive seat. It was a revolutionary putsch; they had "taken over" since—as Jim Morrison said—they "got the numbers." Now, with the suits out of the way, everything would be groovy.

Their maxim had been "trust no one over forty." However, as the ex-hippies reached this august landmark, they forgot their adolescent-empowerment rhetoric. They'd had babies, sure—picturesque as props on their Marie Antoinette play-farm communes—but as their progeny turned teen, they were horrified. Children, it turned out, were a drag; a real inconvenience when one was trying to concentrate in their encounter session or EST training. The "boomers" resented their kids, who signaled their own twilight. When these children grew up and formed rock groups of their own, they were dismissed as twerp pretenders who threatened the primacy of "classic rock." Instead of giving the new generation's music an outlet, the long-haired CEOs went pedal to the metal with Woodstock nostalgia and self-veneration. "The Boys of Summer,"

"Summer of '69," and "We Built This City" were radio rock follow-ups to their previous bouts of narcissism—*Happy Days*; around-the-dial heavy-rotation AOR celebrating the magic essence of the boomer generation, specifically designed to put the kids in their place. The gatekeepers weren't through listening to Neil Young and Windham Hill, and this new music—"punk" and "hardcore"—was obnoxious. It also showed little to no commercial potential.

The hardcore bands often didn't know how to make a chord, let alone understand "songwriting"; they were expected to regurgitate and sit in awe of their parents' culture. They'd grown up with reruns of their parents' TV shows, music, movies, culture, et al. There was nothing created specifically for the punk rockers' generation; the boomers had made nothing for their children because they were extending their own childhood through therapy, self-reflection, religious fads, encounter sessions, and other modes of "finding themselves." The punks lived in the shadow of this massive, self-aggrandizing generation who were high on their own fumes and upset that their birth control pills had misfired; that they now had to raise teenagers of their own.

The bands inevitably reflected this. Hardcore punk songs were sharp, angry, self-loathing, and full of revulsion for hypocrisy. Their aesthetic proposal resonated with young people across America, and a "scene"—i.e., a community and self-sufficient economy—grew, weed-like, despite the music being barred from radio, major record labels, magazines, or any of the promotional tools that would typically accompany such a phenomenon. Thus, the hardcore and punk scenes in the USA, as opposed to their English cousins, were absolutely noncorporate, word of mouth, DIY, and underground—by necessity.

The new groups, however, were still informed by the inherited beatnik and "hip" values of the parent culture. Though they claimed to reject their parents' generation, they aped the anarchic yippie humor and sensibilities of the psychedelic groups. Eventually, though, a band emerged that reflected an entirely new sensibility. When they appeared, the teenage hardcore punk mass recognized them for what they were. They knew they had found a group that was theirs, that represented them.

The group was called Minor Threat.

Minor Threat emerged, fully formed, on the scene in late 1980 with a distinct message, sound, style, and graphic identity. With Minor Threat, the promise of "punk"—a distinct subculture that rejected the hierarchy and alienation of arena rock, and that celebrated amateurism—was manifested par excellence. The punk first wavers, despite their revolutionary affect, had mostly regressed into elitist clichés and major label contracts. Now, in Minor Threat, there was a group who was actually "of the people." Their shows were a total immersion with the crowd, they liked to play first, and their performance was communion, not theater. Plus, their message—"straight edge," aka the rejection of prescribed conventions of adulthood—was novel and provocative. Minor Threat were the proverbial "kids." Glen E. Friedman's *Salad Days* sleeve photograph of Minor Threat sitting on the porch at Dischord House, a caprice of the photographer, became a masterpiece of punk iconography for a group that never set out to create such a thing. This shot, the band on the porch before practice, displays Minor Threat's four distinct personalities, the suburban milieu of second-wave American punk, and the group's unpretentious appeal.

Who were Minor Threat? Unremarkable boys, not related to anyone special. None of their parents owned an oil field or had starred in a Golden Age Hollywood epic. They didn't have high-powered management (or any management at all) or connections to the star machinery of the day. None had starred in a daytime television show as a preteen and hoped to carry their notoriety into adulthood with an edgy new incarnation. Their relatives weren't modeling agency moguls or music industry kingmakers who had signed Joni Mitchell or broke Buffalo Springfield. And yet, somehow, they had created something of special interest to the scene of punk rockers which had sprung up around the world. In fact, Minor Threat were perhaps the definitive "hardcore" group.

"Hardcore" was a reform movement like Protestantism. The term was used to identify the young bands that had distilled the ethos of punk rock to its essential elements: speed, intensity, urgency, defiance, and a sense of subcultural elitism. It was a purification movement that championed a version of punk rock true to the values originally espoused by the music's first-wave participants, musicians who had now strayed into degenerate forms like goth, disco, and new wave. Such artsy and pretentious dawdling held little appeal to the young aficionados who were just now discovering the music and wanted it to embody its radical promise.

In a sense, hardcore was to punk like the Monkees were to the Beatles. As the Beatles got weird, the youth who had missed the boat on Beatlemania wanted a fab four who were still fun, frenetic, and fraternal, as opposed to artsy, orchestral, and adult. Hence, the Monkees, who capitalized on the Beatles's abandonment of their post as envoys of anarchic, antiauthoritarian cheek. Hardcore, though, was different from the Monkees in that it eschewed any hope of success. The Monkees were a canny corporate creation, whereas hardcore music was anticorporate and uncompromising. Written into its invisible rule book—which every hardcore acolyte somehow intuitively inferred—were dictums about what was cool, how to comport oneself, and what constituted "selling out." Number one in the book was contempt for major labels, the music industry, and any group that would sully themselves with corporate association.

Hardcore was rock and roll that had consciously cleansed itself of any aspect that could make it appealing for use in a commercial of any kind. Hooks shouldn't be too poppy. Riffs shouldn't be too catchy. It was an antisuccess ethic. A group was judged by its adherence to these criteria. Hardcore was a perverse snub to square values of success, pragmatism, and status; it embodied a righteousness that only children can pull off with a straight face. Since any whiff of boogie rock, pop ballad, or disco was anathema, hardcore bands engaged in an arms race of atonal simplicity, a nihilistic death spiral that eventually spelled the genre's ruin. But in its beginning, it was exhilarating, fun, radical, and revolutionary. A music of energy and simplicity that echoed the initial appeal of rock and roll, a folk phenomenon proliferated organically by an international congregate of true believers.

At hardcore concerts, these believers—stage diving and singing along—were almost indistinguishable from the bands onstage, and shows were typically pure mayhem. Hardcore was remarkable not only for its stripped-down, faster sound and the slam dancing and stage diving that accompanied it, but also for eschewing the fashion trappings of English punk that had been honed on Kings Road and inspired by McLaren and Westwood's SEX shop. These affectations were mostly rejected by the adherents of the new music who saw them as gaudy and passé, not unlike the Lutherans' disavowal of Catholic frills. Of course, a few signifiers of the punk style were kept as a nod to the parent faith: a leather jacket, a shaved head, maybe some boots. These were mixed with a casual SoCal skateboarder and thrift-store look or, in the case of DC punks and Minor Threat, a louche preppy sensibility. But spikes, mohawk haircuts, and the other baroque indulgences of the British phenomenon were rejected as ridiculous.

Indeed, Minor Threat were much copied for the subtlety of their style. MacKaye's Vans and single-pocket tee—a remnant from his skateboarding days—the Mickey Mouse shirt worn by Brian, Jeff Nelson's wild-man haircut, which revealed the artistic sensibilities of the man, and Lyle Preslar's prep-school getup were no pose. Minor Threat, though, were remarkable for their ferocious approach to the music and performance. Their vision was clear, their message was clear, they were dissatisfied, and their musical assault was irresistible and melodic. Minor Threat struck a chord with audiences across America because their singer was the charismatic leader the movement had been waiting for. Whether you liked their message or not, it was new and authentic. They were a manifestation of what punk and hardcore embodied—the total neglect of their generation. Music wrought by kids for whom nothing had been made and to whom access was denied.

The punks' parents had, of course, defined culture since their appearance en masse on the scene in the postwar period, when the USA was flush with cash, high on victory, and feeling fecund. Punk and hardcore music were an unpleasant disruption to the trip they were on. They were also horrified at the rise of the next generation, who symbolized their mortality, so their neglect at the hands of record honchos wasn't just number crunching, it was natural jealousy, resentment, and confusion. Minor Threat, a band from Washington, DC, were the clearest refutation of the hippie dream that existed.

As a young teen, I saw that Minor Threat were performing with the Damned and another English group at a theater in Washington, DC. Minor Threat's *Out of Step* record had been playing nonstop on the college station I listened to and the Damned had just released their fifth album, *Strawberries*, also on heavy rotation. During the Damned's set, the crew hired to do security got overly rough with the stage-diving punk rockers. This resulted in a riot, with lots of heads broken and people beaten with steel bars and baseball bats. The melee culminated with several members of the security crew facing off with Minor Threat singer Ian MacKaye in the lobby of the theater. I vividly remember gathering with others in a circle to watch this David-and-Goliath struggle as Ian stood up to the deputized security guards/street fighters who were considerably larger than he was. It felt like he was standing up for all of us! Soon, a legion of police raided the theater and ejected everyone except for me; I explained that my brother was coming to pick me up. As I waited, standing alone outside of the now-abandoned theater, the Damned emerged from the front door. We exchanged niceties. "Good show," I told them, "but did you see Minor Threat?" As they laughed about this impertinent comment, my brother pulled up. He was very impressed to see me outside, casually talking to the Damned.

Years later, my band the Make-Up lived and practiced in a row house on Euclid Street in Northwest DC about a block away from that old theater, now gutted and home to a dollar store. Across the street from our place was a halfway house, a hub for a big open-air drug market, and about twenty dealers hanging out on the corner at all times. We became friendly with them since they were always around, and they grew to feel a little protective of us; they called us "the Way-Outs," a reference to a cartoon musical group from the *Flintstones* TV show. One time, a few of the older members of the gang talked wistfully about having worked security for the very same theater production, the cartel that had promoted the Damned/Minor Threat concert which had ended in a bloodbath. They talked nostalgically about how fun it was working security at the punk shows in the old days. The band was not brought to you by Live Nation and security wasn't either. To think that these new friends may have been the ones who inadvertently facilitated my meeting the Damned all those years ago!

Minor Threat's band personality—their wit, tunes, and young energy—made them *the* group of their epoch. The fact that the group never reformed for big bucks or a victory lap—despite countless offers to do so—reveals that they actually subscribed to their espoused rhetoric; that "punk" was supposed to be democratic and inclusive; that the groups weren't the vehicles of elite superstar geniuses, but a format that anyone could utilize to express ideas, pathos, etc. Minor Threat's message, while exciting and attractive, was also particular to their context. When that context changed, the members started other groups, all distinct and with other things to say.

In the song "Minor Threat," Ian sings, *"We're not the first, I hope we're not the last"*; with his patented "old soul" delivery, he's encouraging others to carry on Minor Threat's mission of self-reliance, nonconformity, creativity, industry. More than the idea of "straight edge," the example of the band is perhaps what resonates most.

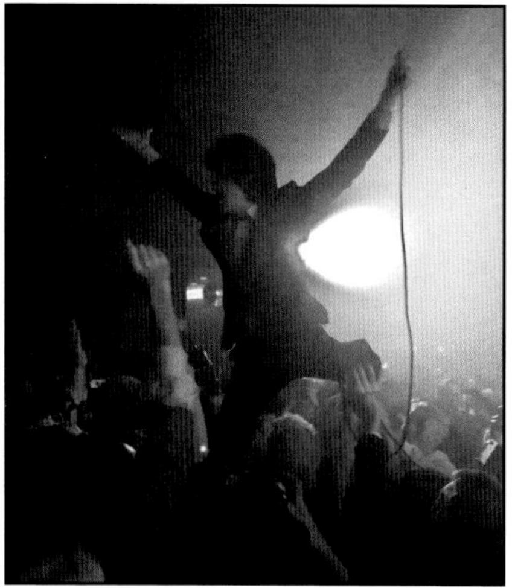

IFS in the crowd at a reunion performance of the Make Up.

Introduction

by glen E. friedman

Punk rock was serious, it was idealistic, and it was angry, but punk rock could also be as fun as *anything*. It was youth-generated, like most great new and original music.

No parents were around to speak of or see at punk rock shows in the late '70s and early '80s. Now there are more punks, more people thinking for themselves, and more people trying to motivate and change the thoughts of others with their creativity, just as I have always hoped for. Of course, there's also more poseurs, people just looking to impress or be cool, etc. So what—as long as there are more of the real ones, we're okay.

Minor Threat formed at a time when that term "hardcore" became a thing, but really they were a punk rock band. They had melody and they were aggressive and they had a good time too! Besides the incredible anthems they poured out one after the other as a bunch of teenagers, there was an "everyman" feel to this group. When the lead singer Ian MacKaye was onstage, the audience really saw *one of their own* up there. He had the energy, spirit, and presence of the crowd around him. But as much as he was on their same level, he was different because he rallied energy and enthusiasm in the room like no one else.

I had already met Ian at CBGB on December 26, 1981, before I knew anything of Minor Threat. His brother Alec's band the Faith were opening for Bad Brains. I met them and others from the DC crew who made it up for the show. They were all very friendly and cool. They knew me because they were fans of skateboarding, *SkateBoarder* magazine, and my DogTown roots. Although they were fully dedicated punks, they would not deny their love of skateboarding and the early outsider perspective skating afforded them. The transition from skateboarding to punk rock was an obvious one at the time. May I remind you there was no such thing as punk rock or hardcore when we all started skateboarding, it was a natural progression from one culture into the next; the transition was almost flawless for teenagers coming of age in the time we did.

Truth be told, I didn't get it when I heard the first 7" from Minor Threat. I was sent money from a pen pal of mine who I met at the Del Mar skate ranch (he had designed the skate ranch logo—he later became known as the artist Pushead). He was even more of a weirdo than the rest of us. He came from Boise, Idaho, and he would send me money in Los Angeles to get him records at Vinyl Fetish in Hollywood or Zed Records in Long Beach. He wanted the new stuff coming out that you couldn't find anywhere else. Before shipping him his records I'd give them a spin on a turntable. He asked for the Minor Threat debut record. I got it for him. I played it—it was okay. I admit that record at the time did not make a real mark on me.

A half a year later I heard their second 7" extended player and it knocked me out. When I listened to the song "In My Eyes" with Ian yelling, "*What the fuck have you done?*" and the chorus, "*It's in my eyes, and it doesn't look that way to me,*" I was floored and fired up! I went back and gave that original EP another listen (from tapes the same friend sent me after he got his goods). I felt the fool by not recognizing the fury and intensity and sharpness of that record the first time around. I was now a Minor Threat fan, on my way to becoming an ambassador and propagandist.

Once I discovered this new friend's music, I wrote to Ian with admiration and appreciation. It was odd for me, I had never written a "fan" letter before, and even though we had met and I had spoken on the phone with his brother a few times, I was compelled to actually write him. Minor Threat's records were important, life-affirming, authentic, and inspiring. I wanted to be a part of what they were doing. I wanted to help spread the word. There were not many places to do so back then, but with a camera and a big mouth, I did what I could.

When I finally got to see them play, it was a hydrogen bomb of excitement on the stage and in the crowd. The venues became river rapids of motion, and sing-alongs with almost every lyric. It was truly a changing of the guard from the older punk rock crowd to the new hardcore punk rock. Unlike some of the most popular bands of that moment, they were not even a couple of years older than us, they were the same age and younger, they were a mirror of the audience in every way.

They too were fans of the music and scene, they too were having fun and at the same time were dead serious about it.

I first made pictures of them on July 3, 1982, at the Alpine Village Barn in Torrance, California. It was an incredible show, and in my opinion Minor Threat owned the night, but everyone onstage that evening killed it.

I went to the East Coast later that summer to visit my father, and just a month after the LA show, in August, I saw them play on their own "turf" at the 9:30 Club in Washington, DC. I brought my camera and made one of my all-time favorite photographs at this gig (the image that appears on this book's cover). The performance, the crowd, the intensity were astonishing.

The next time I was to make live photos of them was at a phenomenal show the following Christmas school holiday in New York City at the famed CBGB during the end of 1982. Minor Threat were late (now as a five-piece band, the new, albeit temporary bass player, Steve, was added and Brian moved to second guitar), *way* past their allotted time to play due to problems with their van. The gig was one of the early "hardcore matinees" at CBGB, and they almost did not get to play. But after some negotiations, they were allowed fifteen minutes just to keep the crowd from rioting! The crowd had been waiting and waiting, and when the band finally arrived onstage, the powder keg of pent-up energy was explosive and uncontrollable. Those fifteen minutes were somehow stretched to a half hour. New York City punk rock was never the same after that show, it was now gonna be hardcore or nothing at all.

In April 1983 they came to Los Angeles again. They played at an old roller rink out in the San Fernando Valley. By this point in time I was busy managing Suicidal Tendencies, who were also on the bill, so I was not making pictures that night, just worrying if the bands were going to get to play at all in this new venue or if the police were going to shut it down. Both Minor Threat and ST played incredible shows. ST solidified their reputation outside of their own neighborhood that night by bringing their out-of-control fan frenzy to another territory. But it was Minor Threat, three thousand miles away from their hometown, that had everyone singing every lyric.

The following day I invited the group to come meet me at the Kenter Canyon Elementary schoolyard, one of the hallowed skate spots for the out-of-towners to see and experience for themselves where some of the foundations of skateboarding were forged. I had a session planned to shoot pictures of skateboarding freestyle innovator and prodigy Rodney Mullen. We got an eventual *Thrasher* cover from this day too (the January 1984 issue), and moments of this excursion exist on a *Flipside* video fanzine (Volume 2) that featured clips of the show the night before and even some footage of us all skating (you can find it if you try).

That evening, Minor Threat played in a little club that was literally underground: Cathay de Grande, a really dark place with no raised stage to speak of separating the band from the audience. I didn't shoot the gig that night, but I enjoyed the show without my camera, and before they left town we made some group portraits near where they were staying.

That summer I went down to DC to see a Faith show, but I missed it due to a horrible flight delay. That sucked, but the next day Ian brought me to a local ramp spot out in the woods somewhere in Virginia for a great skate session. We made photos and did an article for *Thrasher* magazine about Ian and Henry's old skate crew and the current dudes shredding down there. That article actually ended up being *Thrasher*'s October 1983 cover story.

Later on, when we got back to Dischord House (a group home and the HQ of Ian and Jeff Nelson's independent record label), and before Minor Threat had a practice in the basement, we made photos of them on the porch and in the front yard. After this day, Minor Threat only played one more show and then broke up permanently. One of the photographs ended up on the cover of their last record, the *Salad Days* 7" EP.

Since those days, Ian has become one of my very best friends and collaborators. We work together on projects, and hang with each other's families. When we're in the same room or talk on the phone, the conversations never end.

This book is an homage to the great band that inspired and continues to inspire people of all ages around the world. What you see here is the best of the less than two hundred exposures in total I made of them on 35mm black-and-white film. (I only shot black-and-white because there was little interest at the time in hardcore punk from any publications, let alone those that printed full-color.) If you're a Minor Threat fan you have no doubt seen some of these, but you haven't seen most of them. It's "in my eyes" and this is how it looked to me, when we were all "out of step with the world."

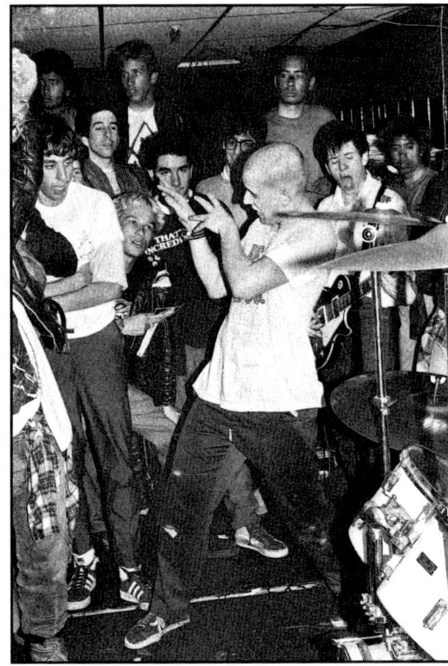

Minor Threat at Cathay de Grande.
Ian trying to put a hex on me, 4/4/83.

Photo by Kevin Salk.

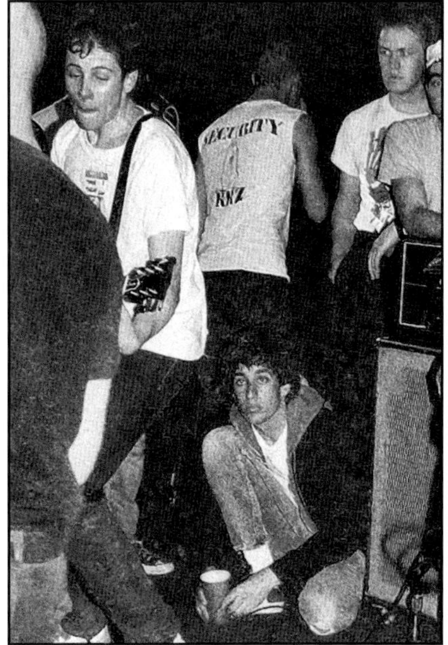

Minor Threat at Rollerworks.
Onstage by Lyle's amp, 4/2/83.

Photo by Marla Watson.

July 3, 1982
The Barn at Alpine Village
Torrance, California

Ian MacKaye - vocal
Lyle Preslar - guitar
Brian Baker - bass
Jeff Nelson - drums

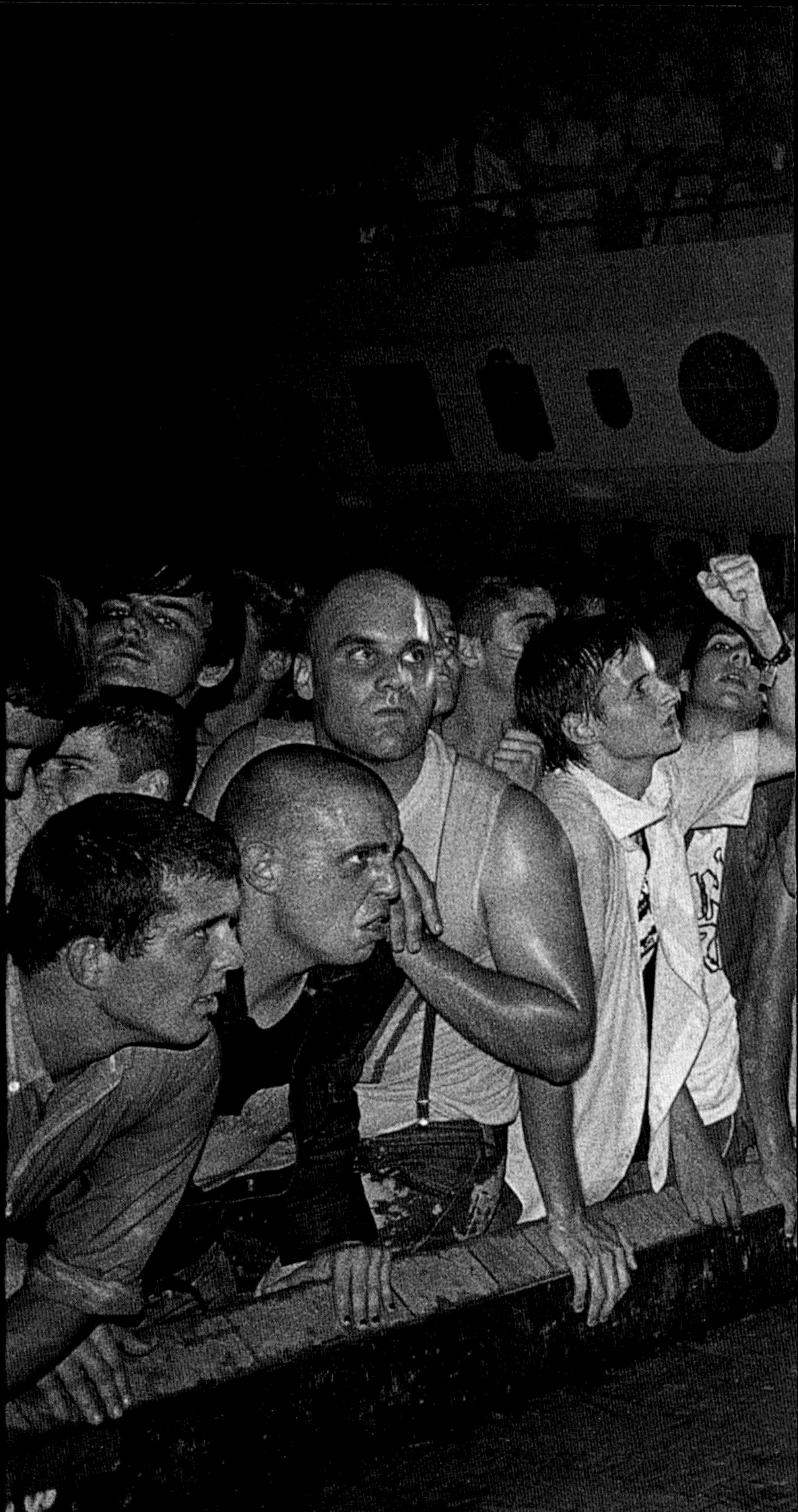

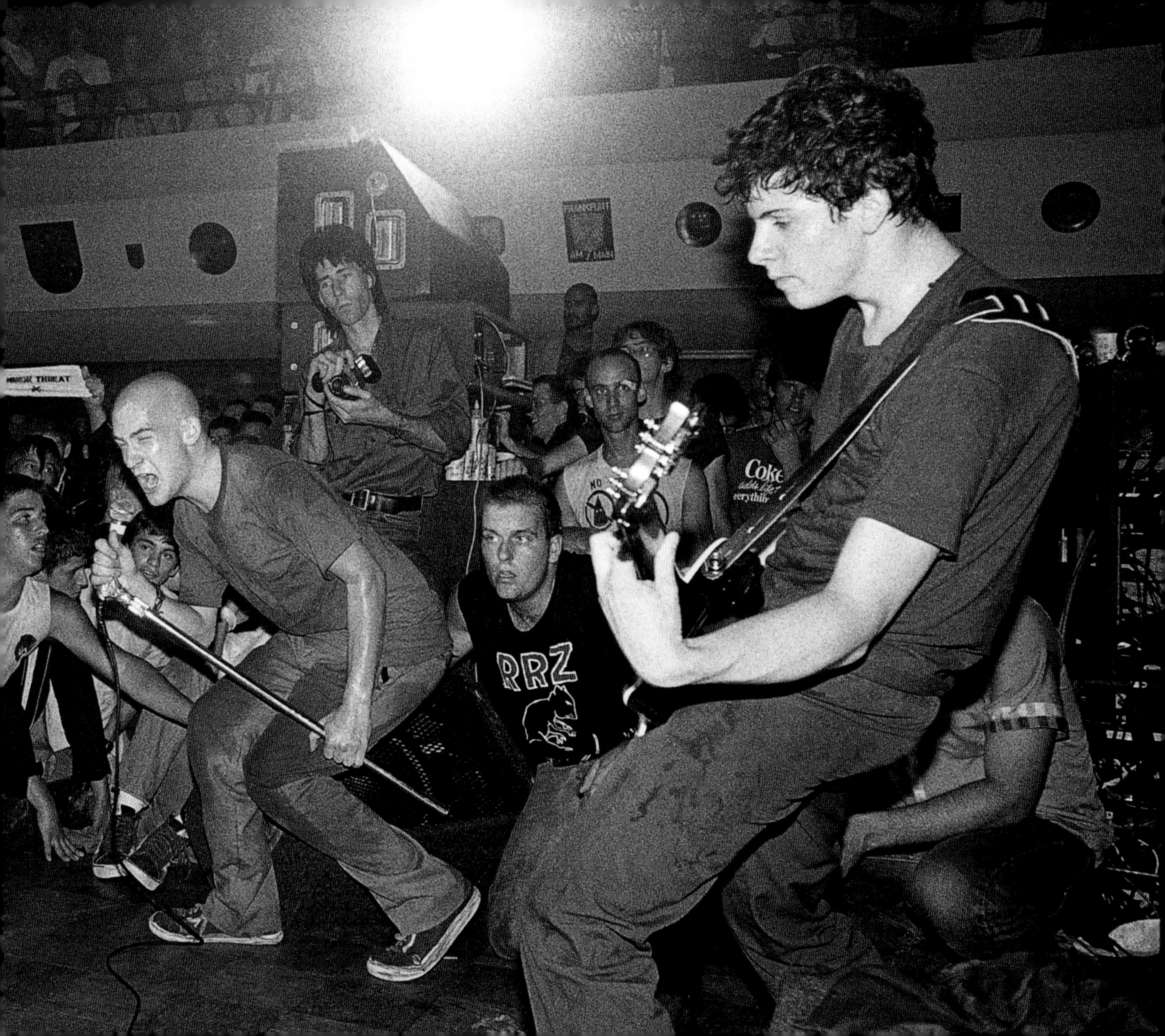
THREAT
RRZ
Coke

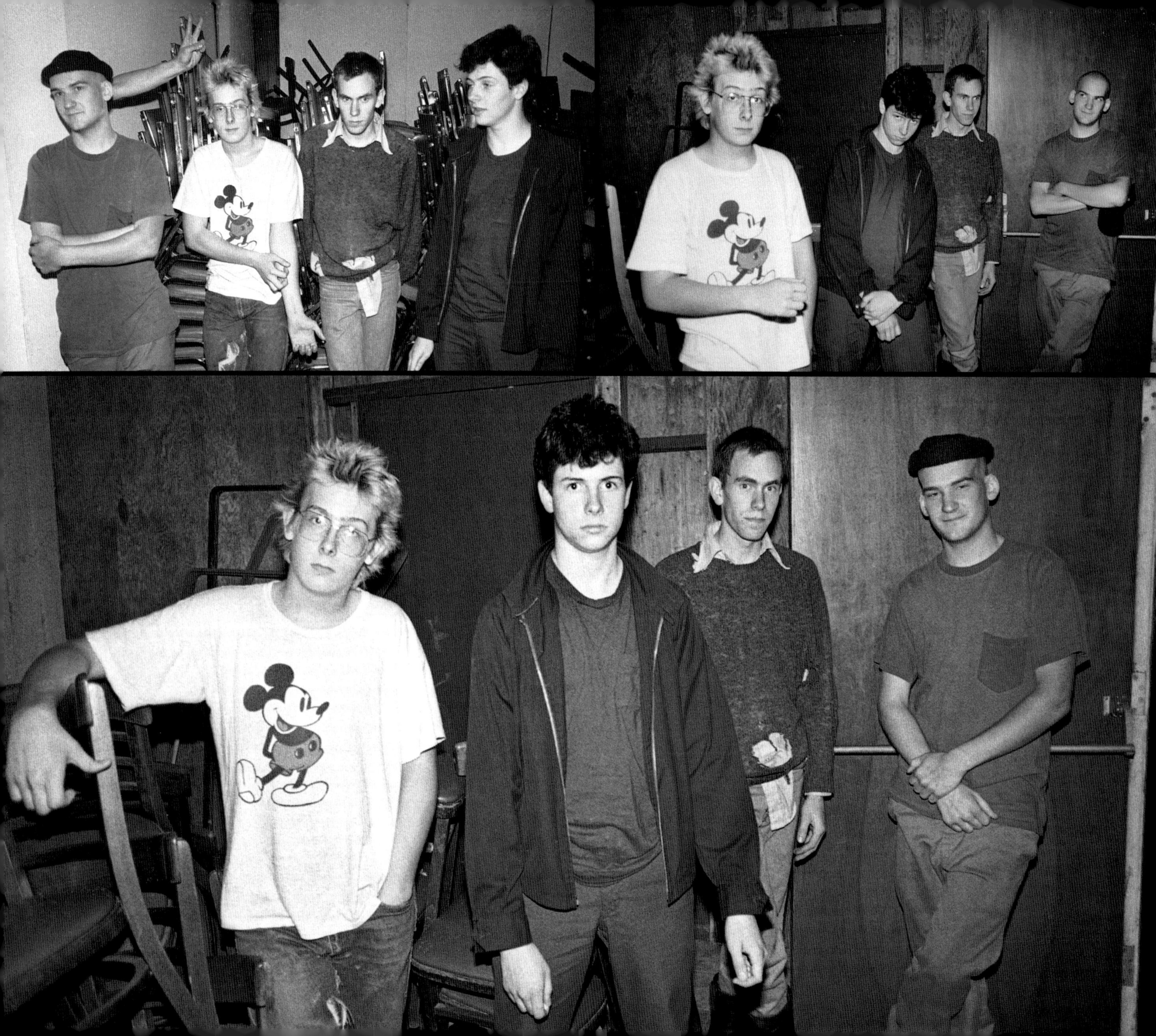

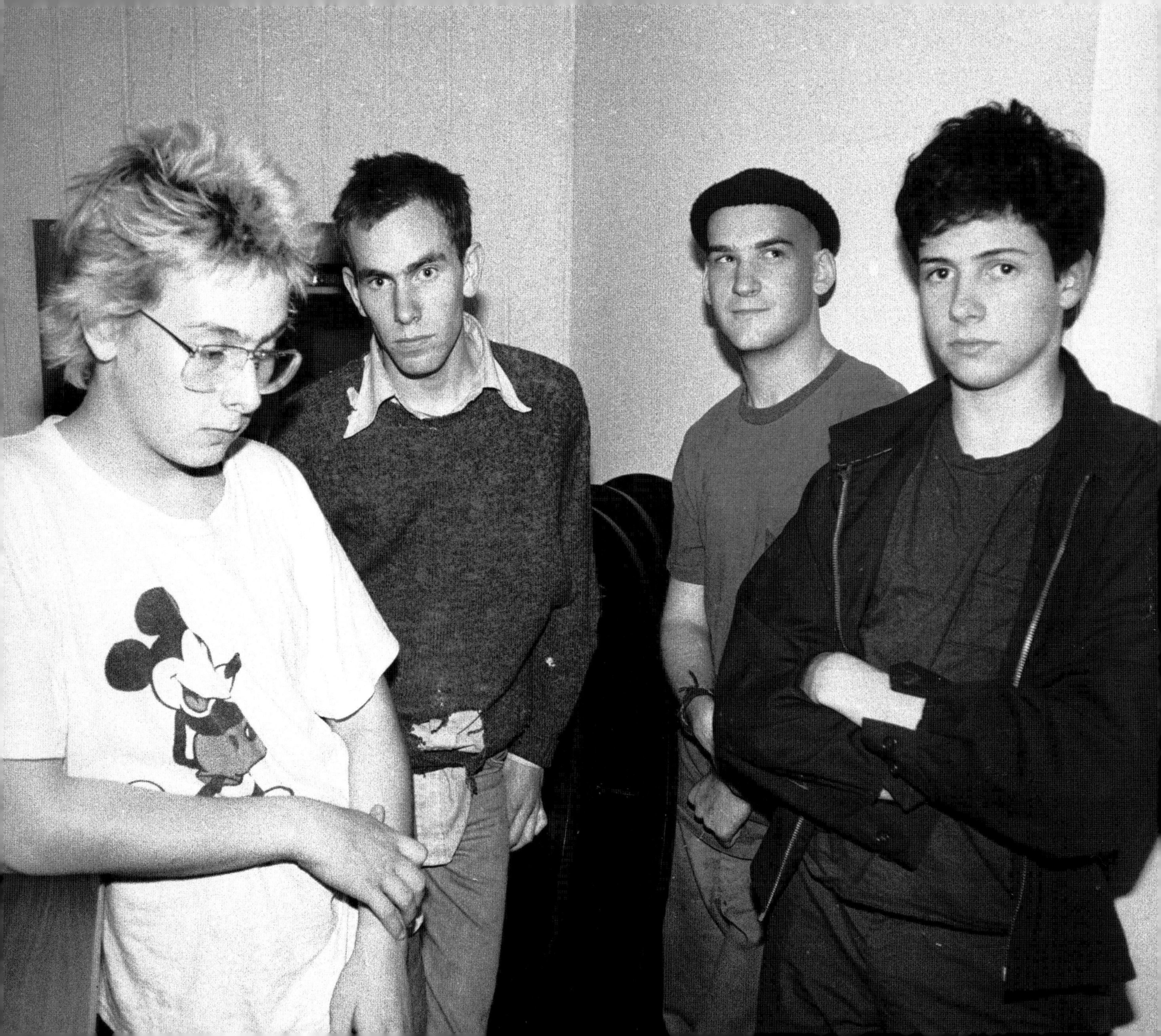

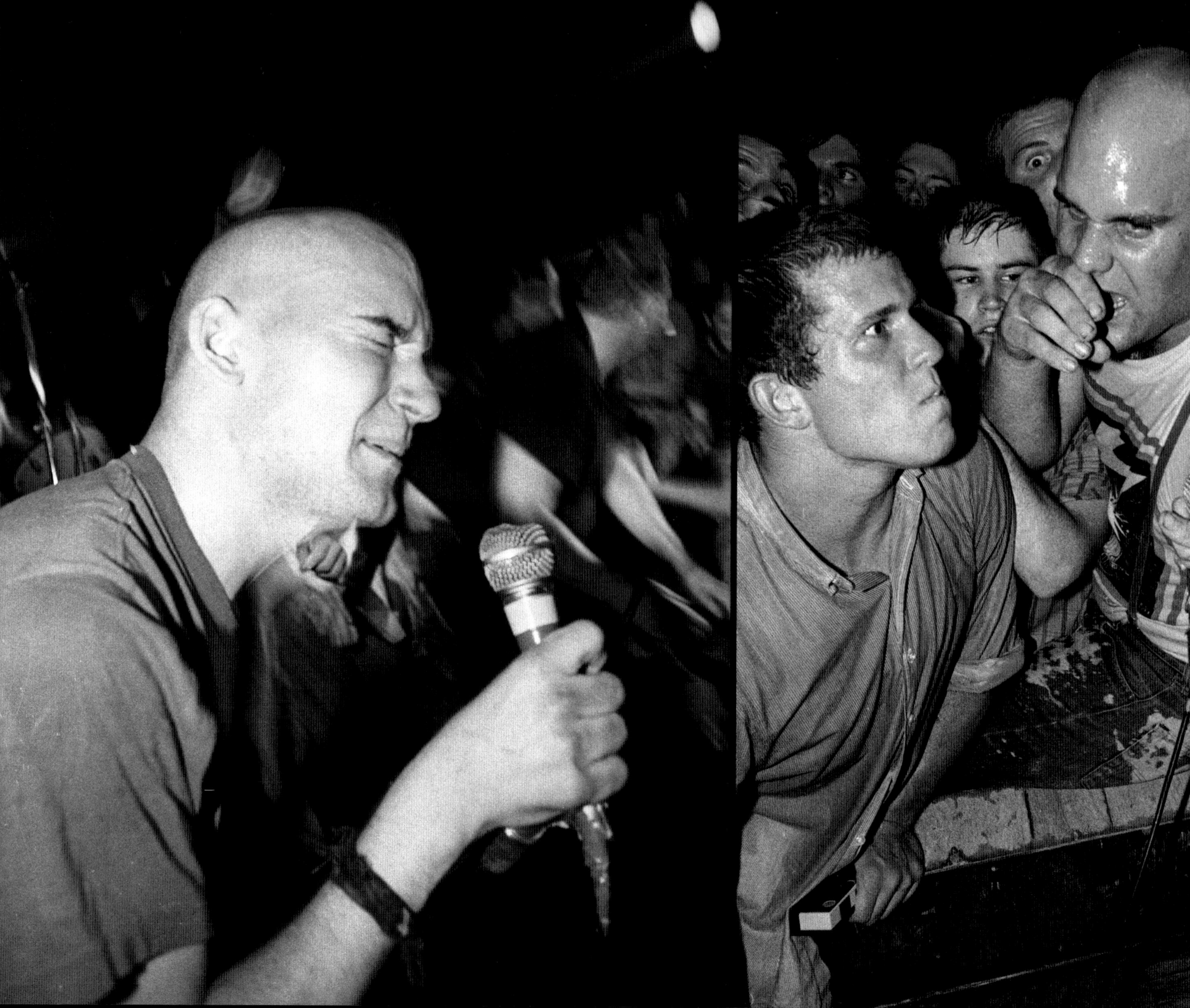

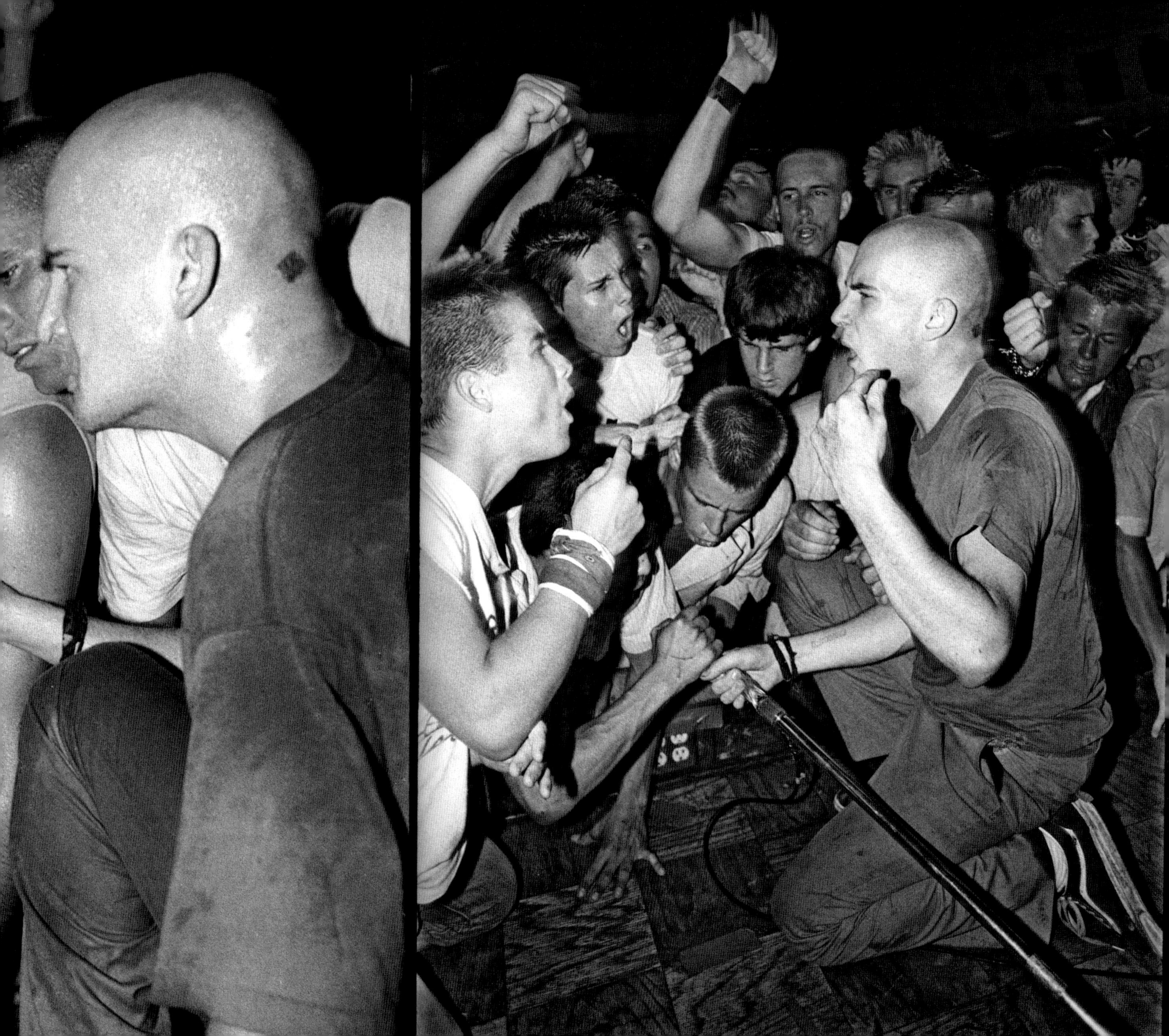

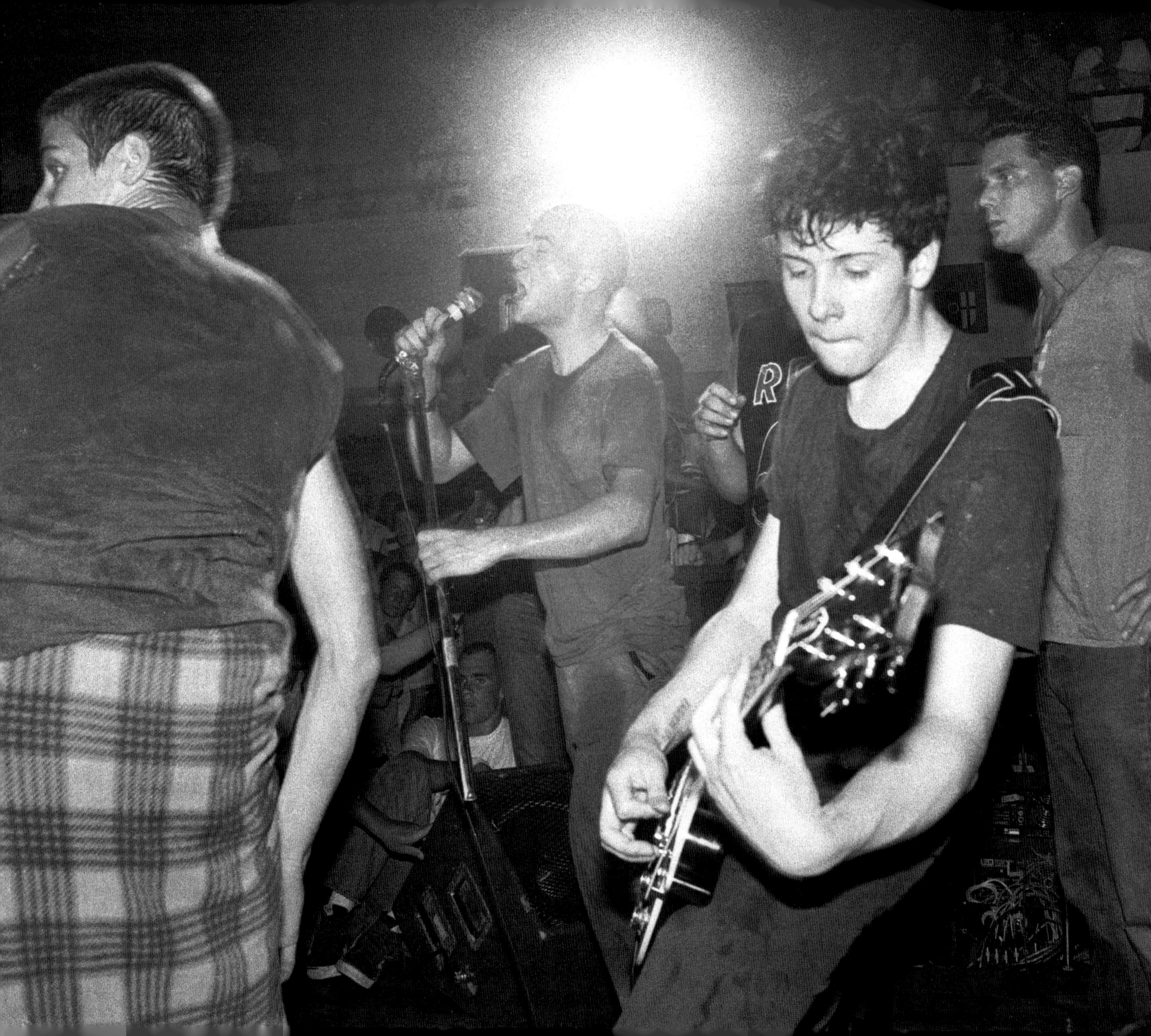

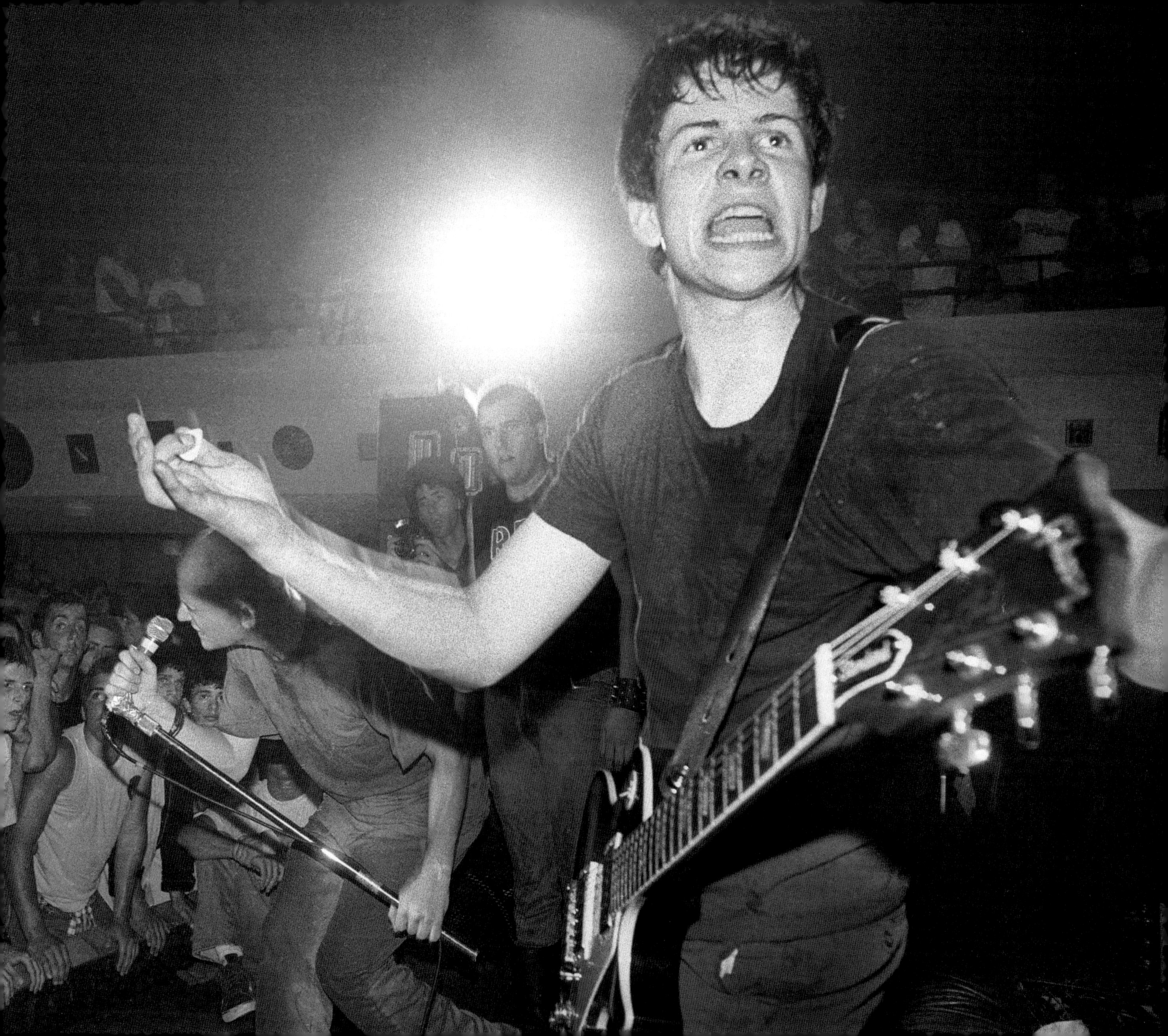

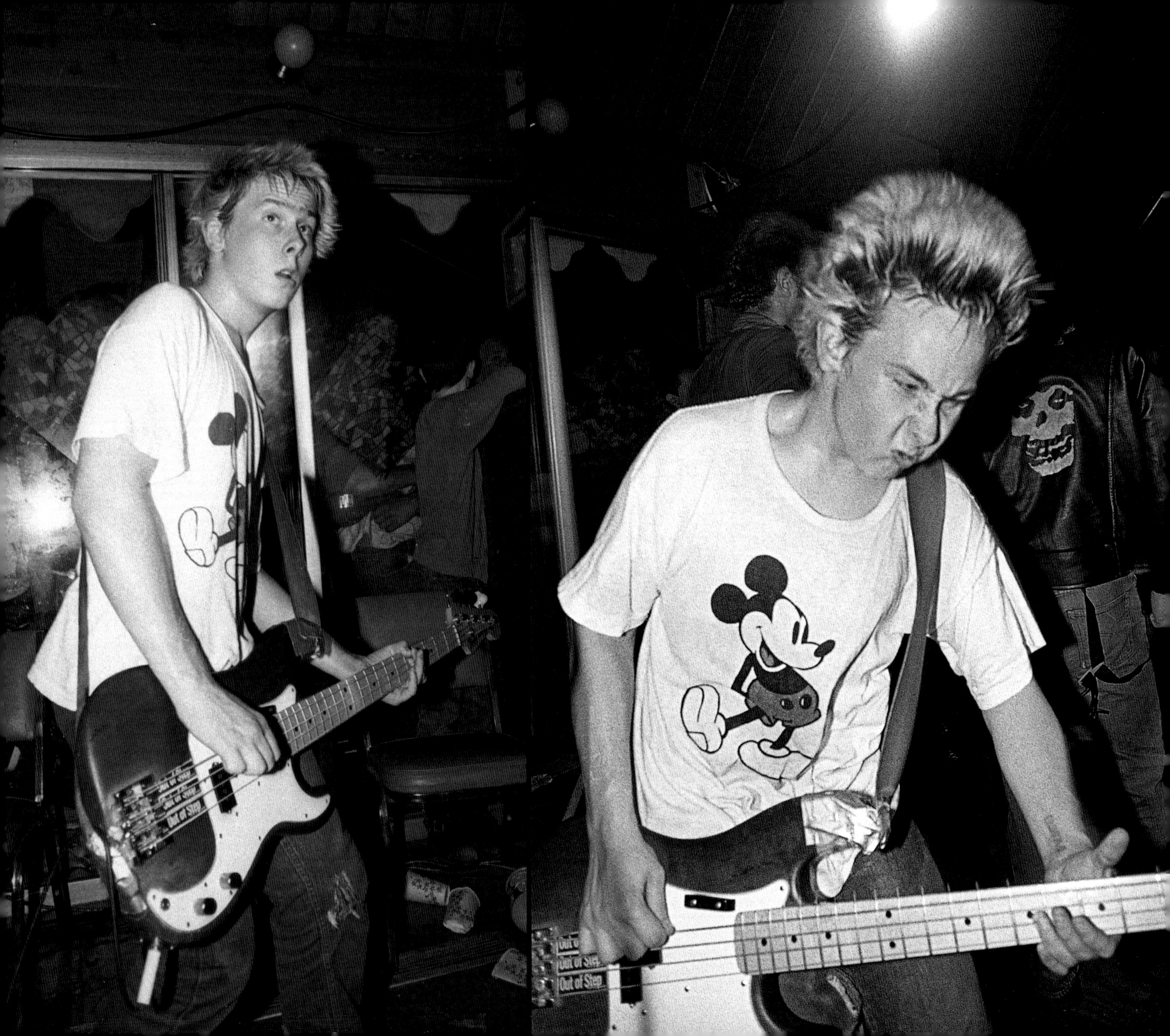
Out of Step
Out of Step
Out of Step

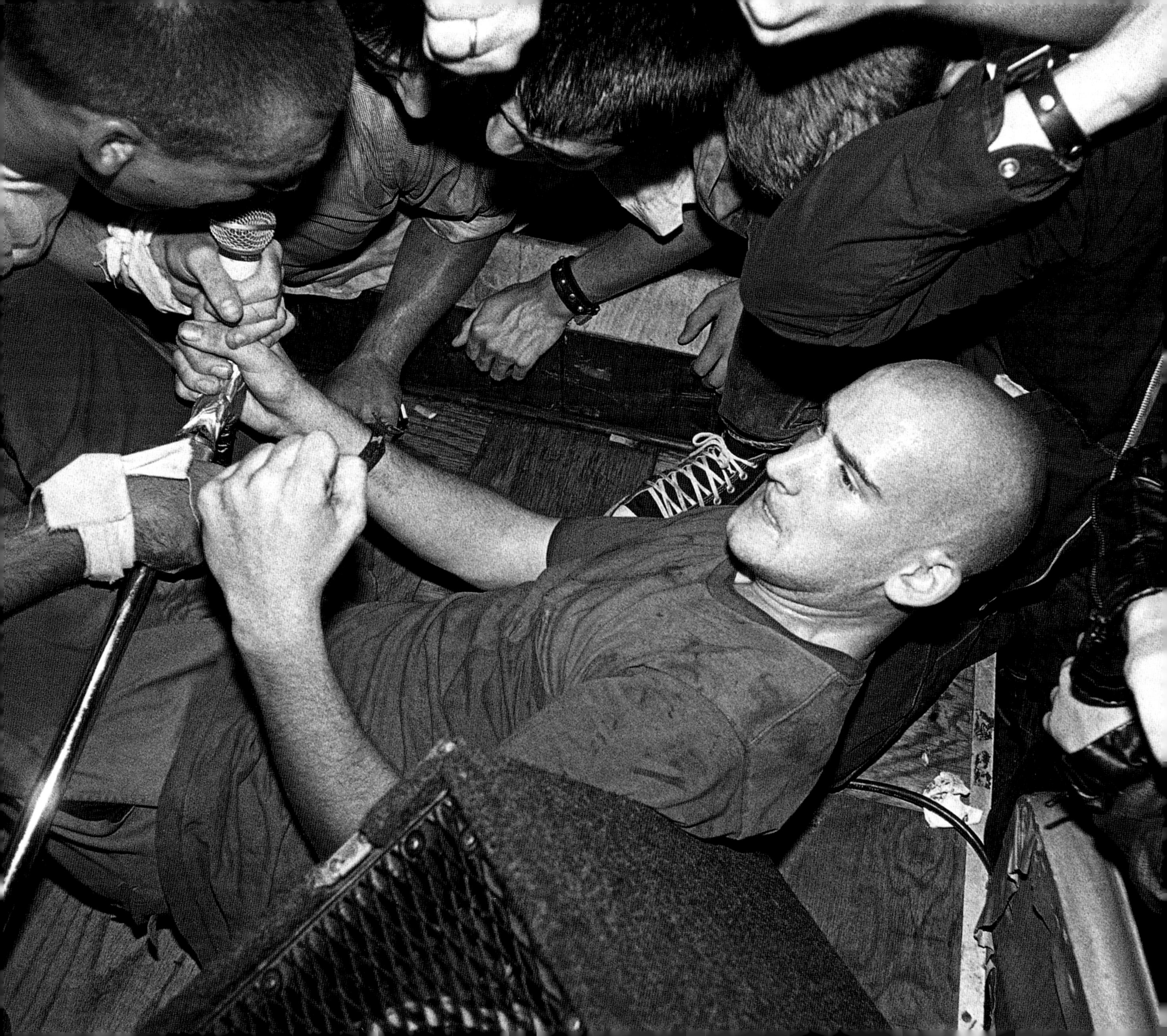

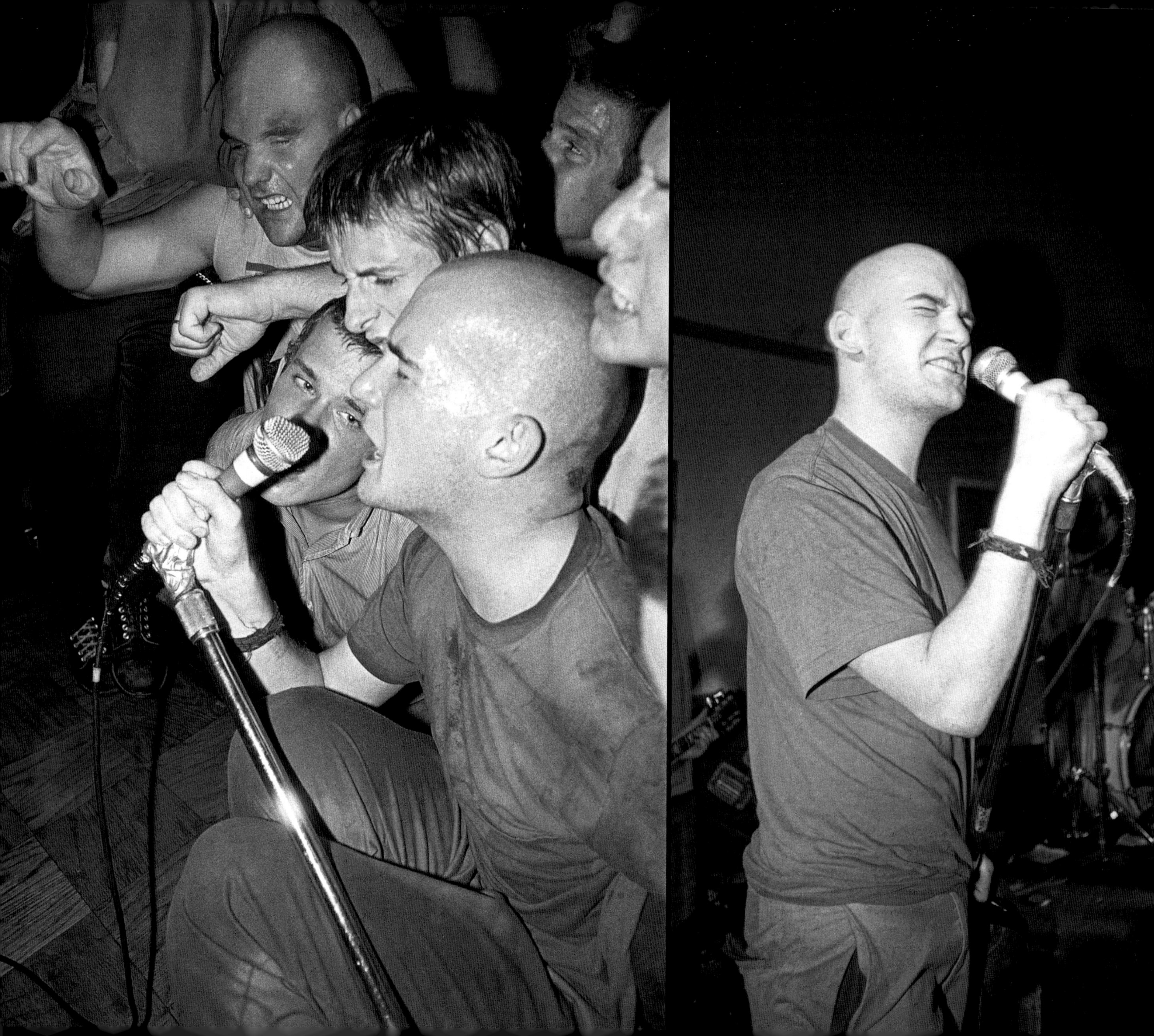

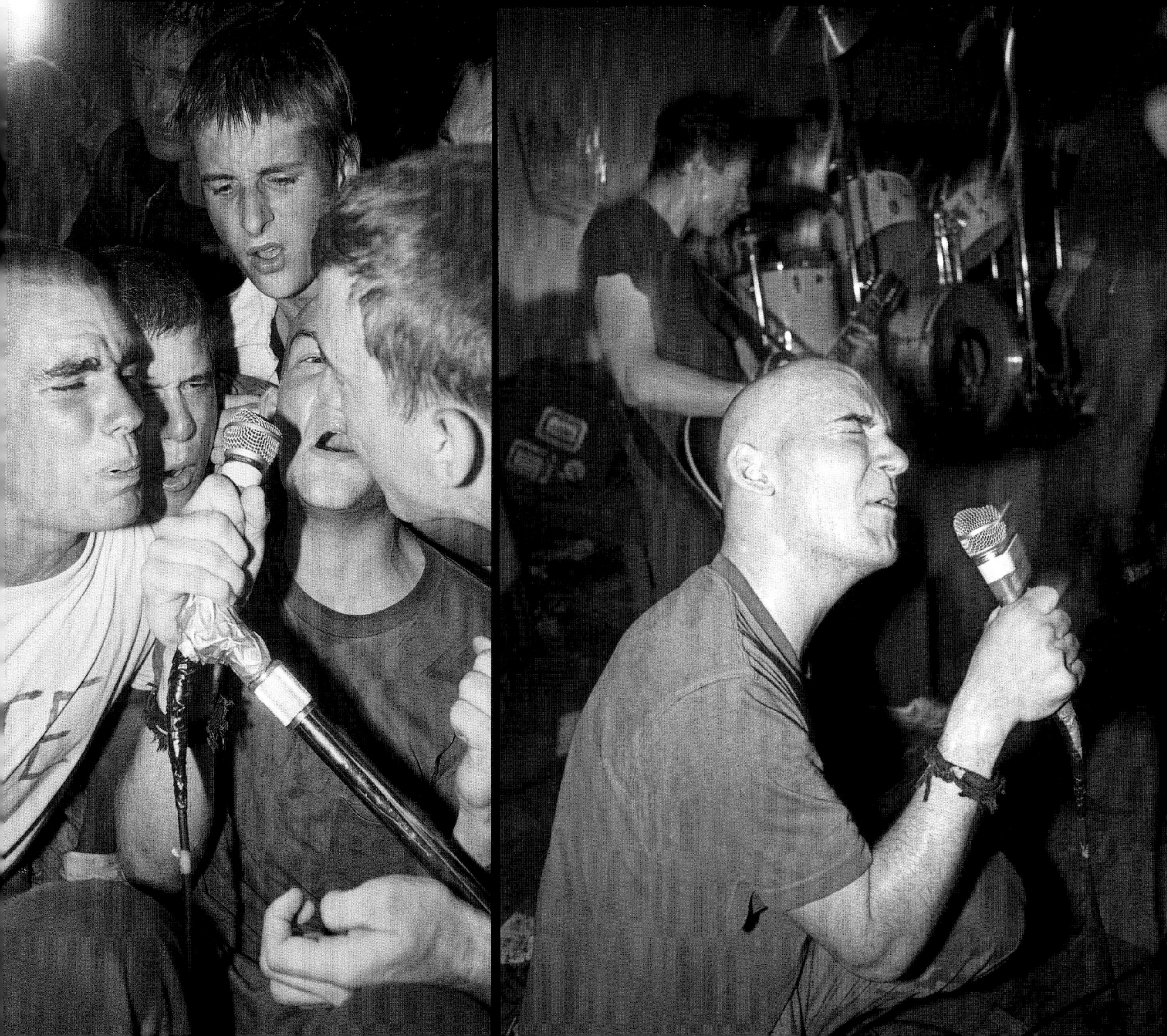

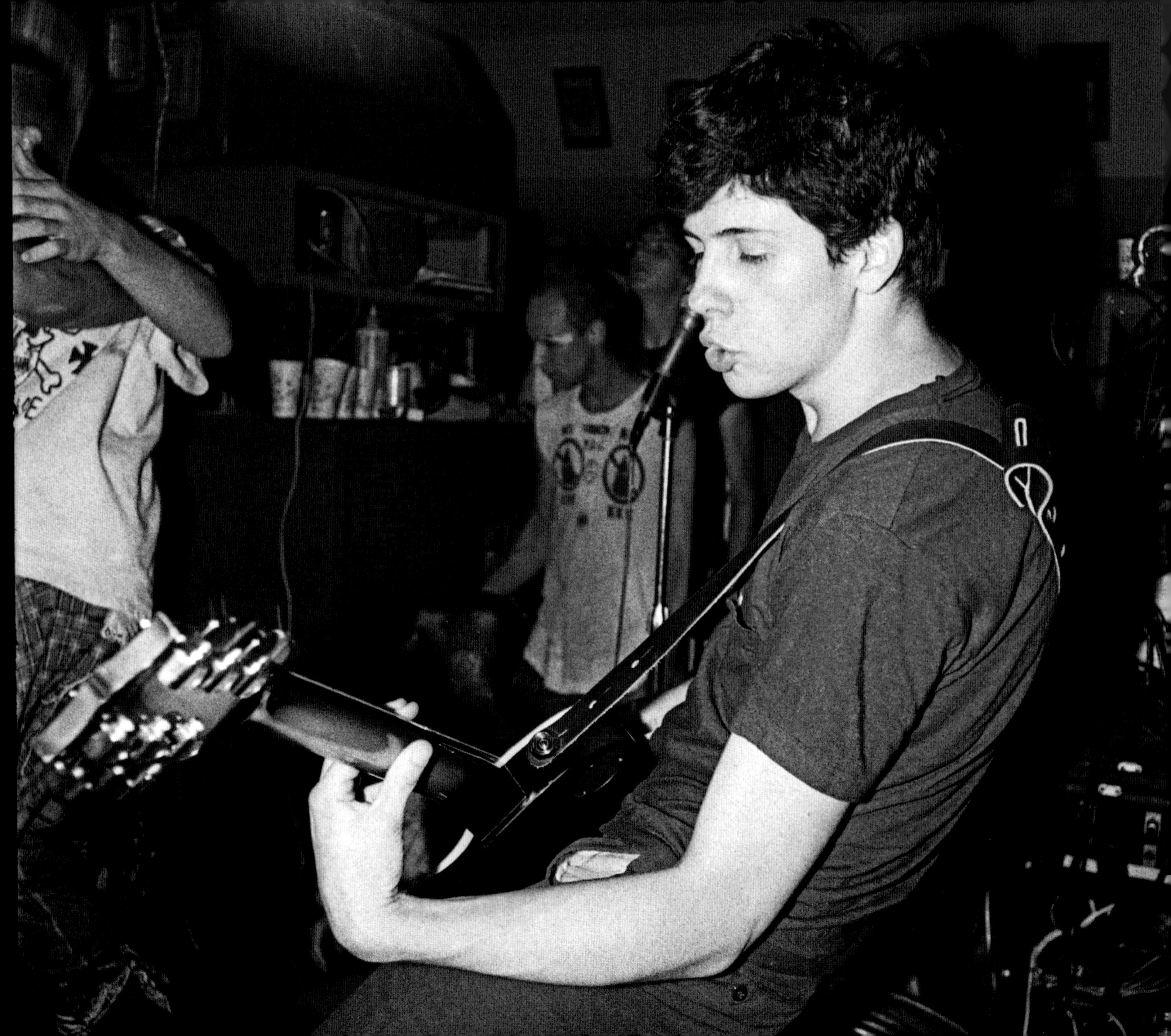

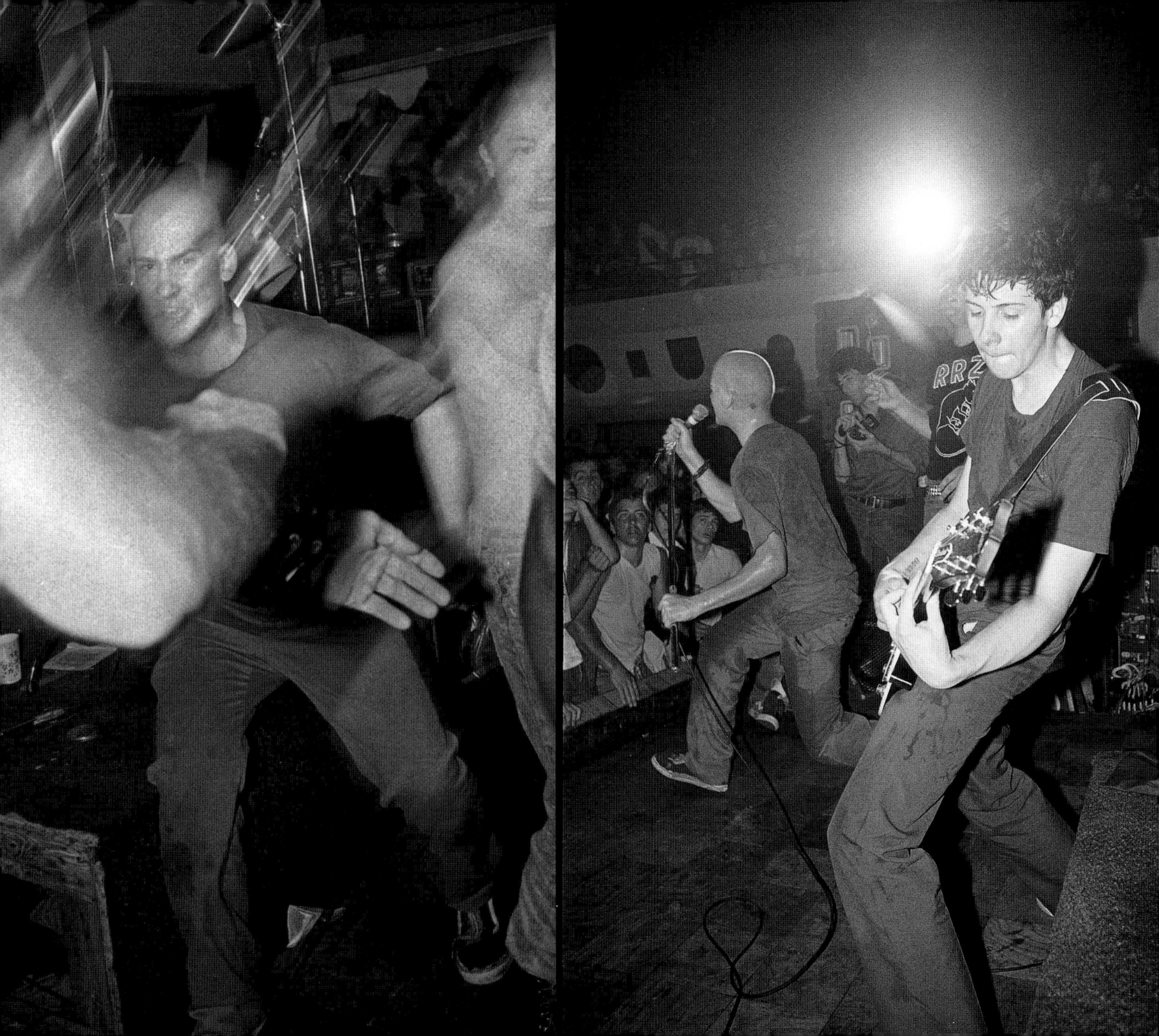

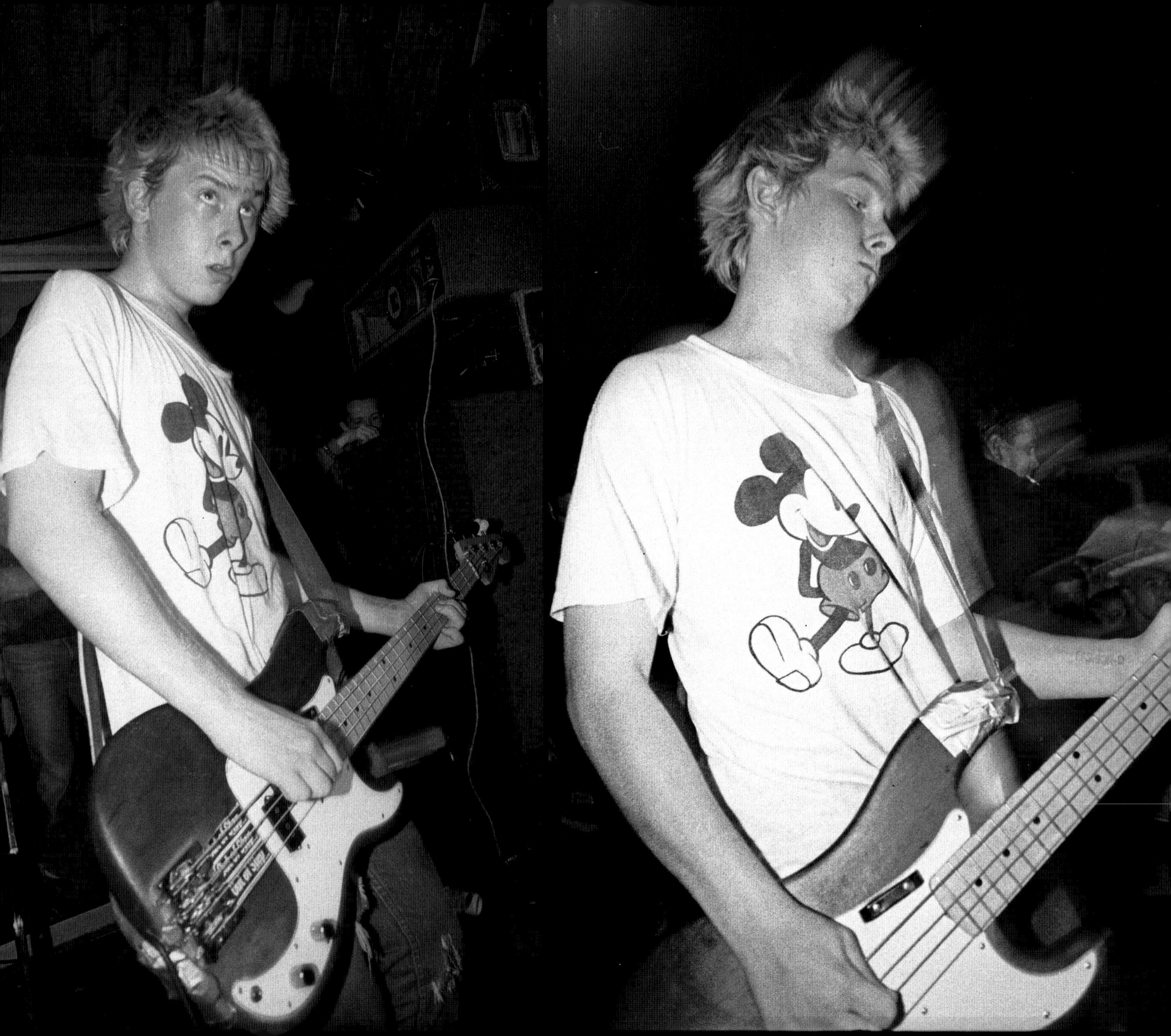

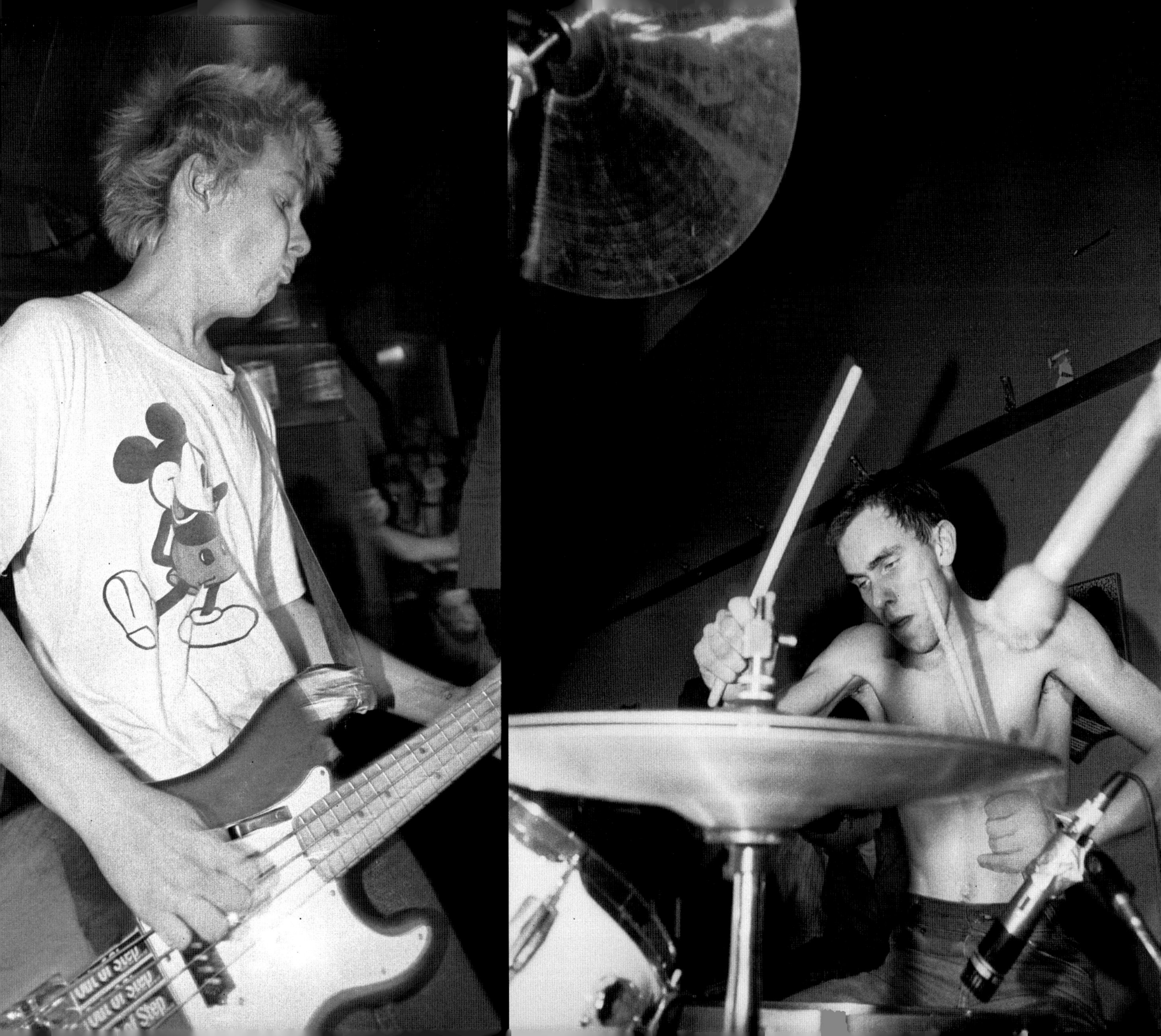

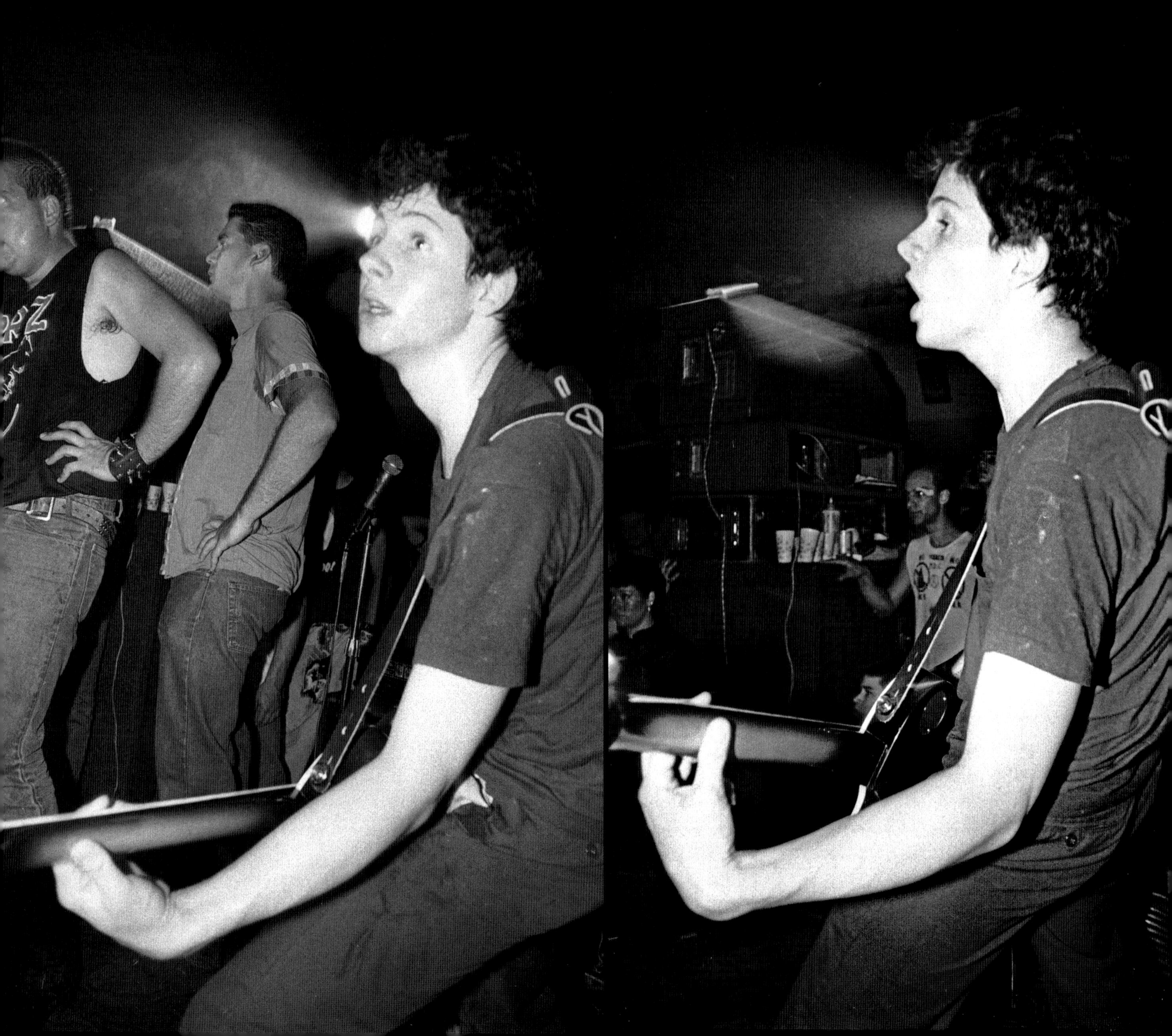

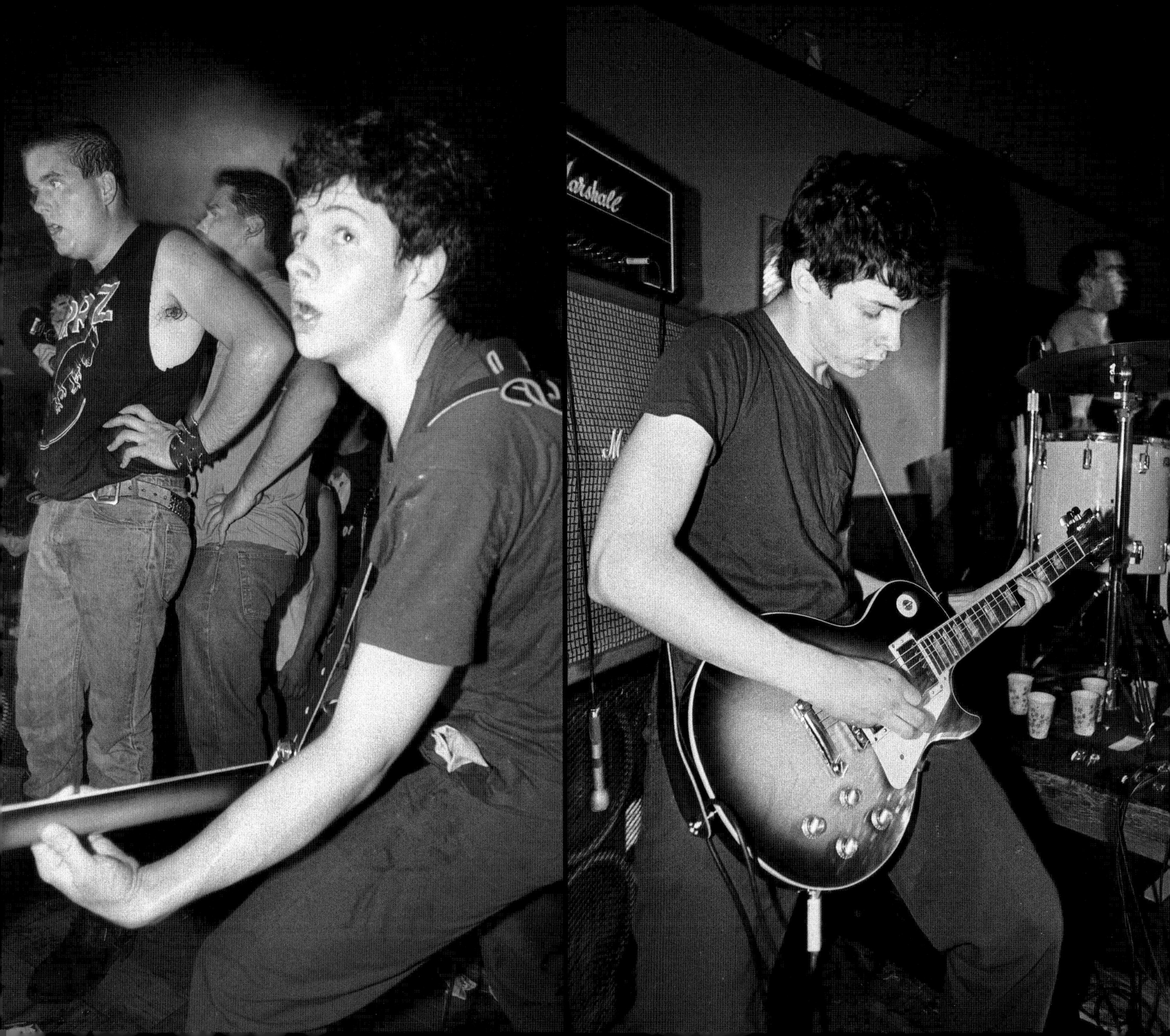

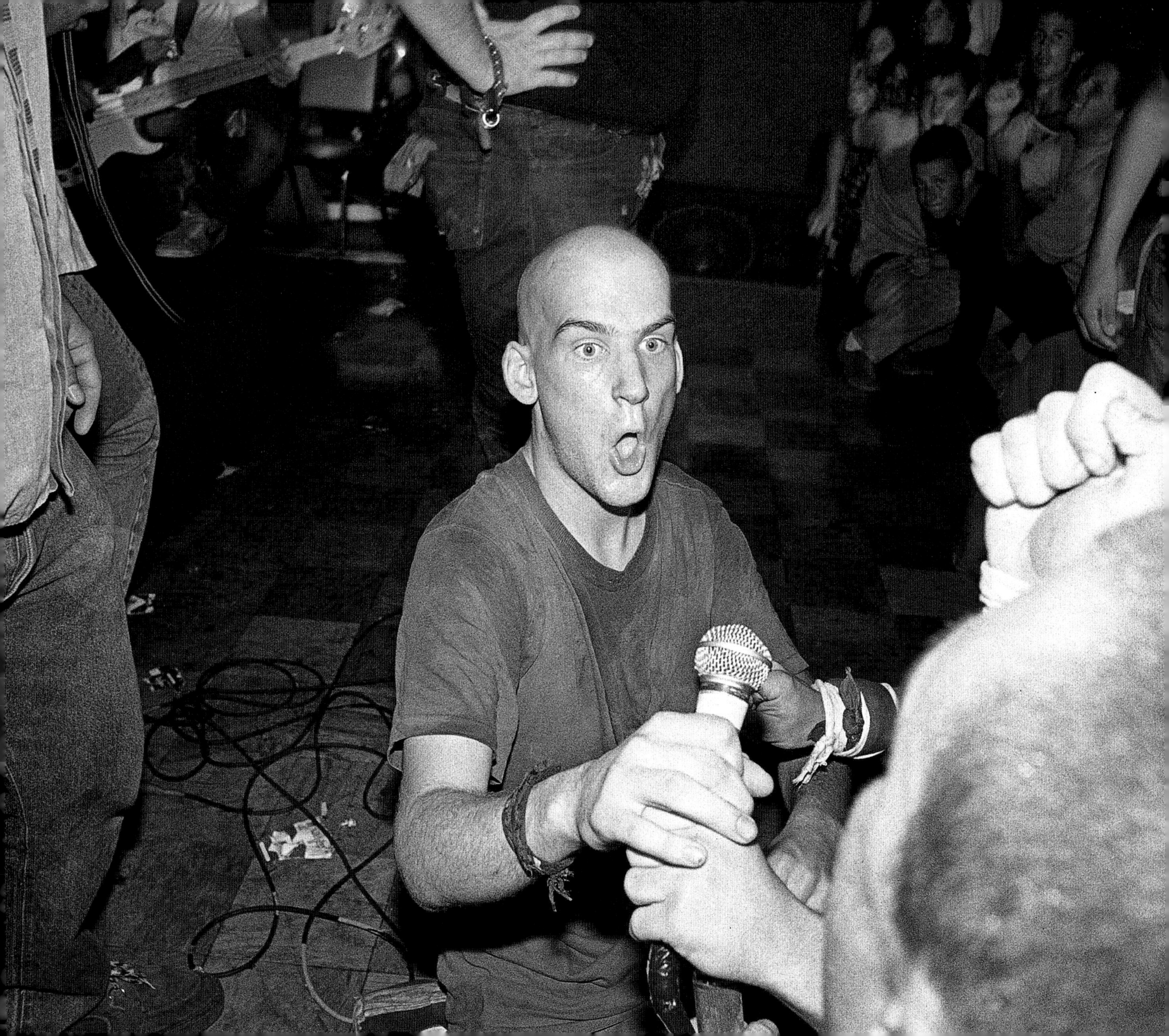

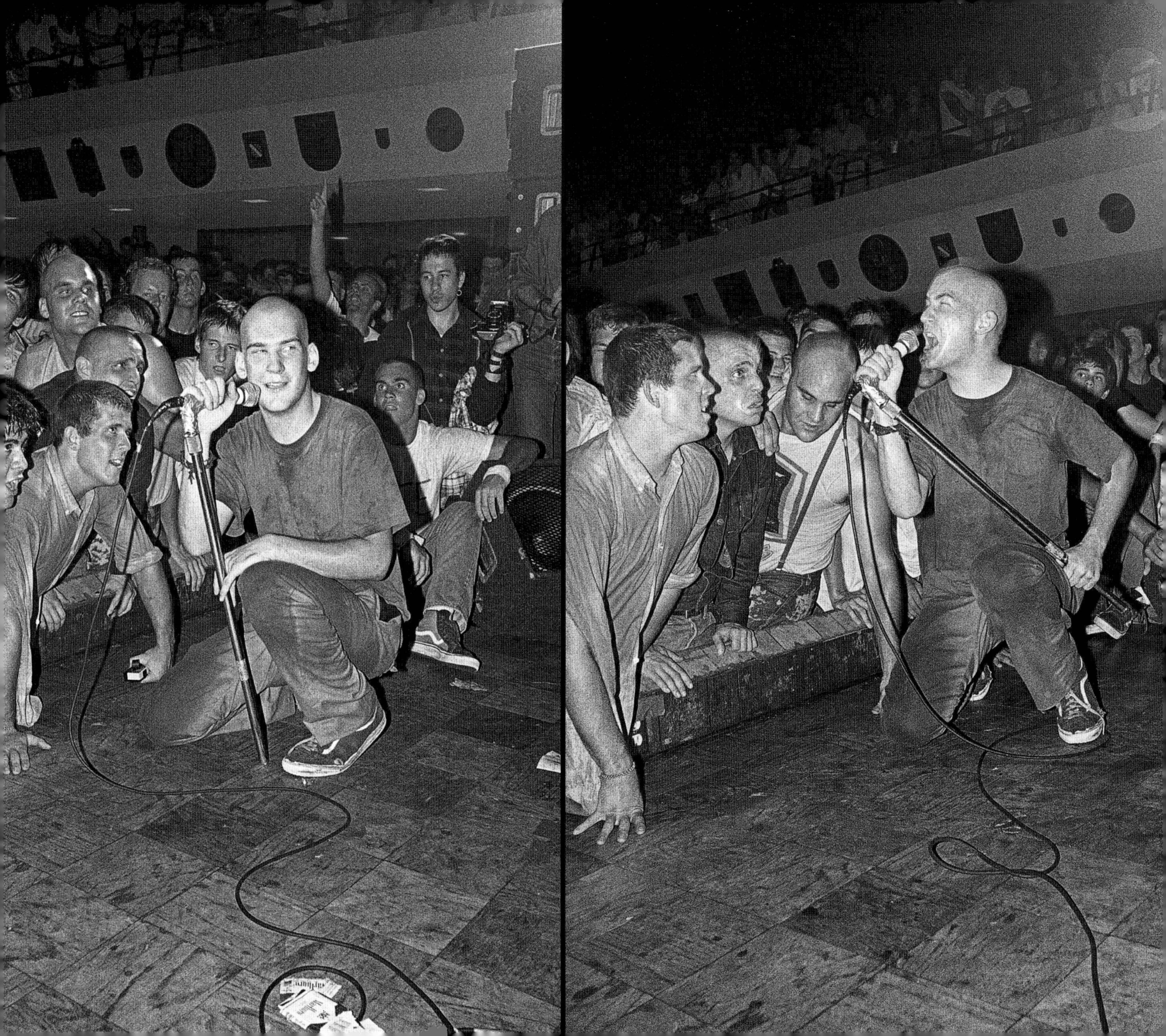

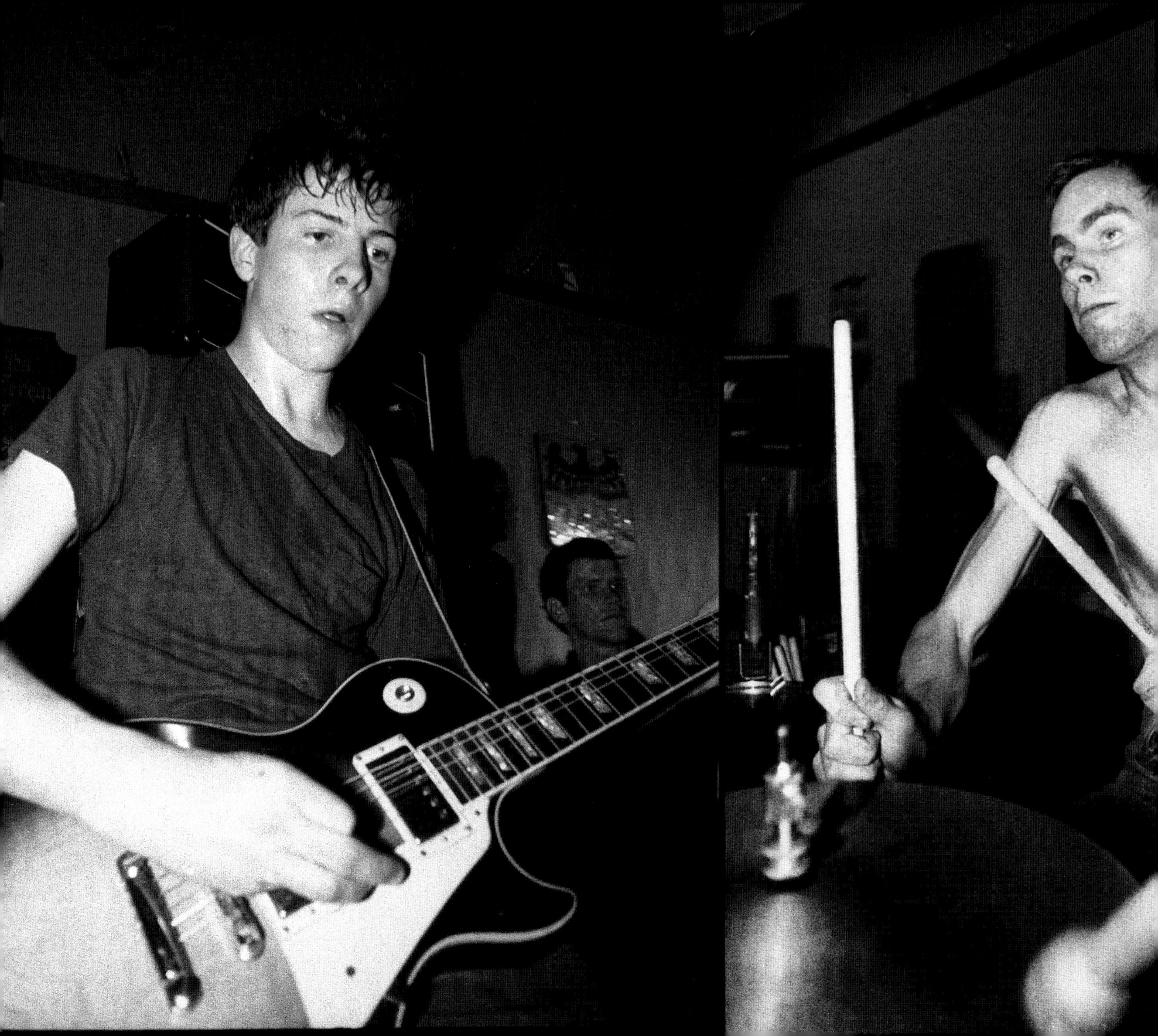

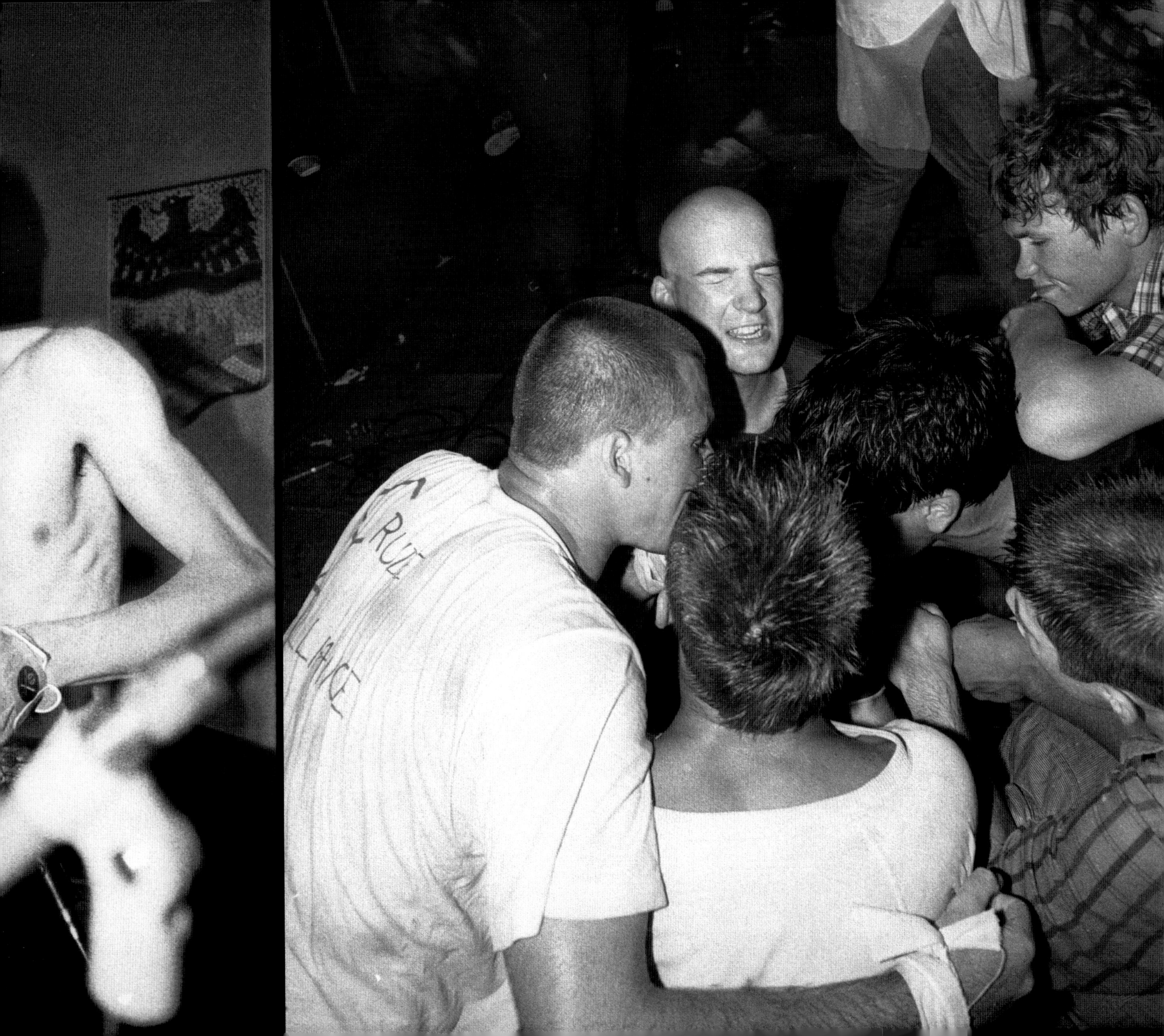

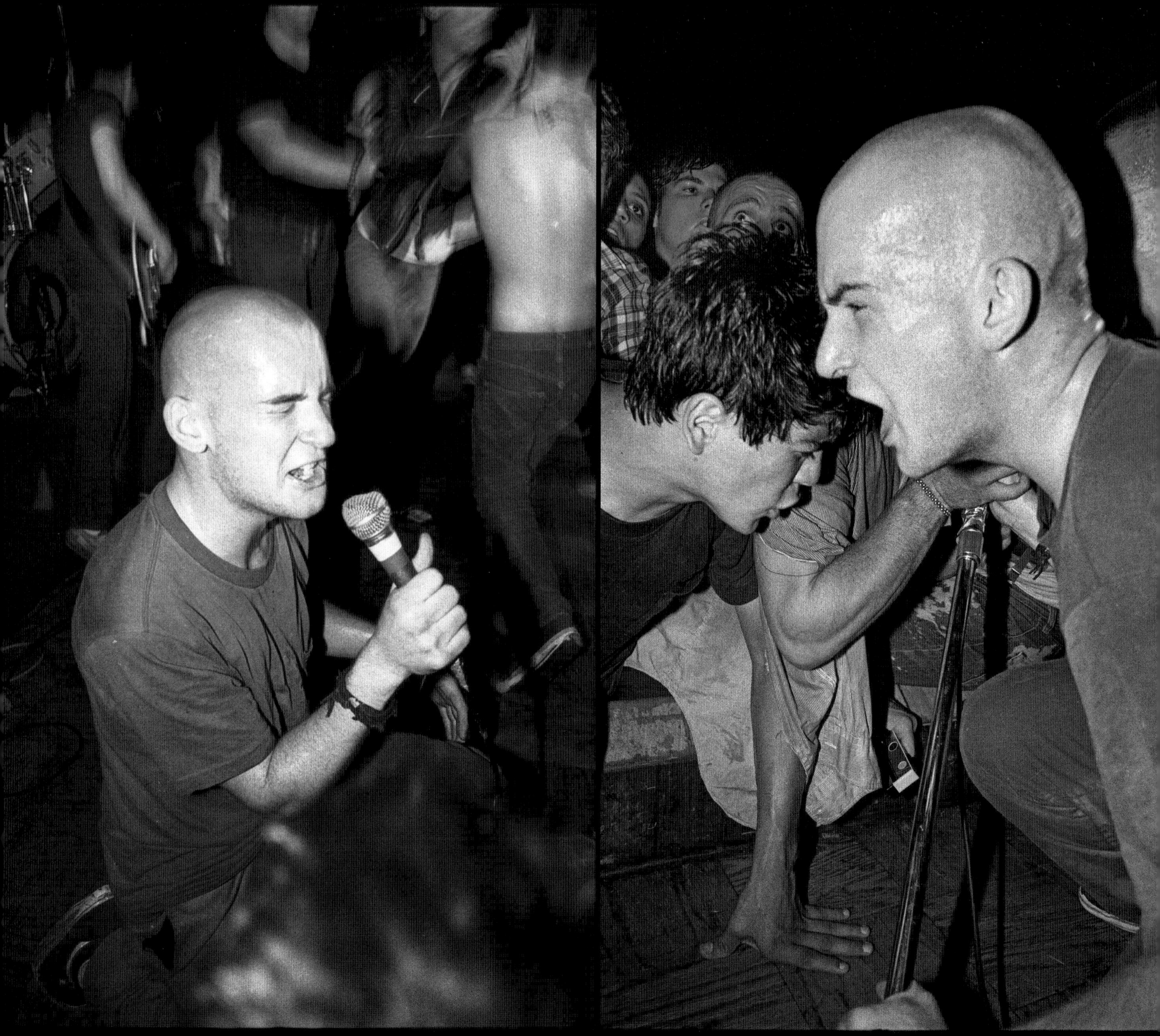

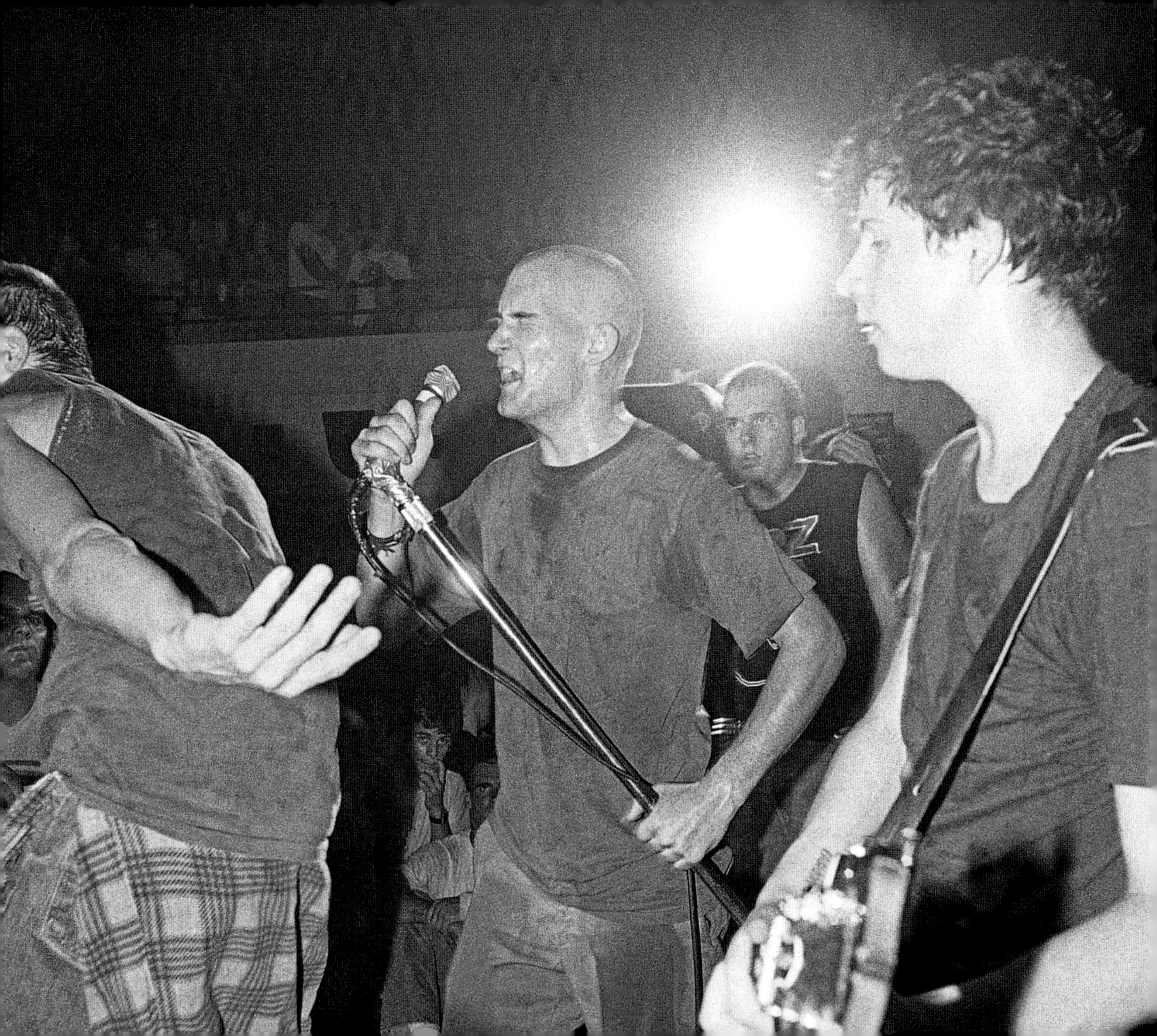

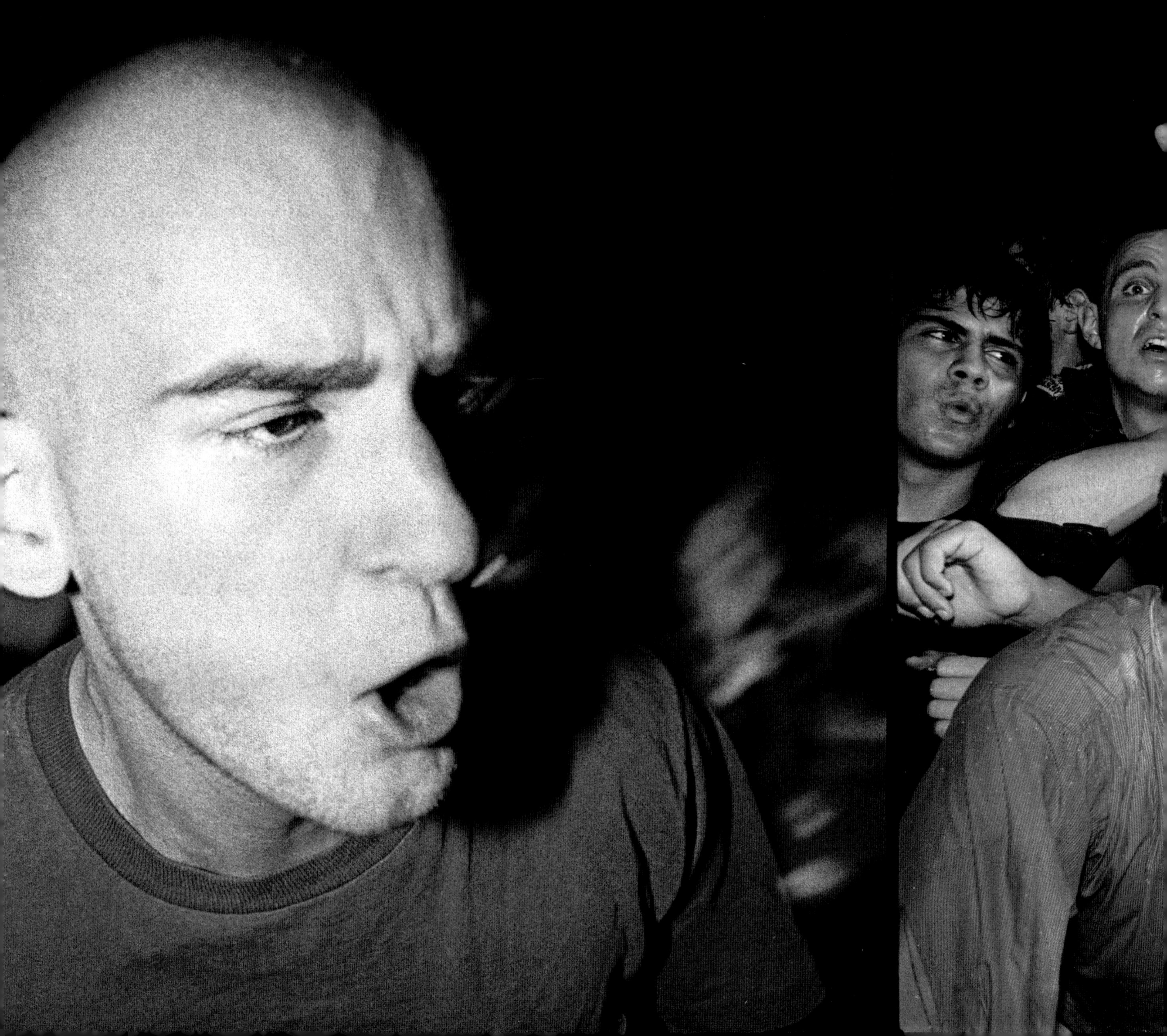

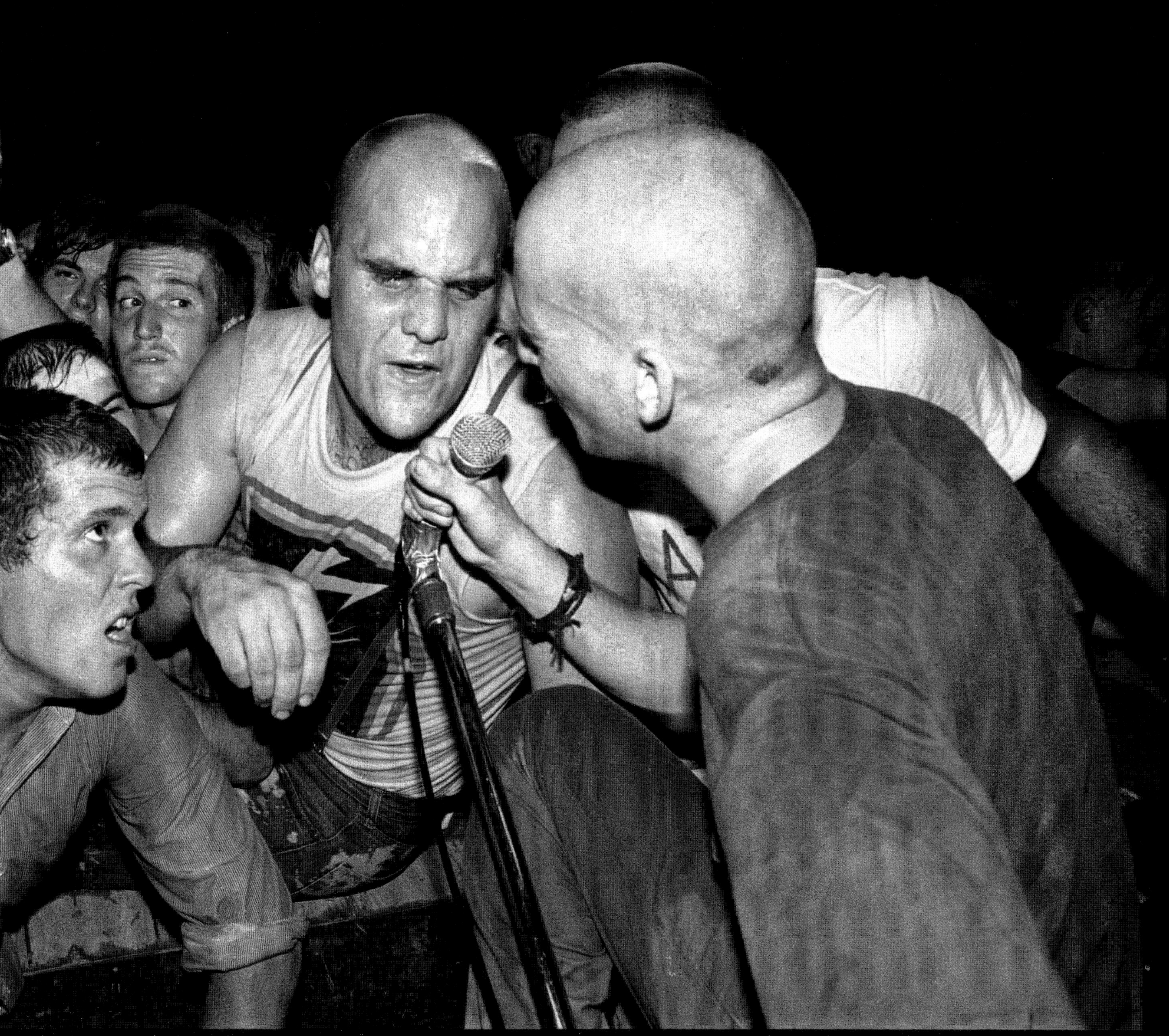

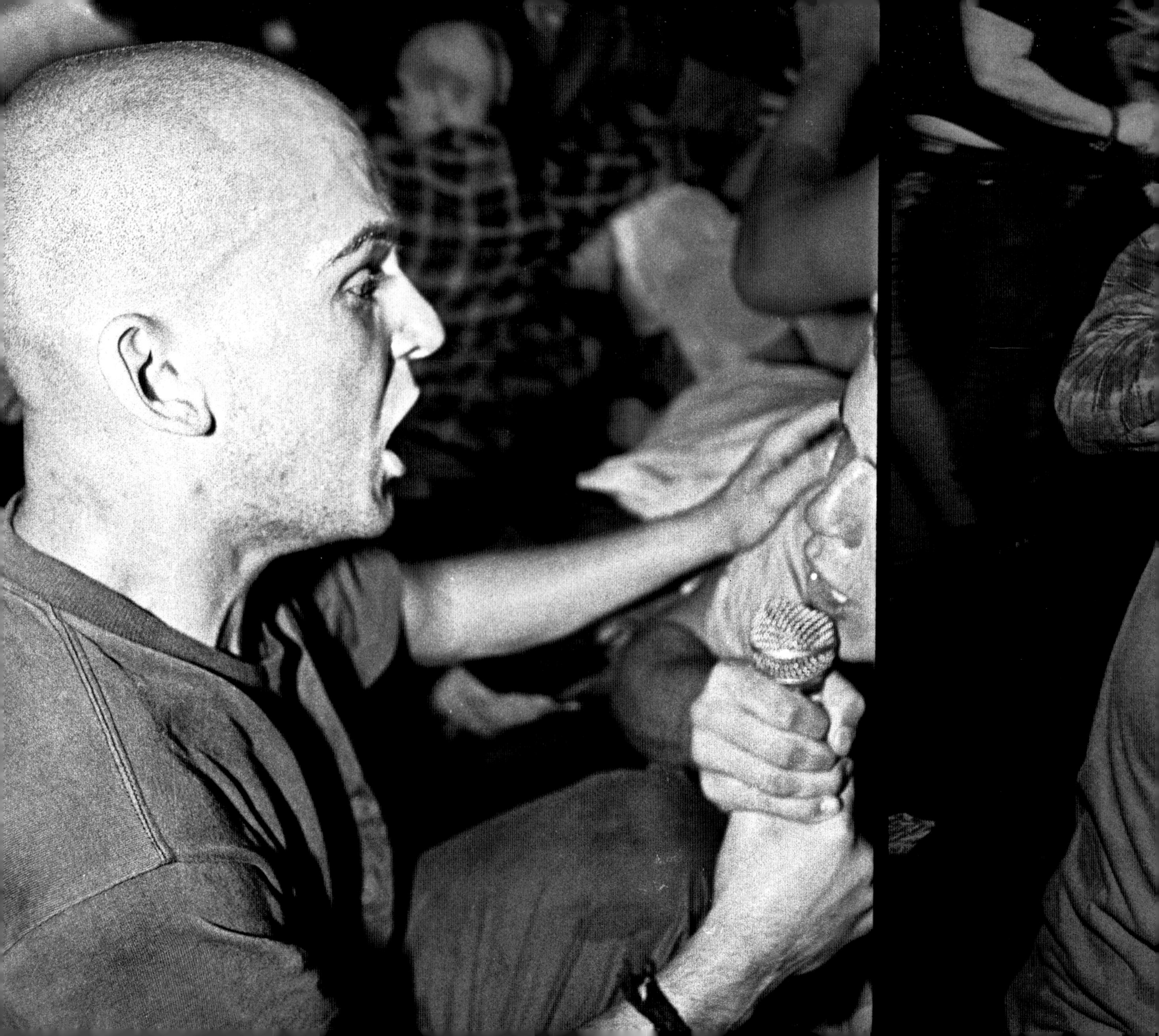

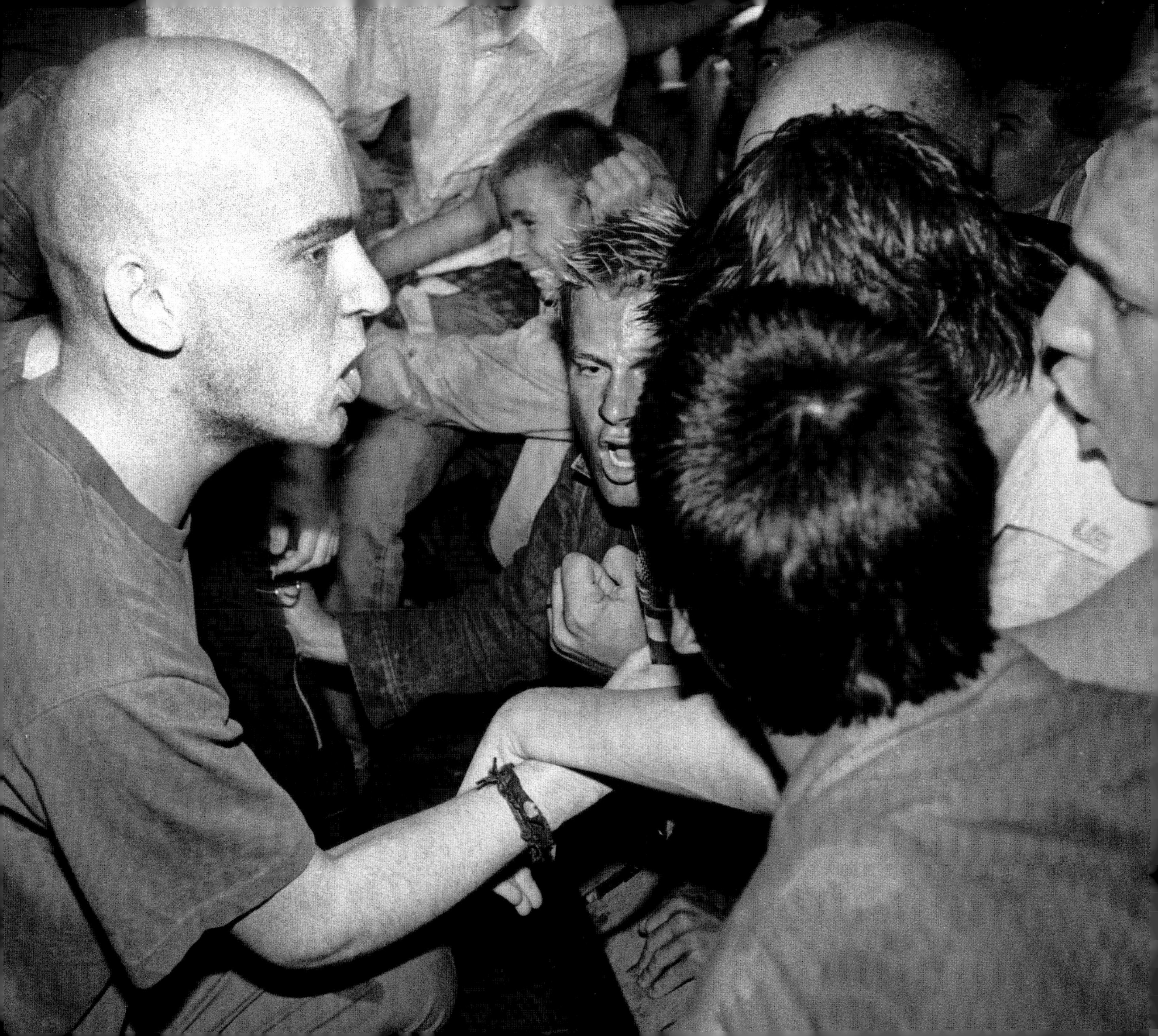

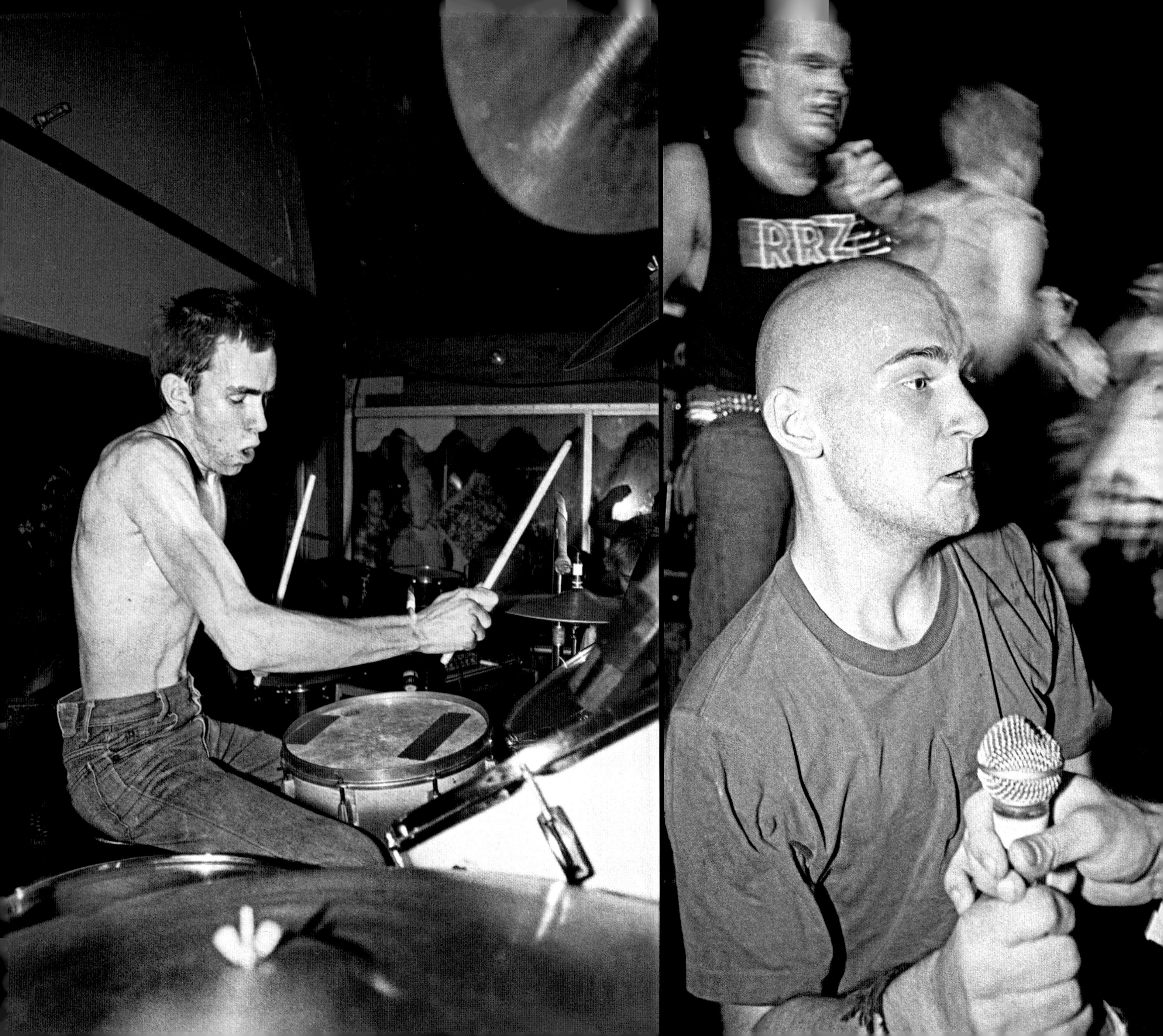
RRZ

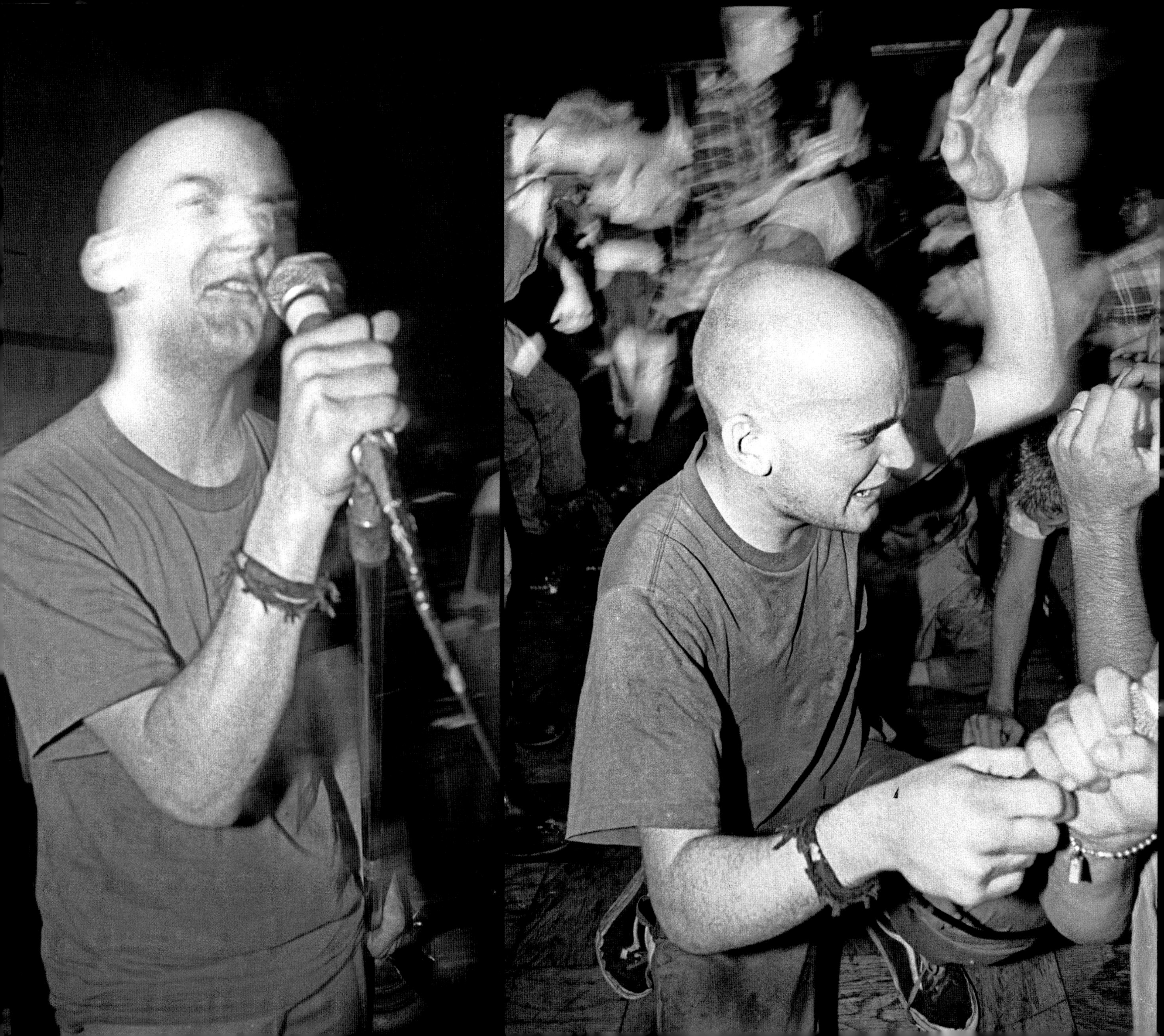

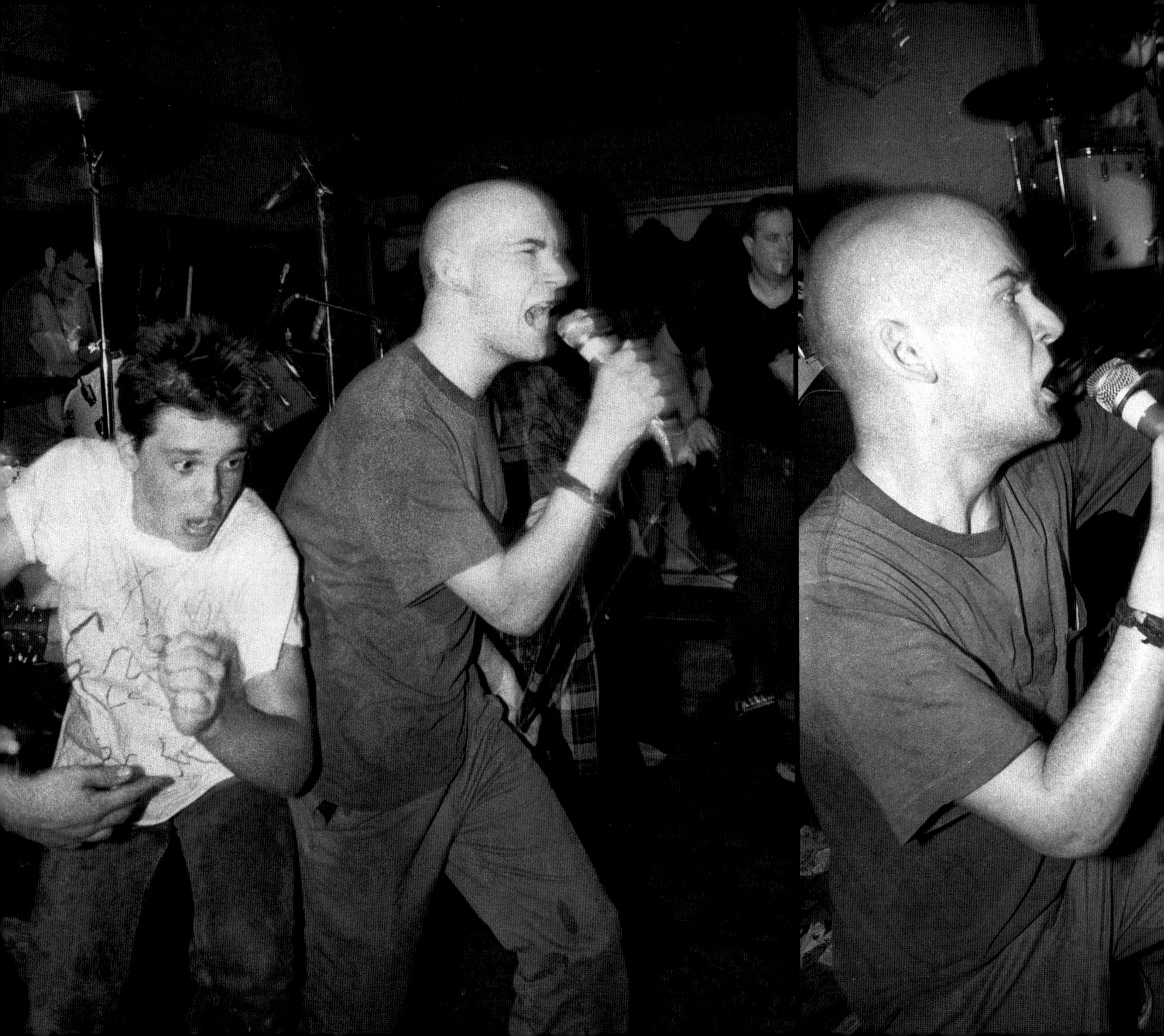

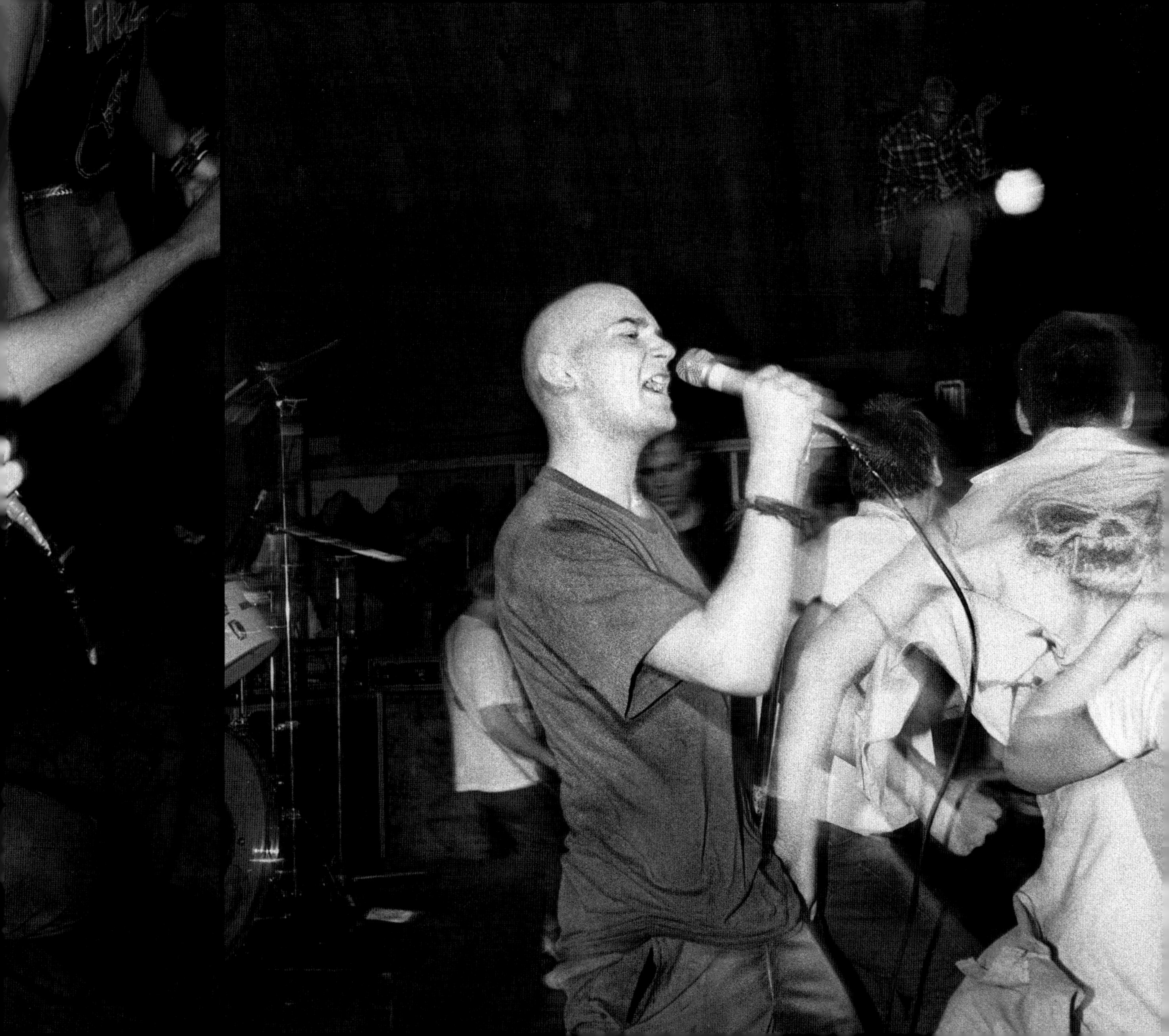

Jeff, Ian, and Jello before the show.

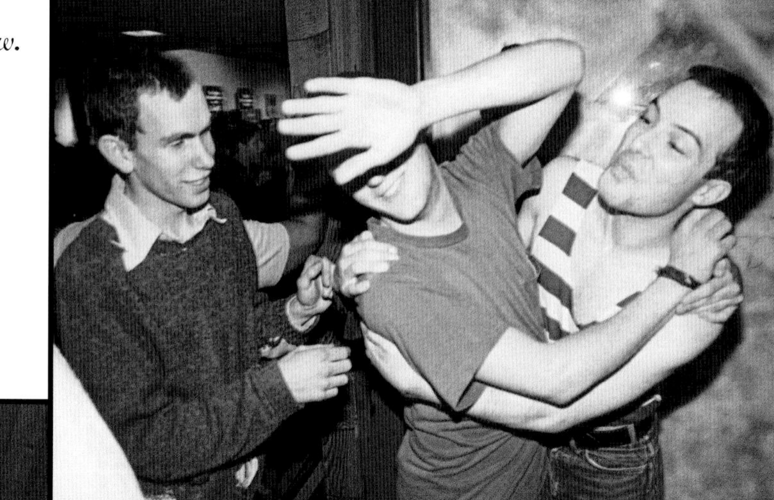

Dead Kennedys set.

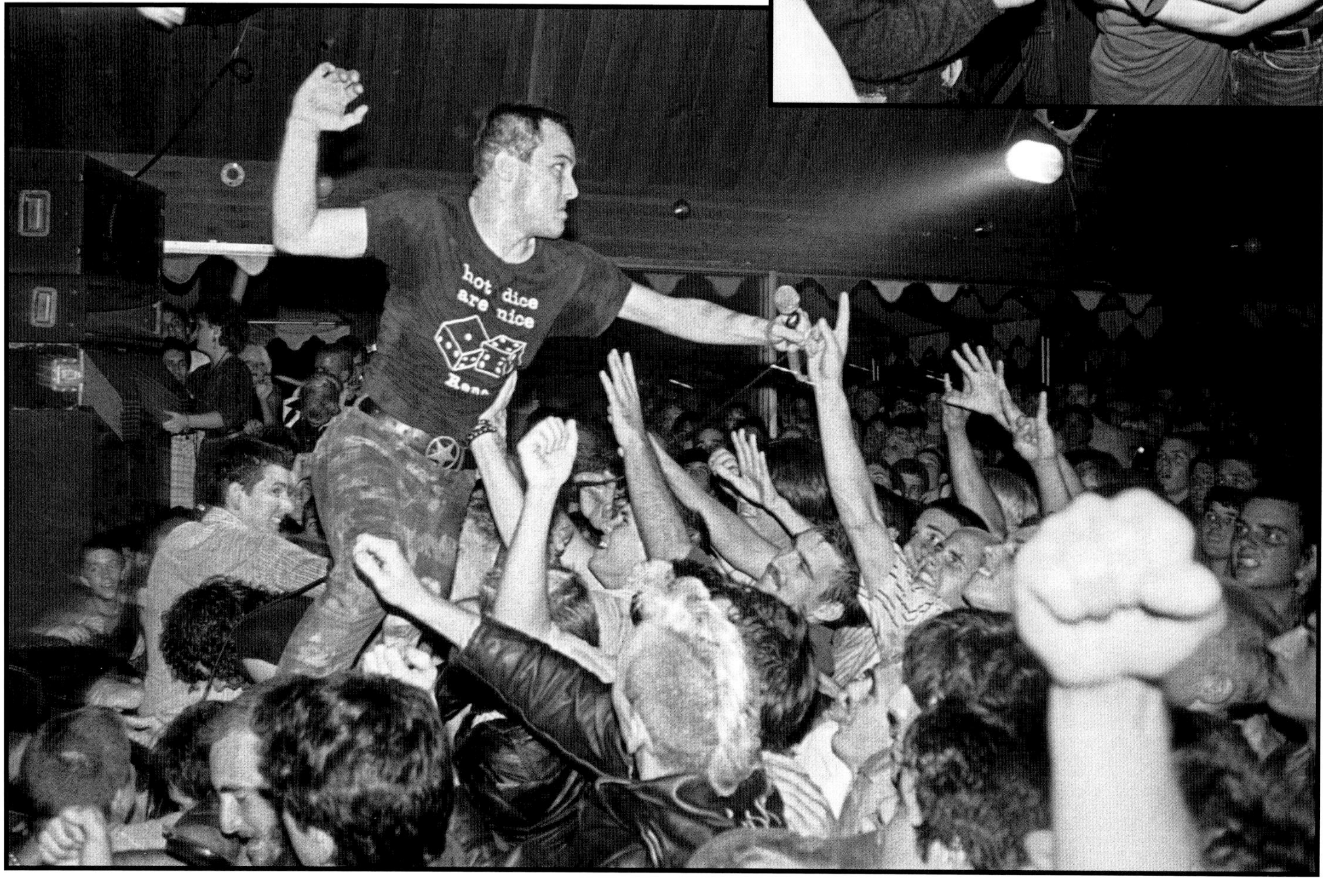

What a show! What a weekend!!

Dead Kennedys, Minor Threat, and three near-total unknowns—MDC, Zero Boys, and a "real people" punk band whose tape I liked called the Detonators.

The atmosphere and energy in the room was so positive and full-on, you could FEEL it! Not the usual tension from all the macho shit. I don't think I saw a single fight.

This night was all that and more. The crowd welcomed the Detonators, who still had Mike Mooney as their lead singer. I'm not sure they'd ever seen anything like this before.

Nor the Zero Boys. Fresh outta water from Indianapolis; supporting that all-time classic *Vicious Circle* album hardly anyone knew or heard. One note, and the crowd went wild. Dancers and divers zoomed all over the stage. Paul Zero (Mahern), still a teenager, looked like he was just trying to keep it together, and not get swept out sea. For all I know, he might have been shaking in his shoes. The crowd loved them, they held their own. Smiles and respect as far as the eye could see. As good as anyone on the West Coast, and the people knew it.

Next up—MDC. A harder sell. Slow intro, then the fastest, fiercest hardcore most people there had ever seen. The audience stood there wide-eyed, jaw-dropped, and dumbfounded, for at least a song or two. Then everyone went crazy again.

Then the band we ALL came to see, Minor Threat! And the place REALLY erupted—thrashing, rippling bodies gone wild, all the way to the back wall.

Plus, the sound was OUTSTANDING everywhere in the building. Great sound, even good sound, was such a rarity back then—especially in the rented halls and barns who'd have us. Even the monitors worked. Thank you, Rat Sound! A big older guy with a cigarette, who worked for Fear, expertly ran security from stage right, clasping his hands in a stirrup, so all the stage-diving hordes could get a running leap and let fly.

Minor Threat and the whole DC crew were already fueled by the fire, PMA, and the stage energy of the Bad Brains, before they even saw Dead Kennedys or Black Flag. And like DOA and the above, they could really really PLAY.

And WE had to follow.

When you go out and play after something that amazing, two things can happen. Either you stiffen up and get nervous, and actually do get blown off the stage (which Minor Threat sorta did to us two nights earlier in San Francisco); or the adrenaline takes over because you're already UP, if not possessed, and you rise to a whole other level. The crowd takes you even higher, no drugs needed; and the sounds and spirit of all become one.

I still think we won the night, by the skin of our teeth. One of the best shows, top to bottom, I ever saw. And damn near the best show Dead Kennedys ever played.

Thanx, everybody!
—Jello Biafra

August 1, 1982
9:30 Club
Washington, DC

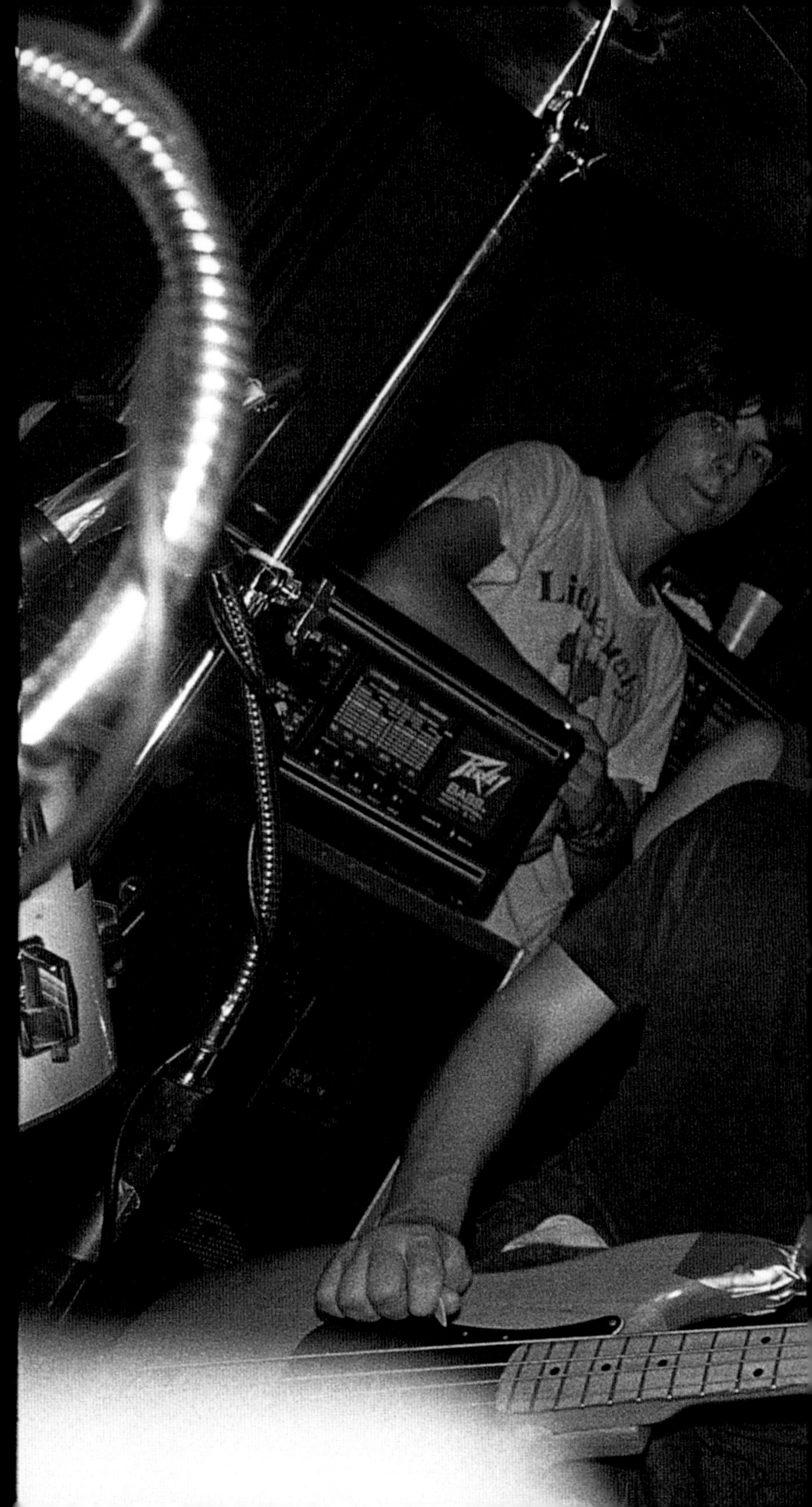

Ian MacKaye – vocals
Lyle Preslar – guitar
Brian Baker – bass
Jeff Nelson – drums

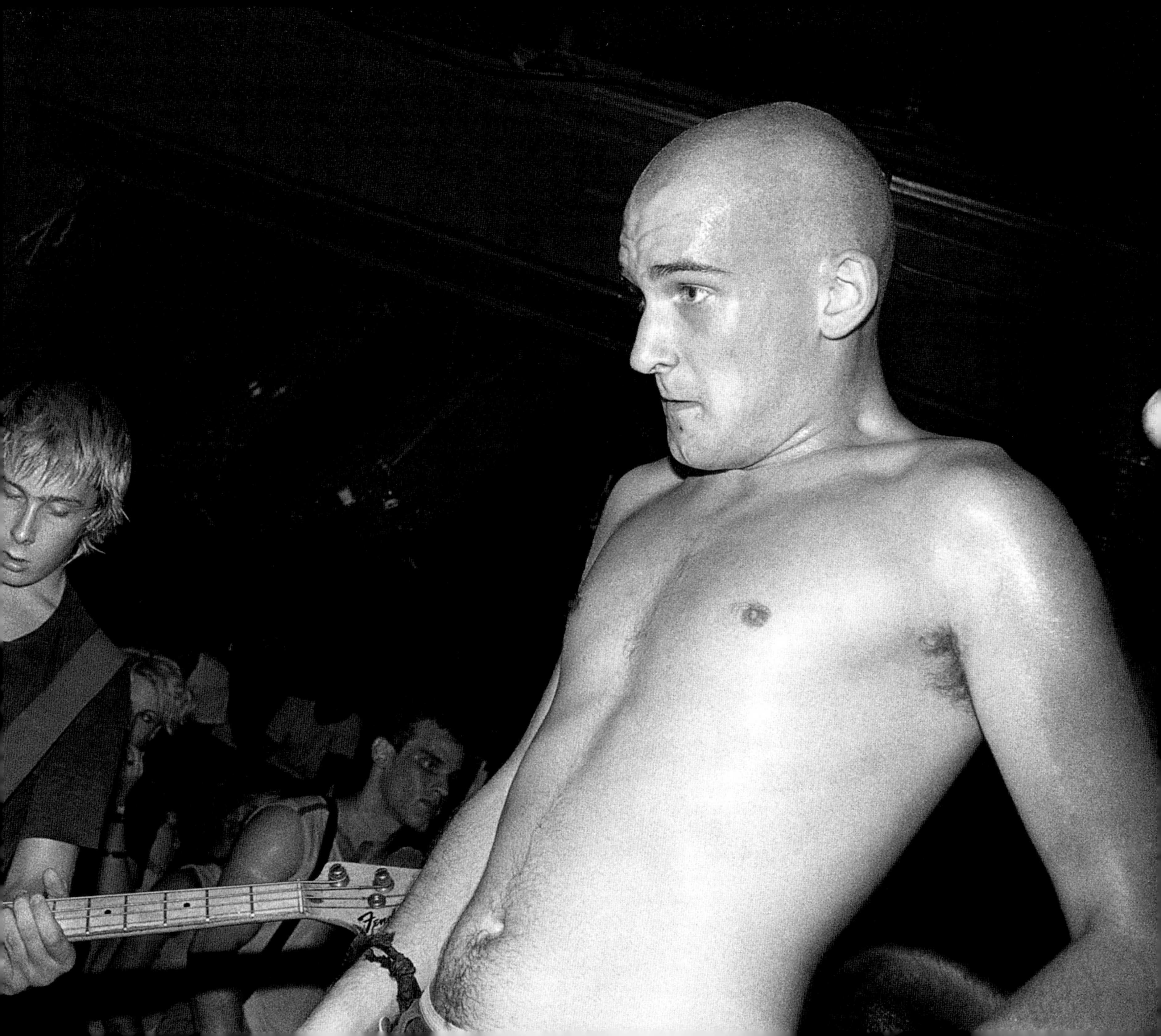

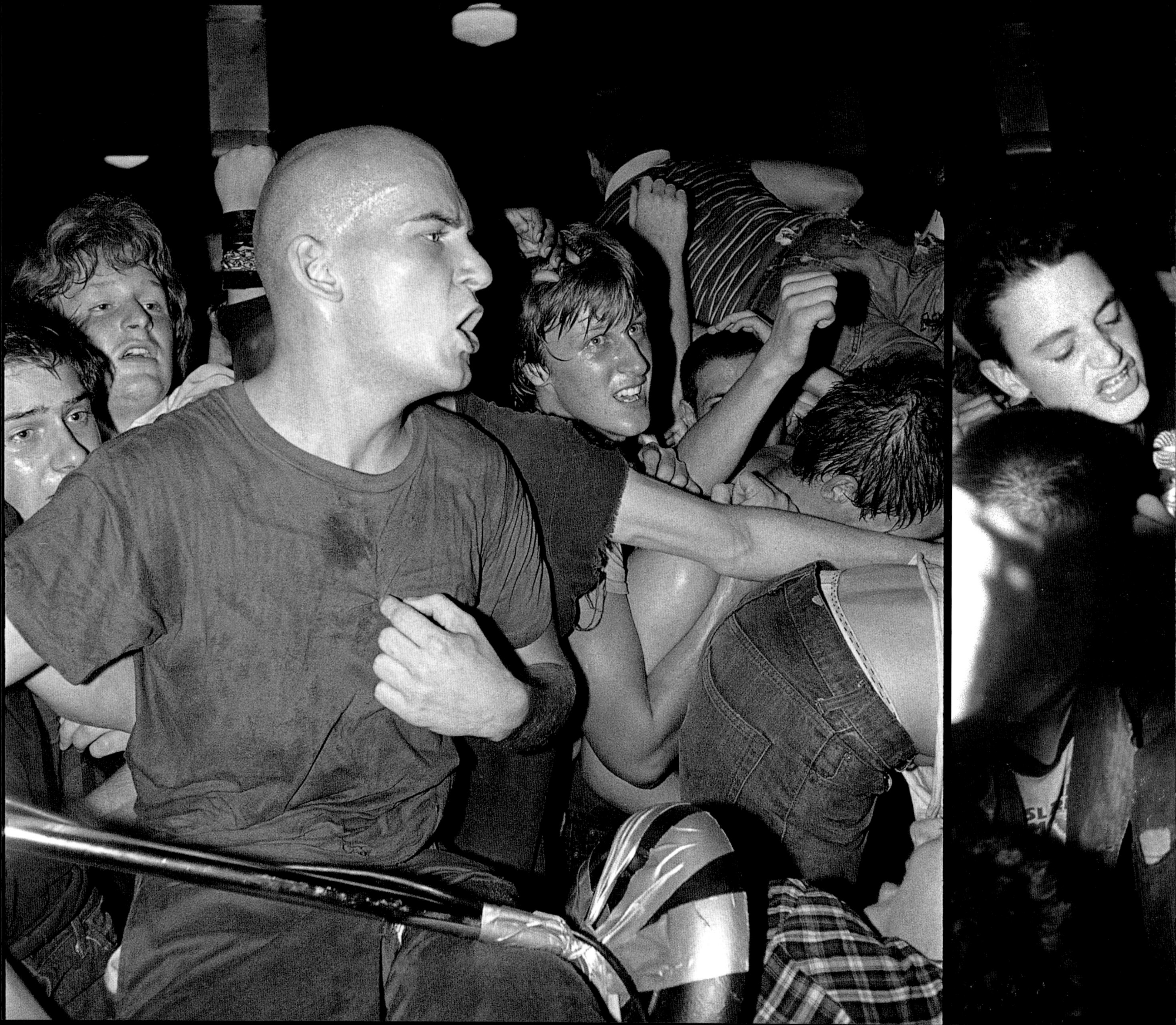

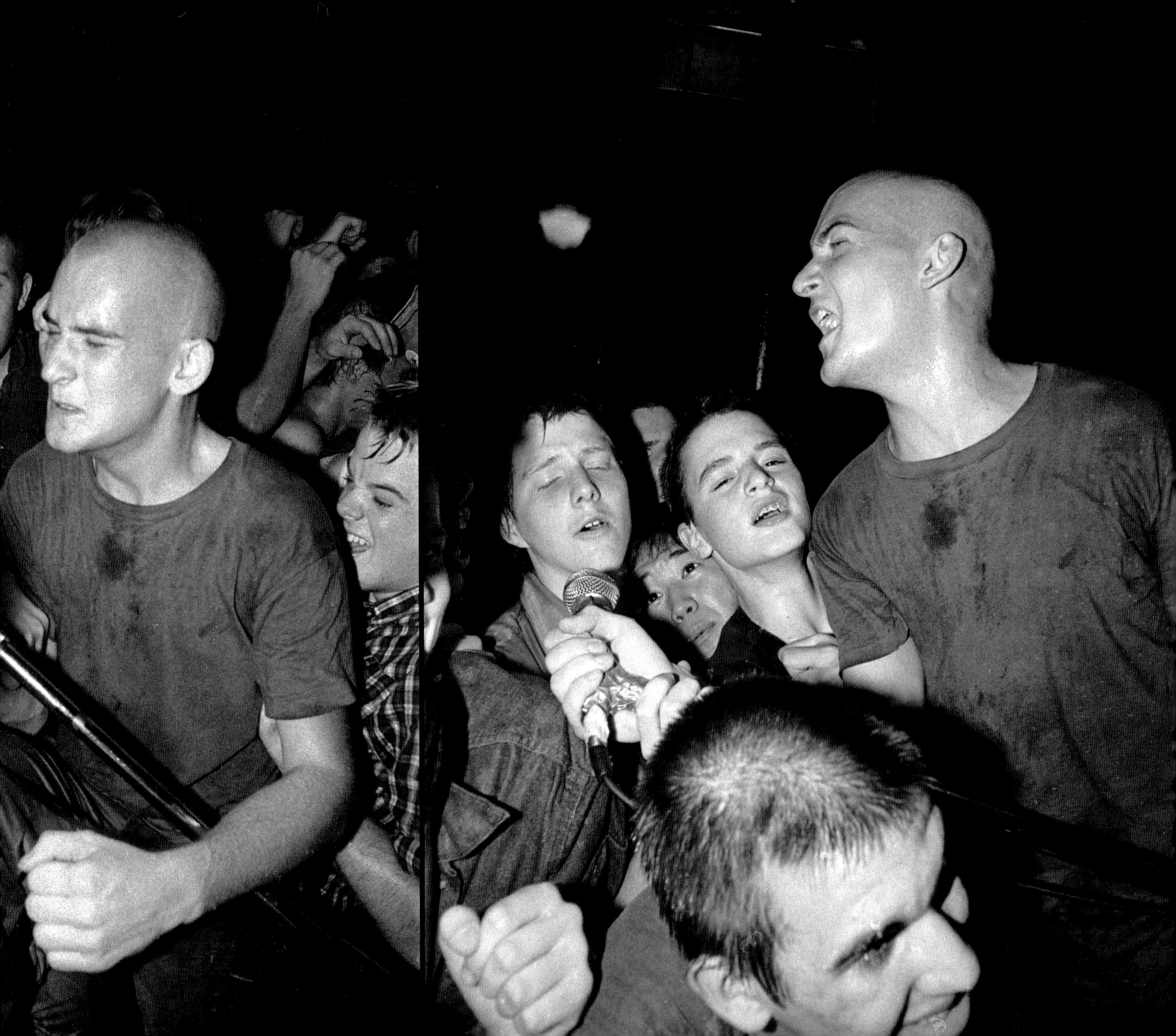

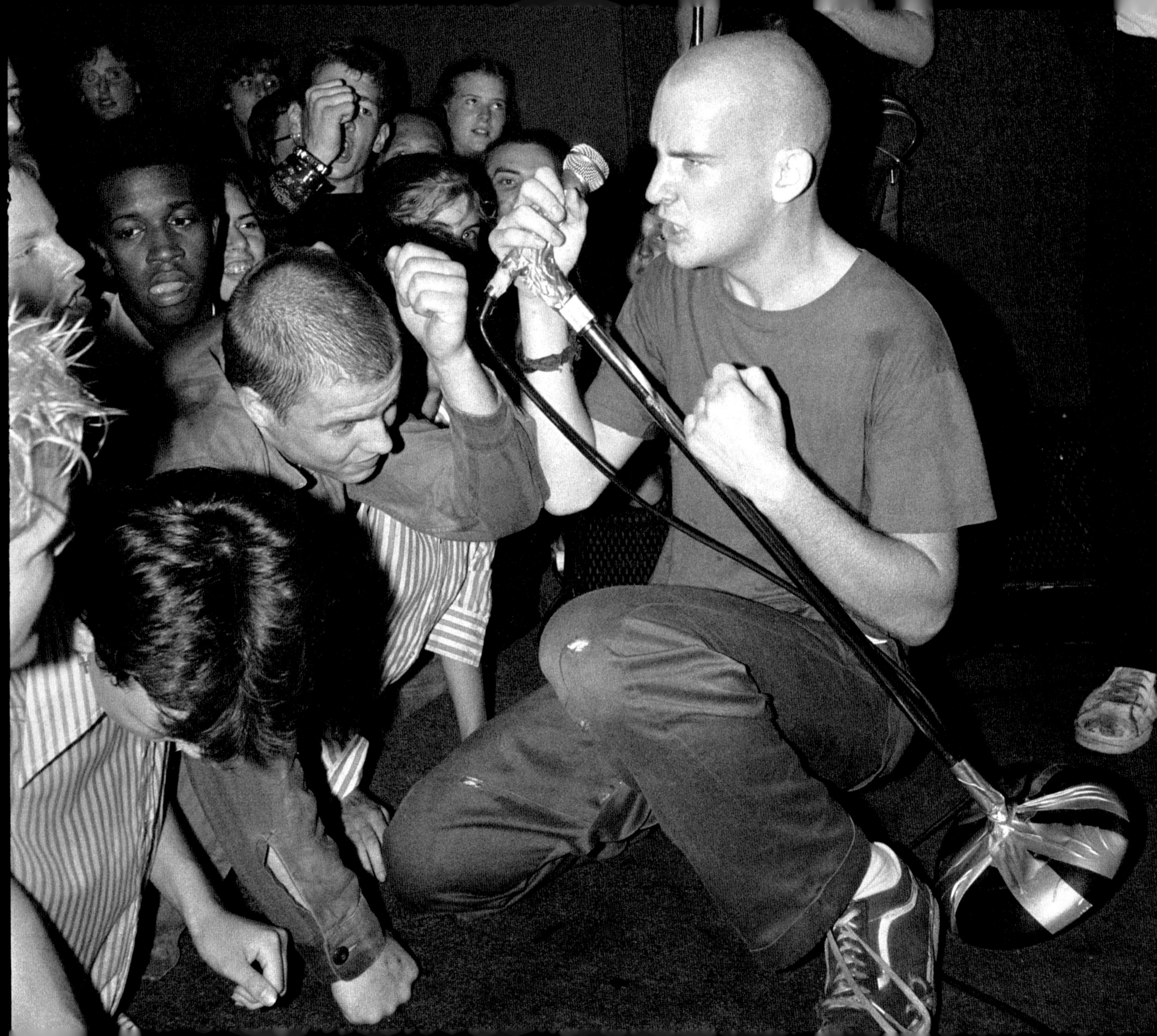

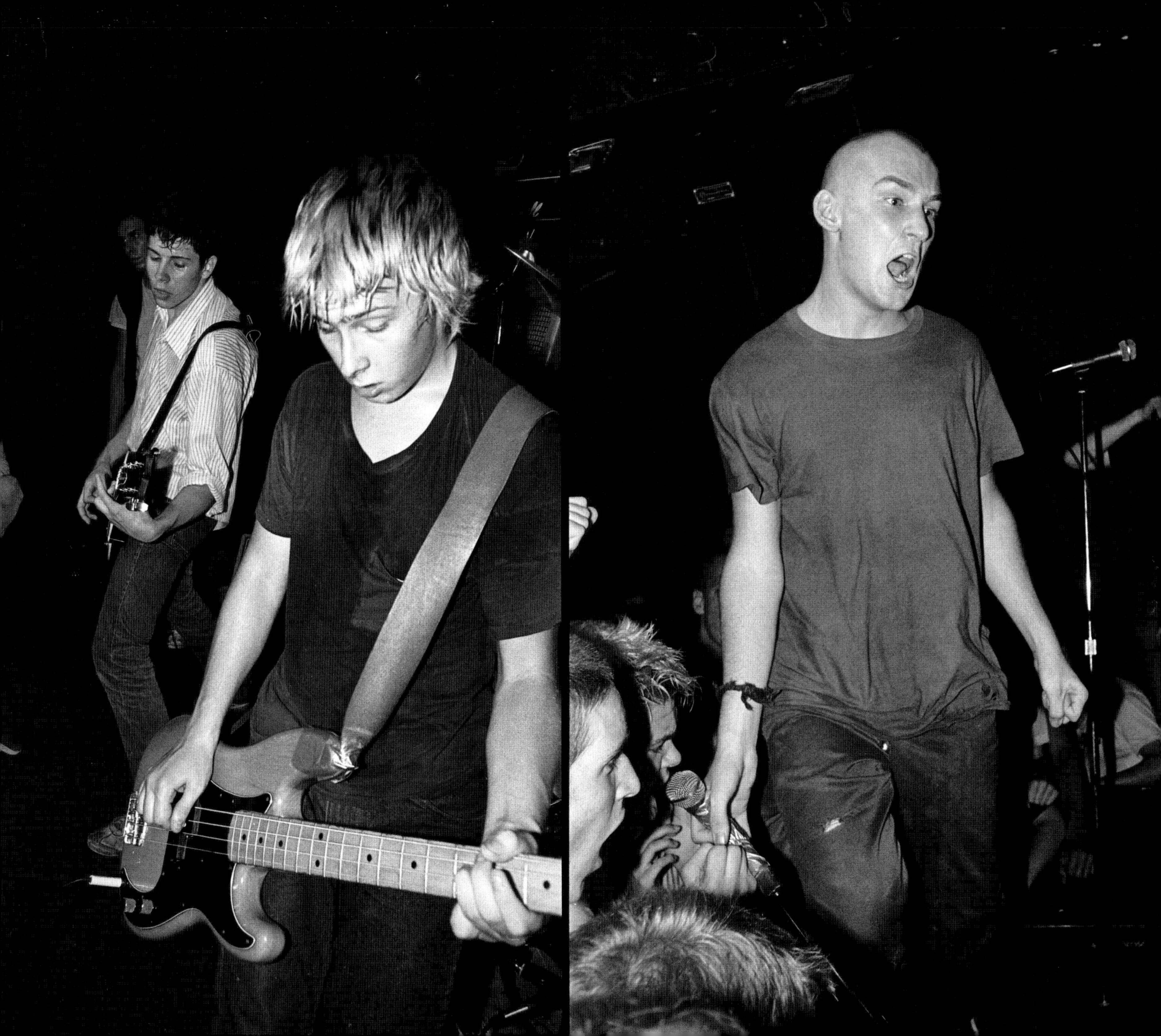

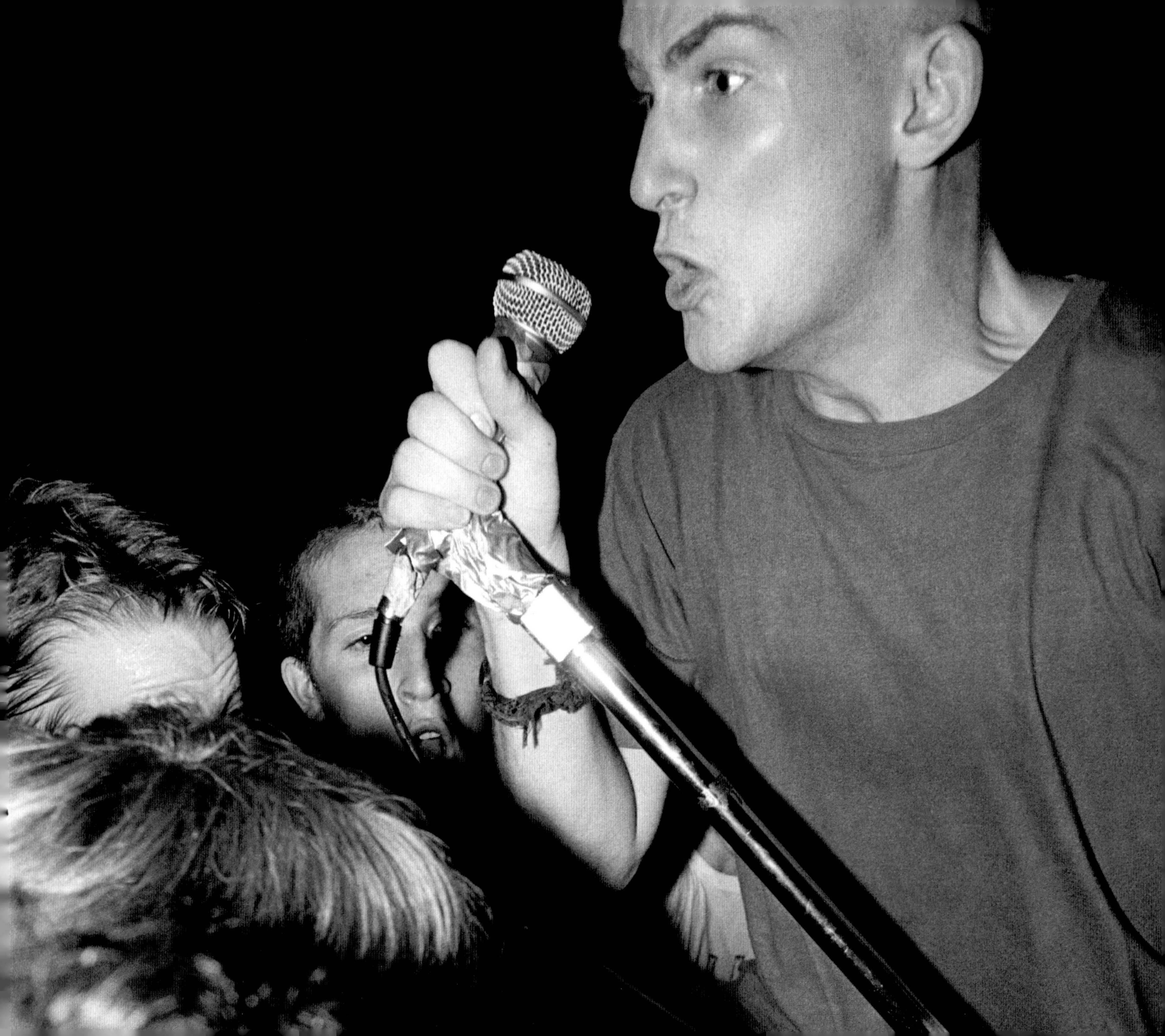

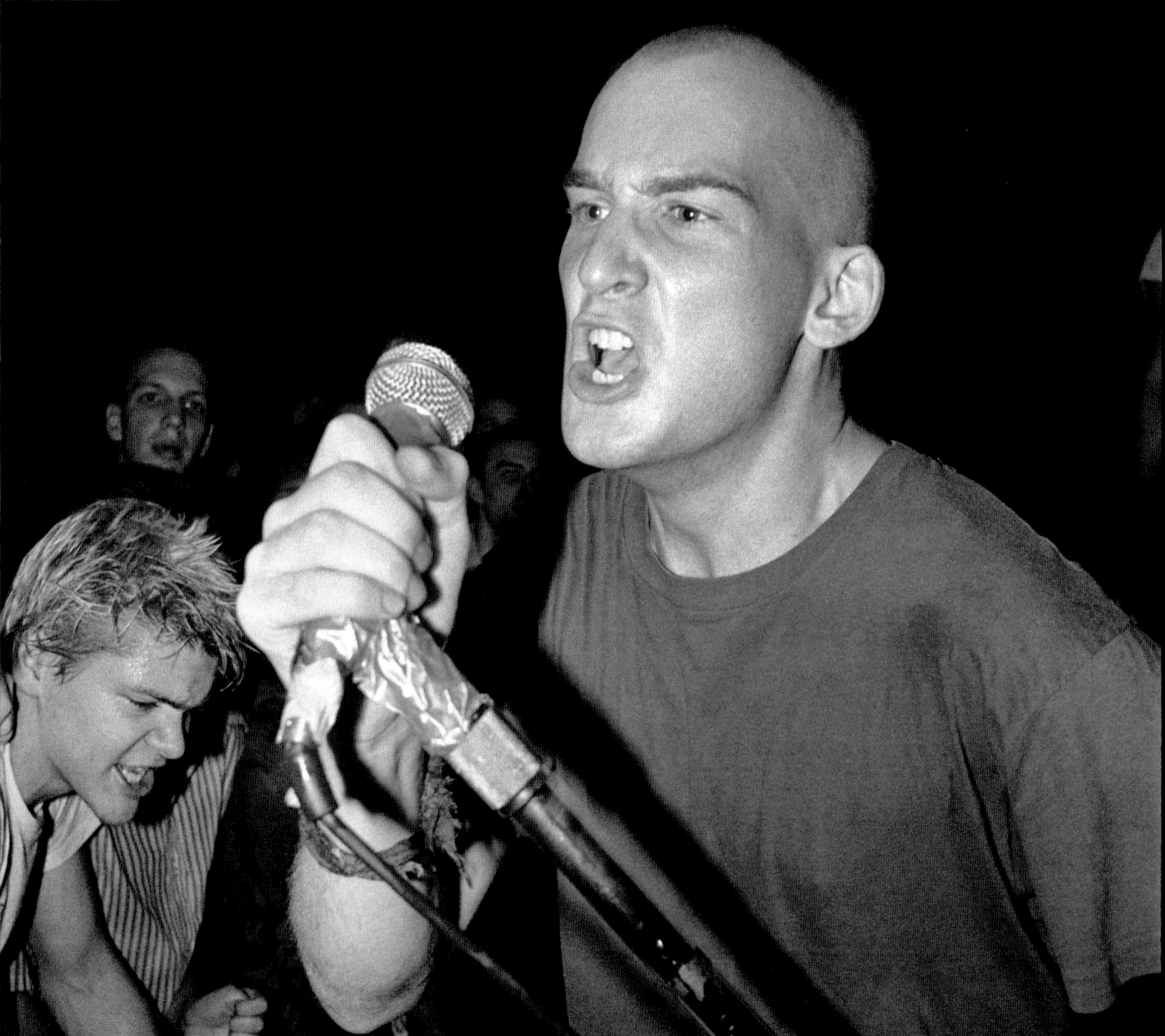

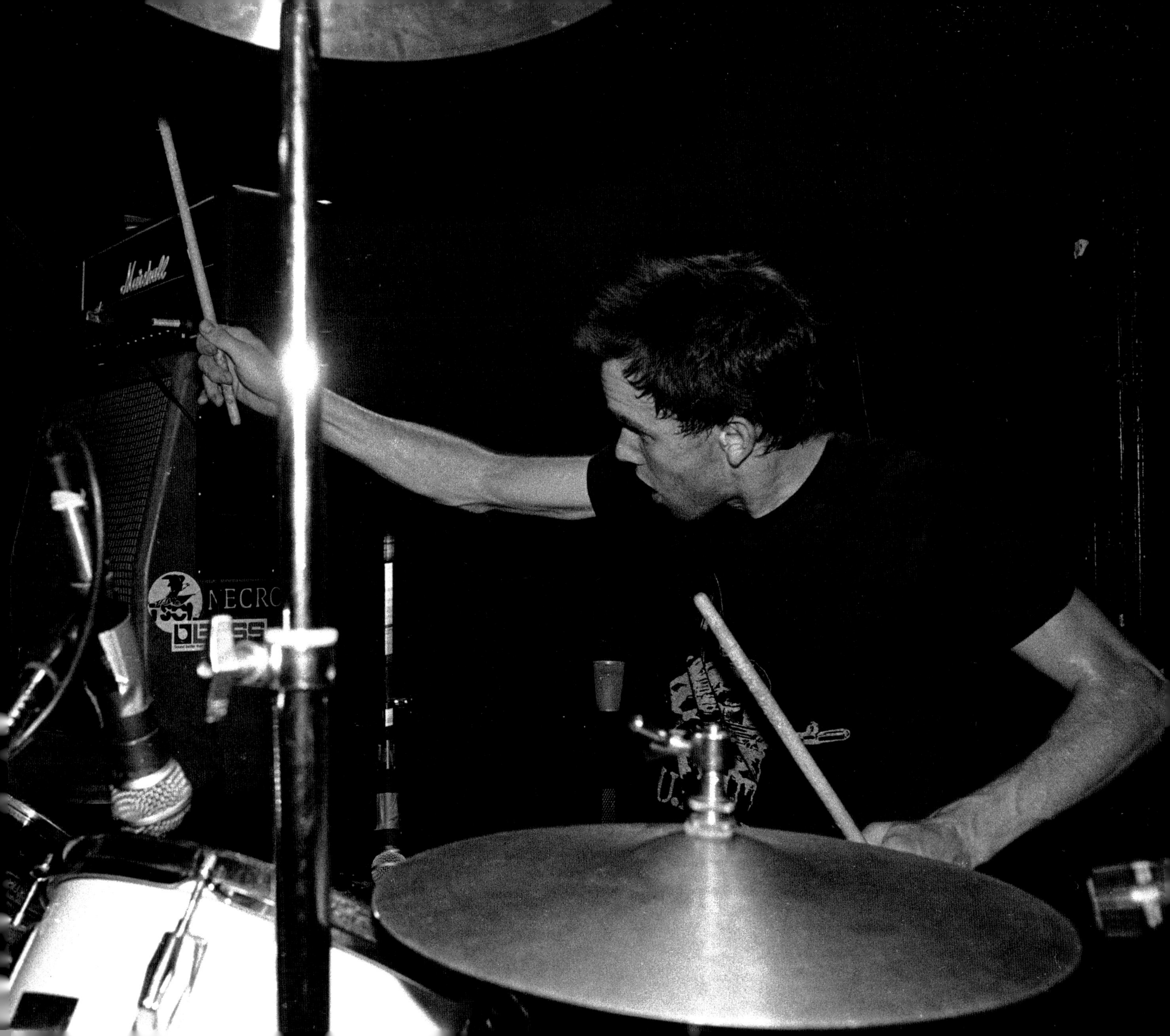
Marshall
NECRO

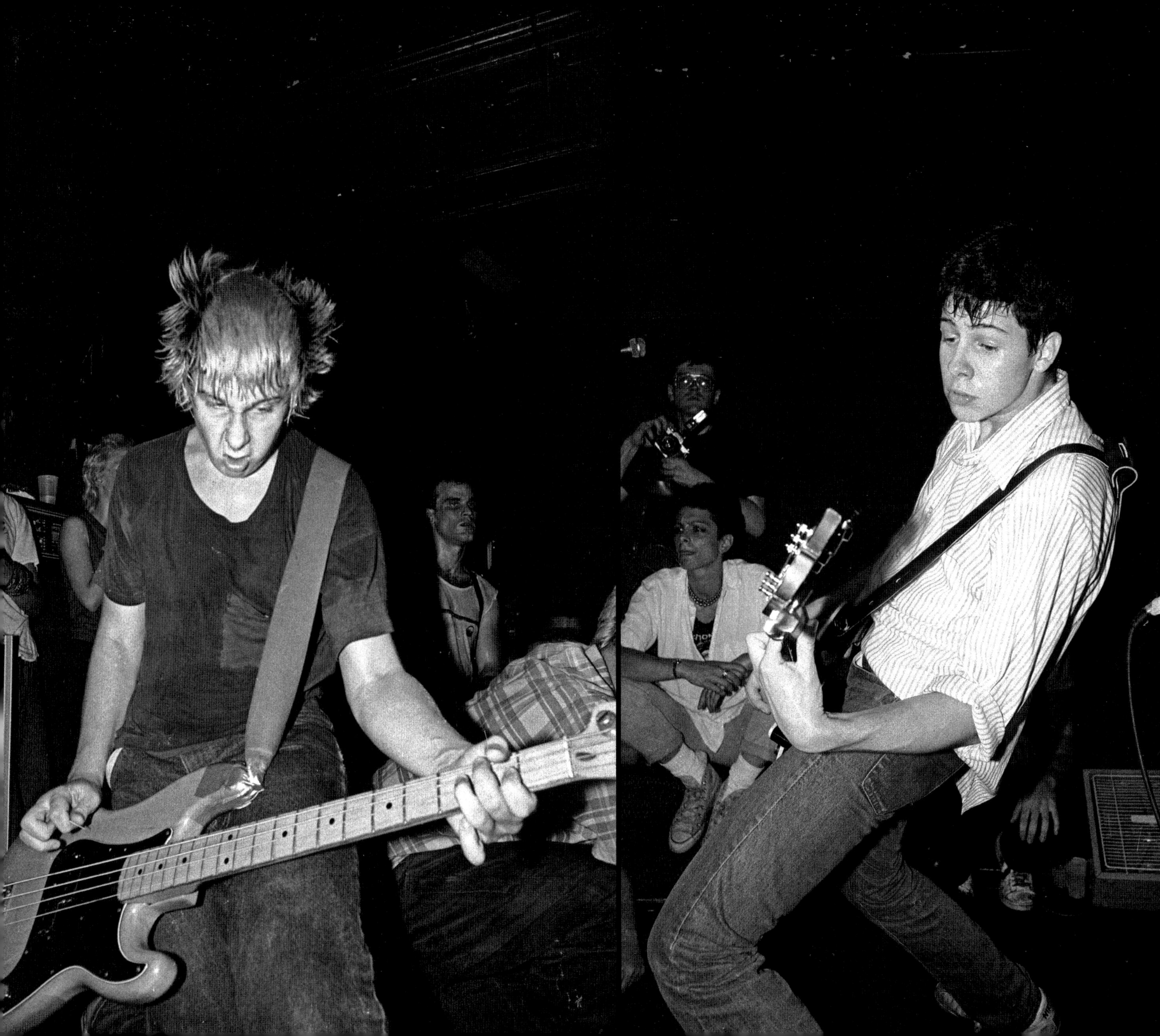

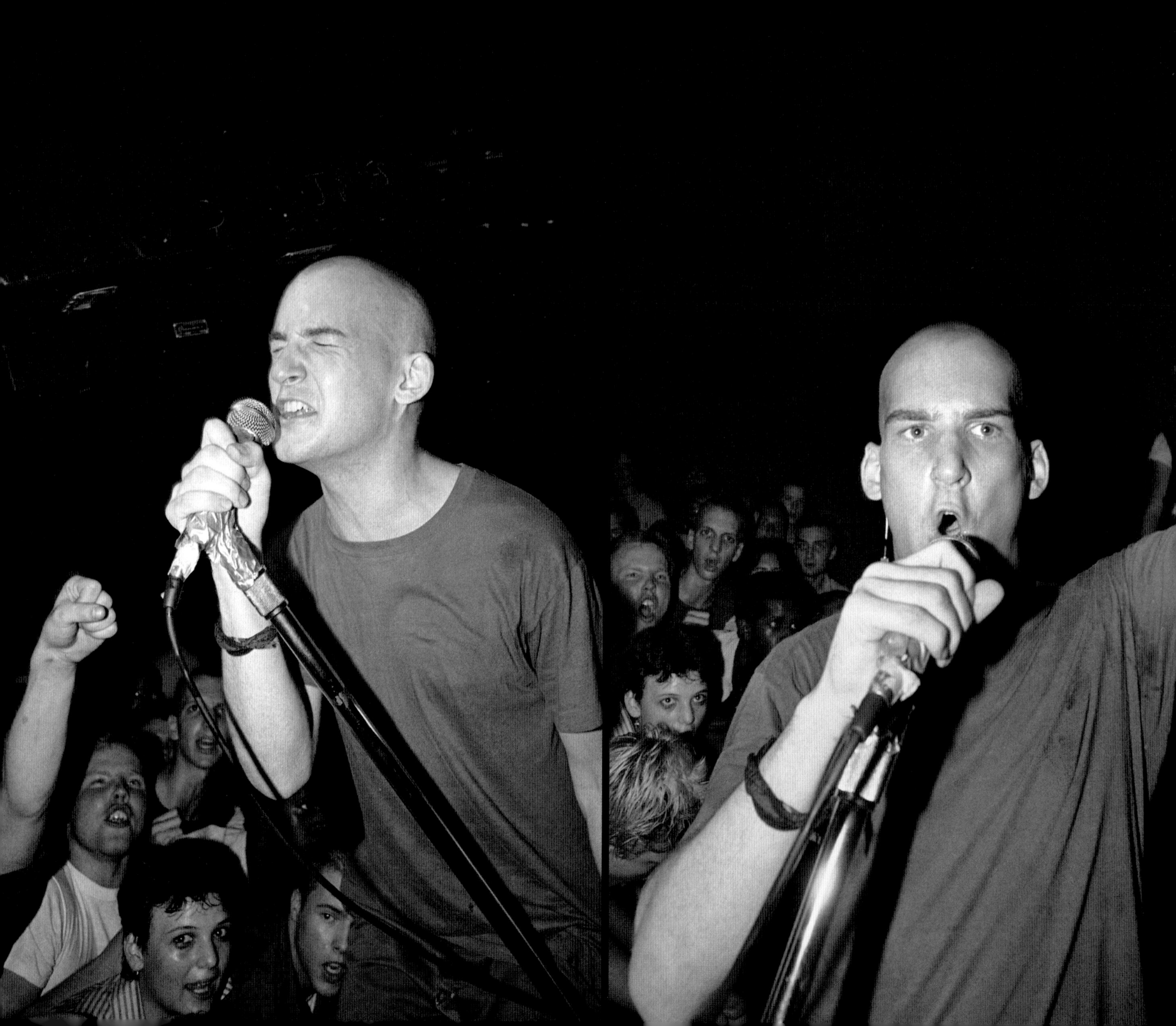

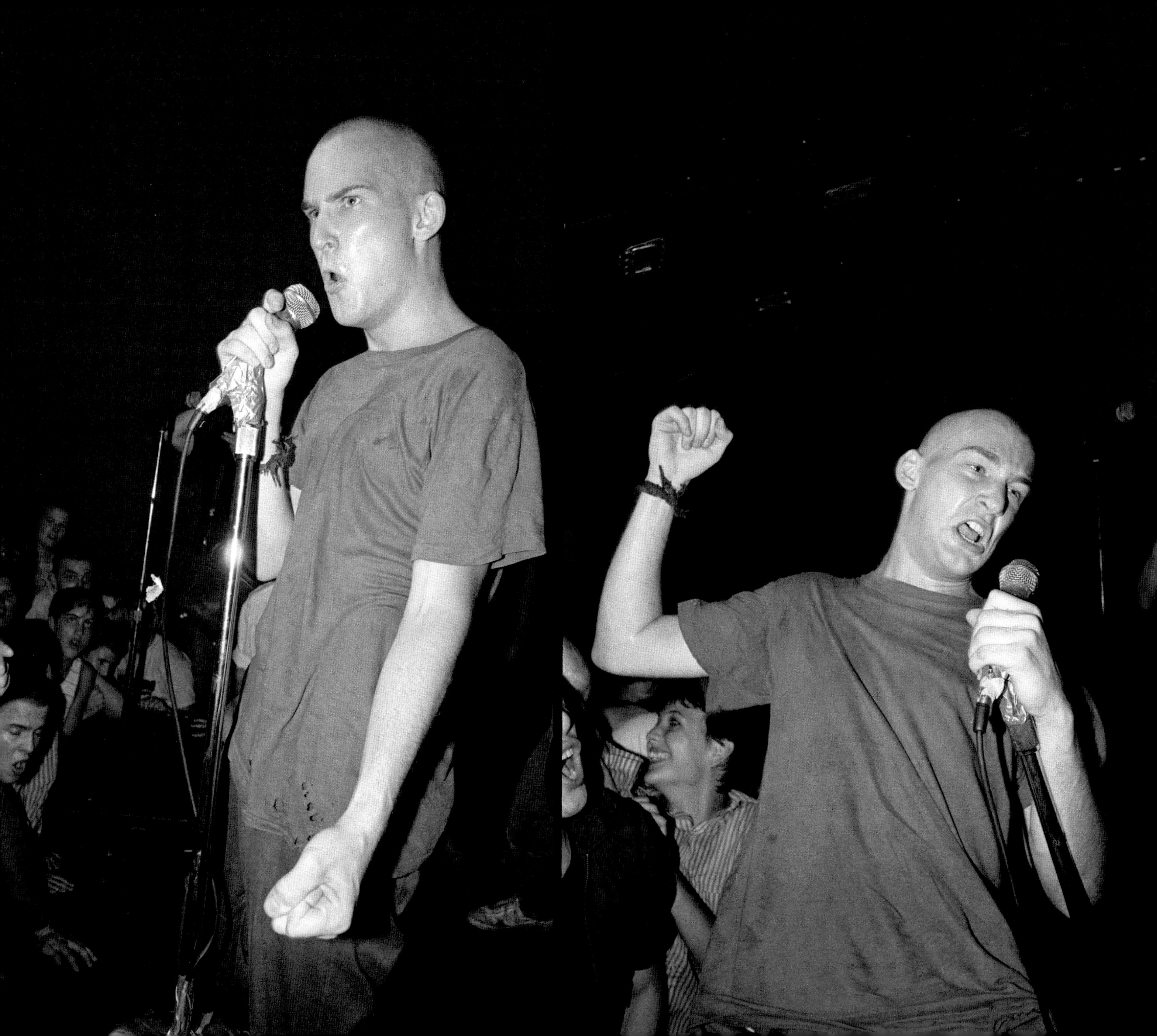

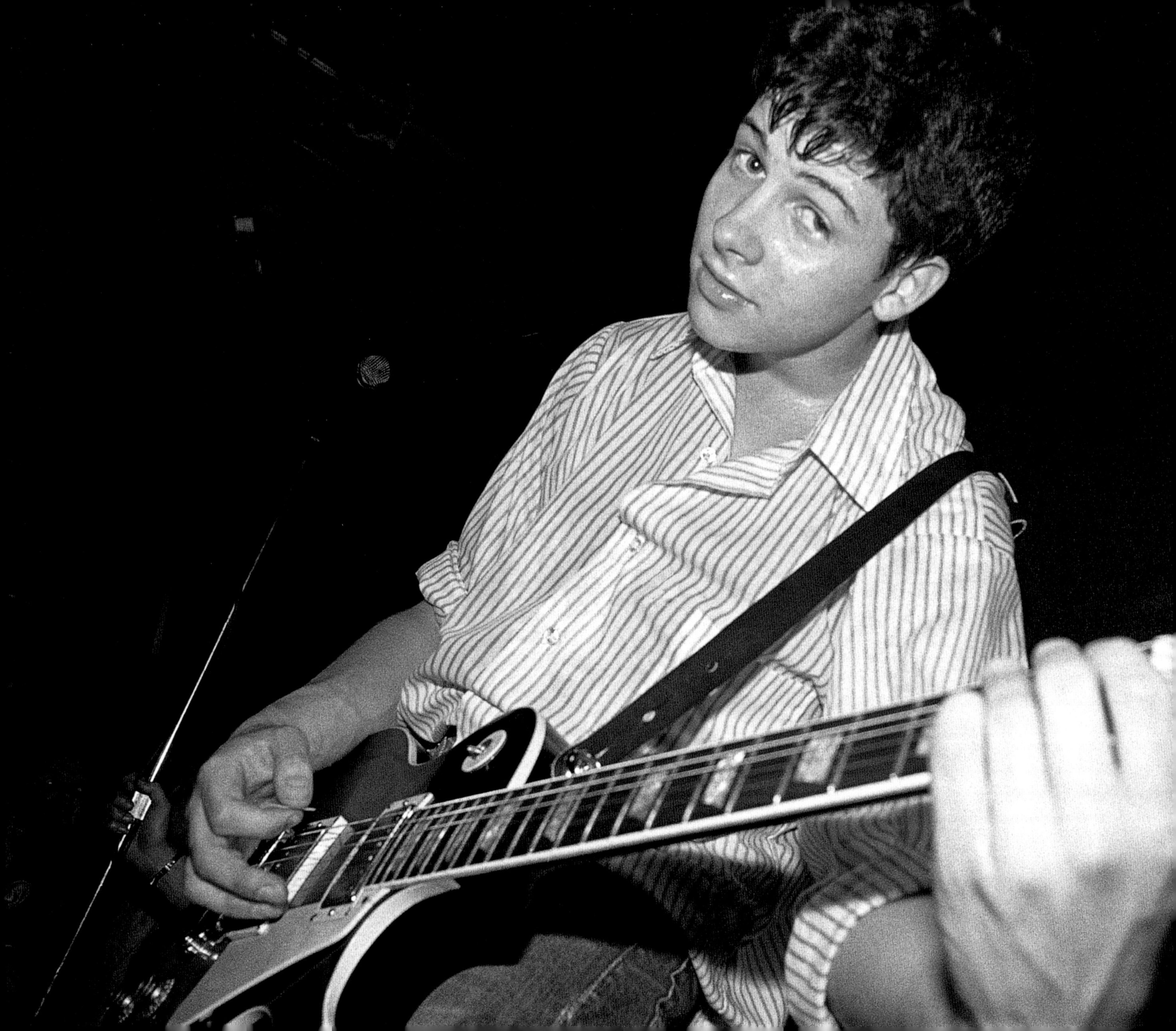

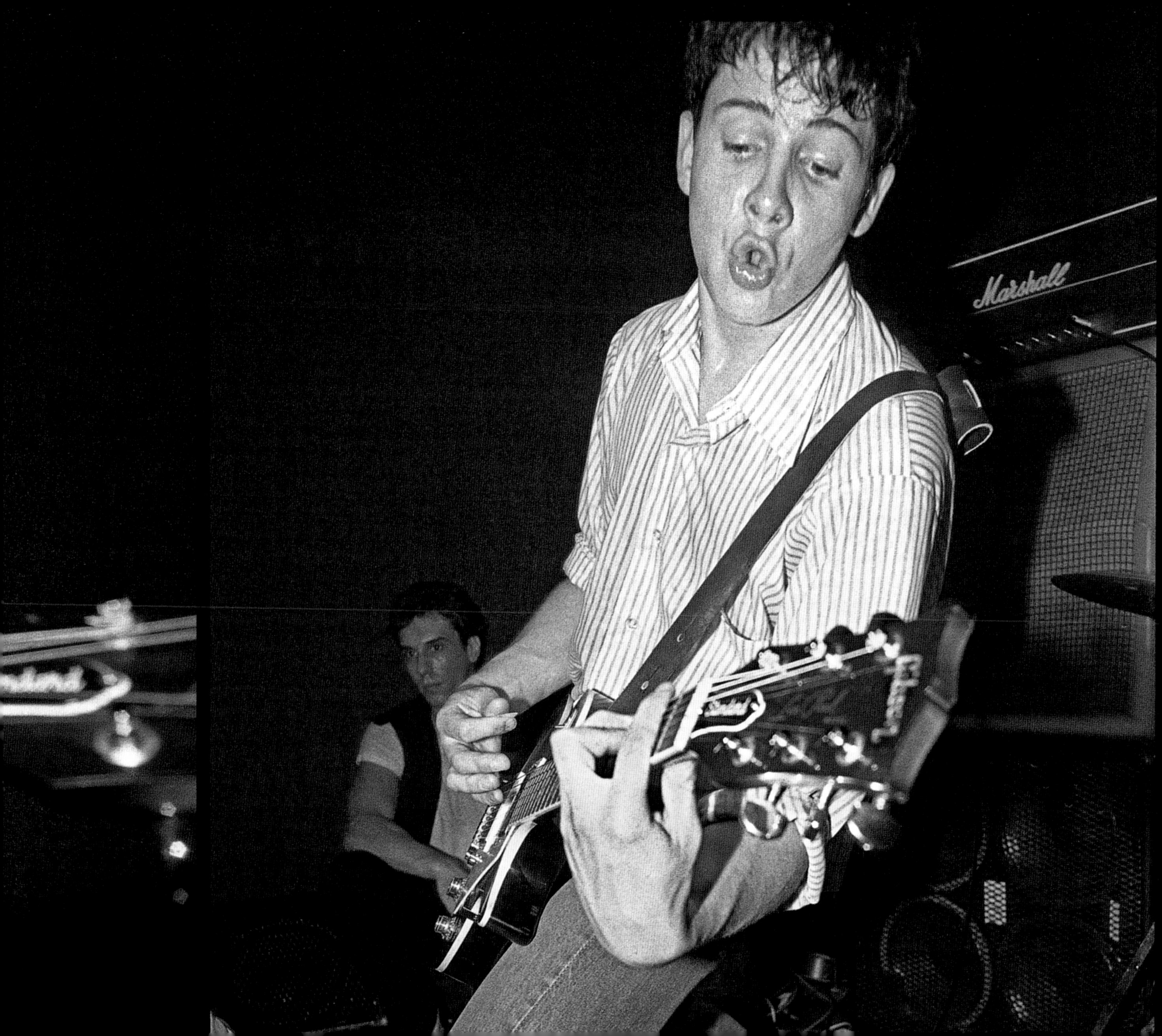
Marshall

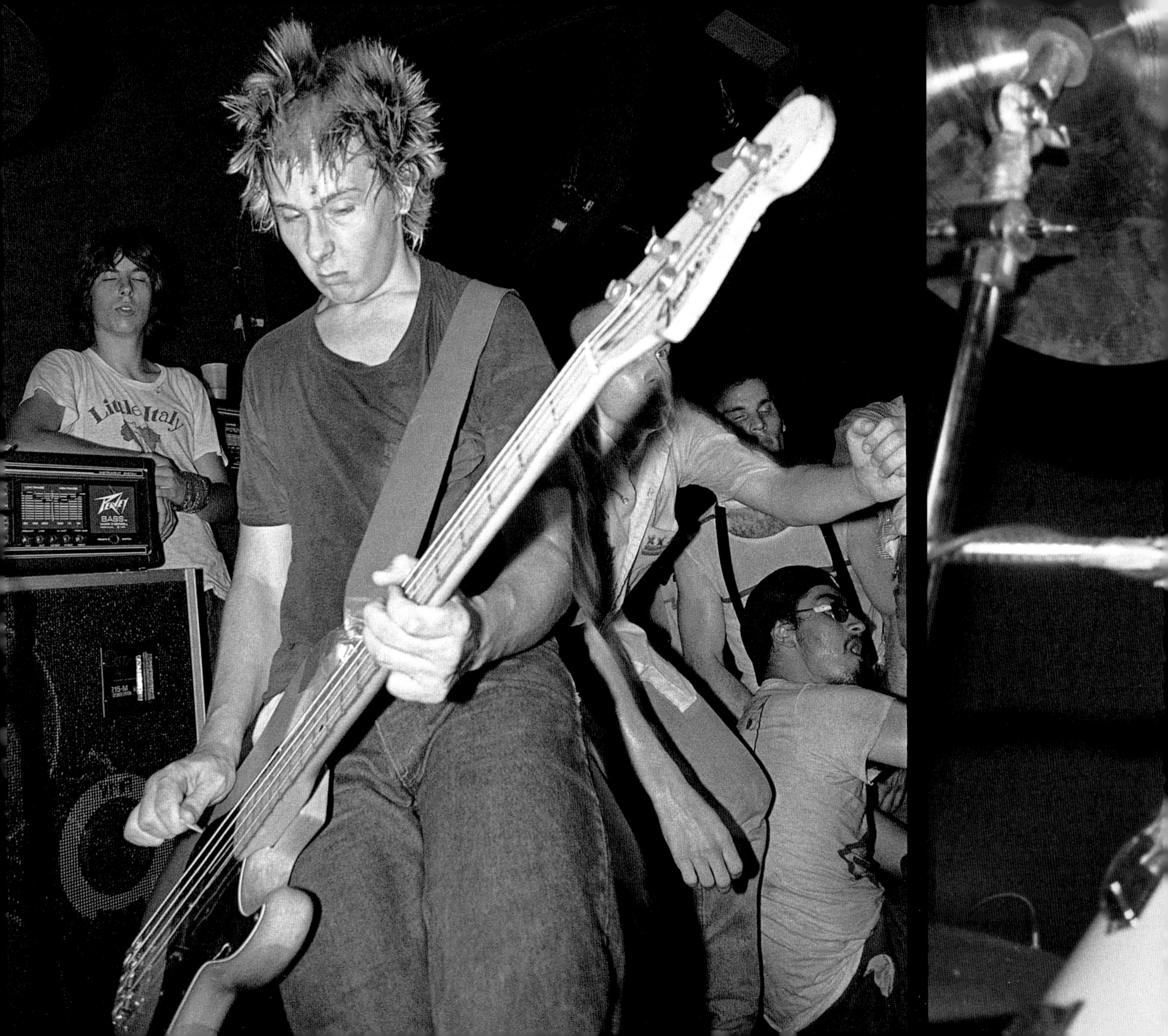
Little Italy
Peavey
BASS
215-M

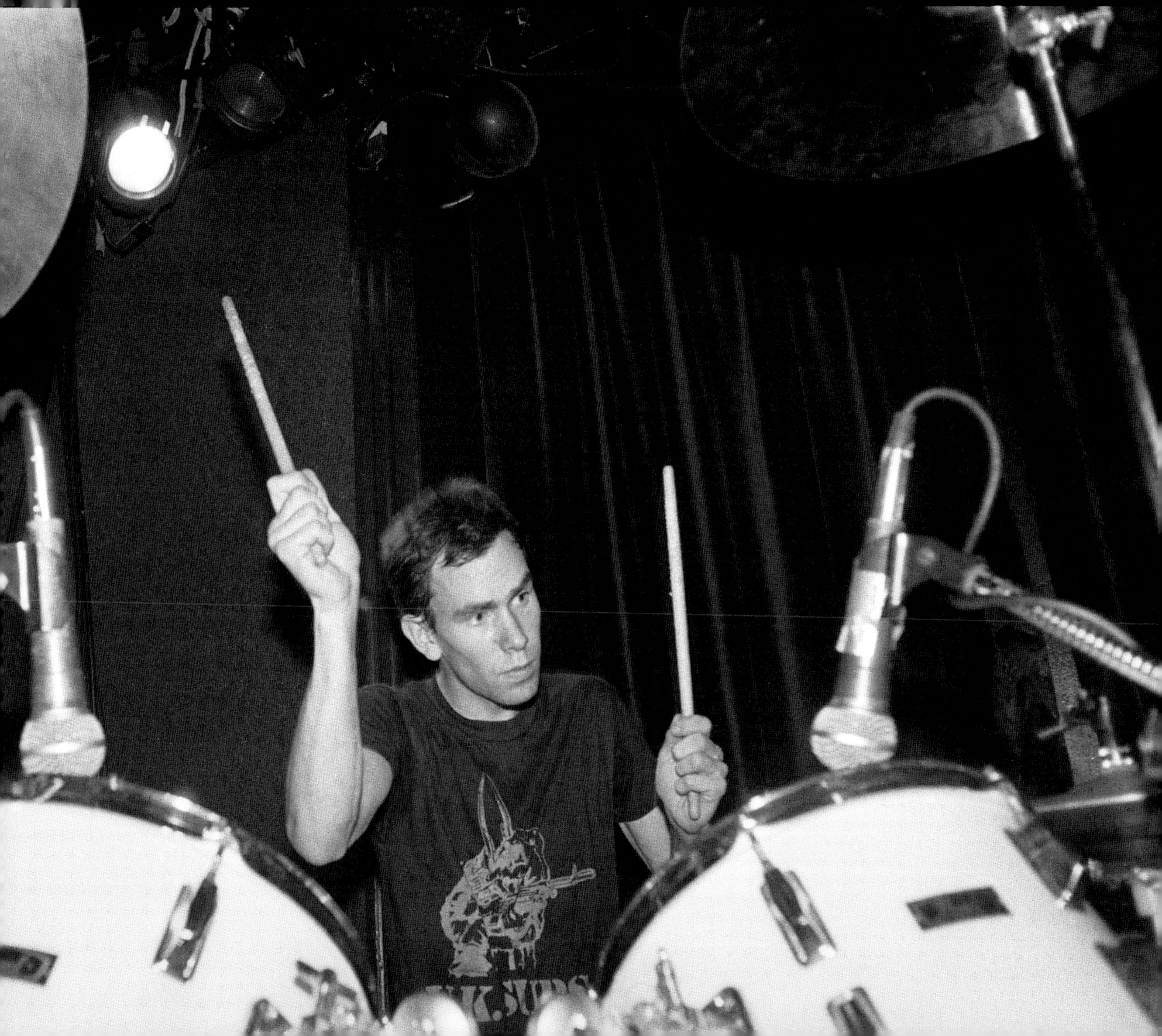

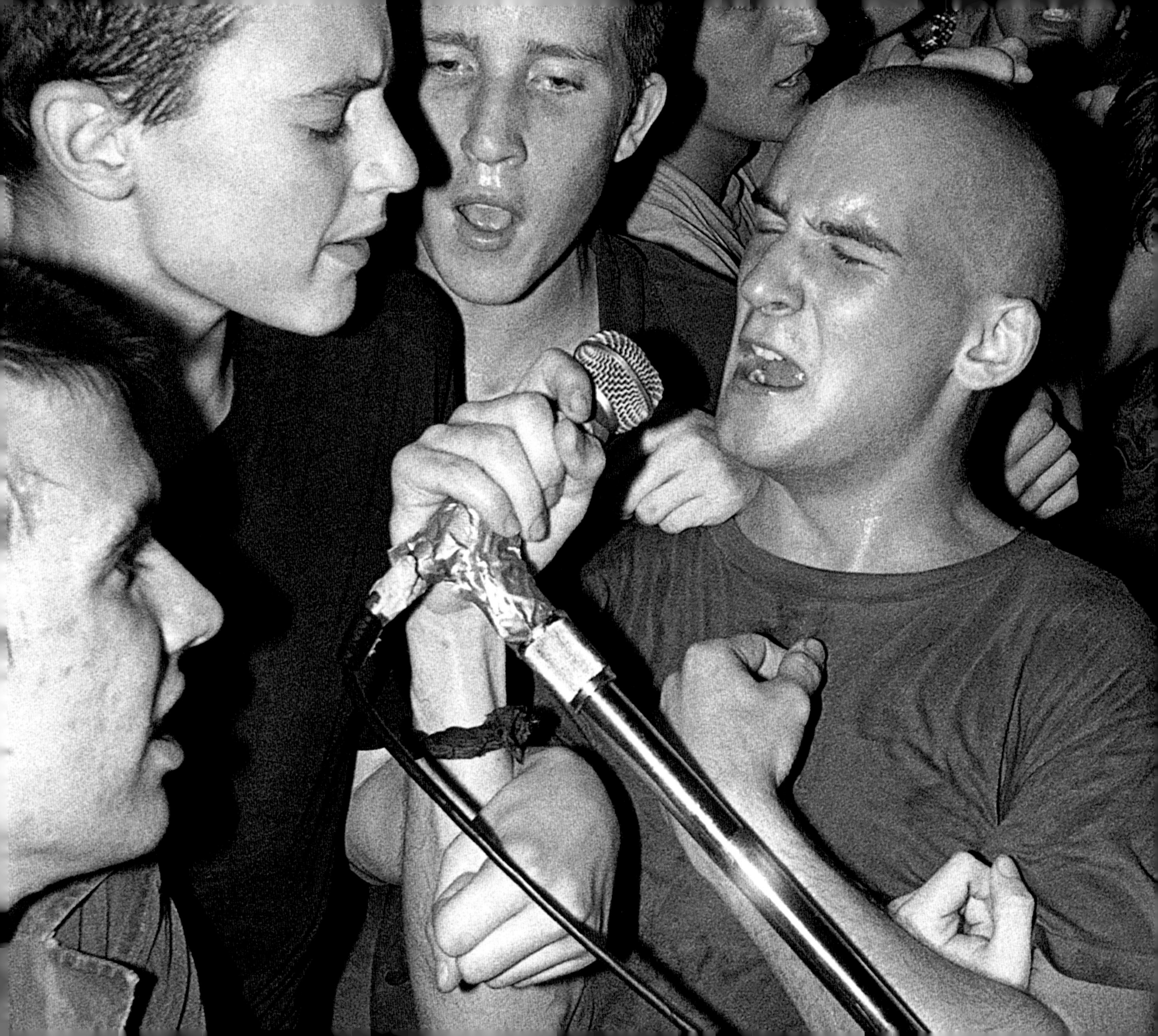

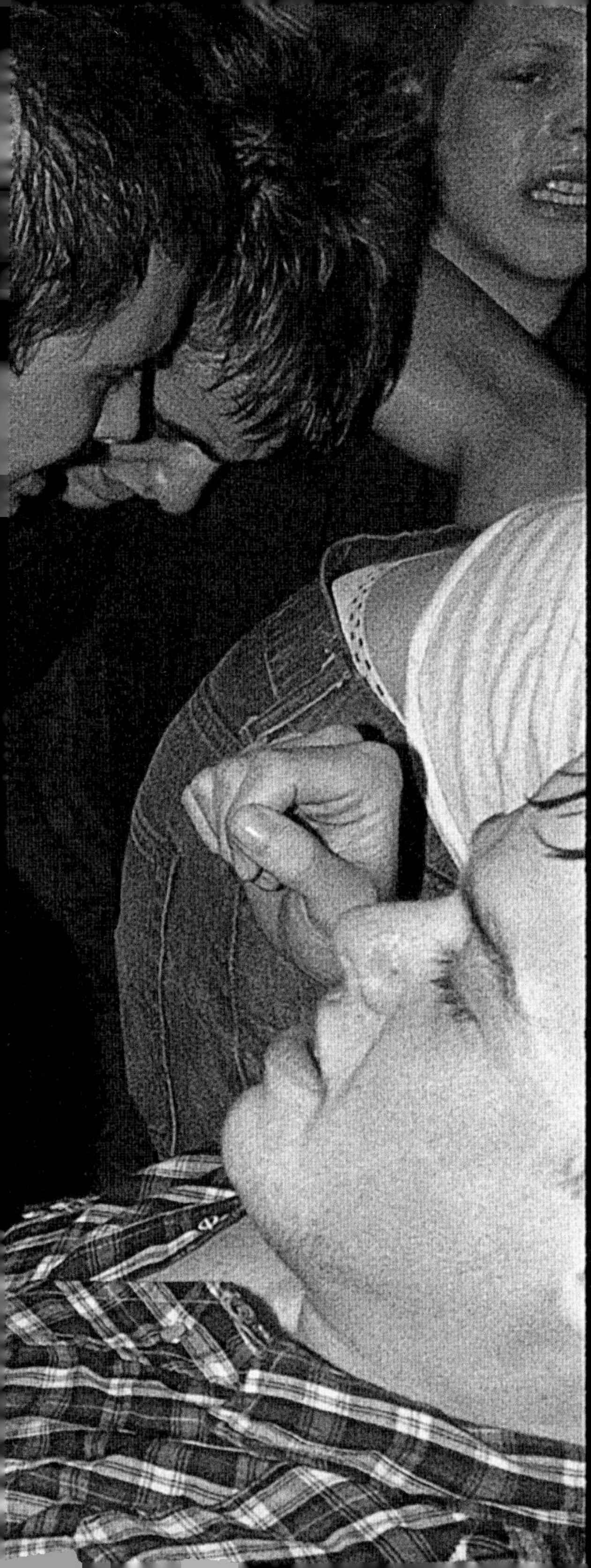

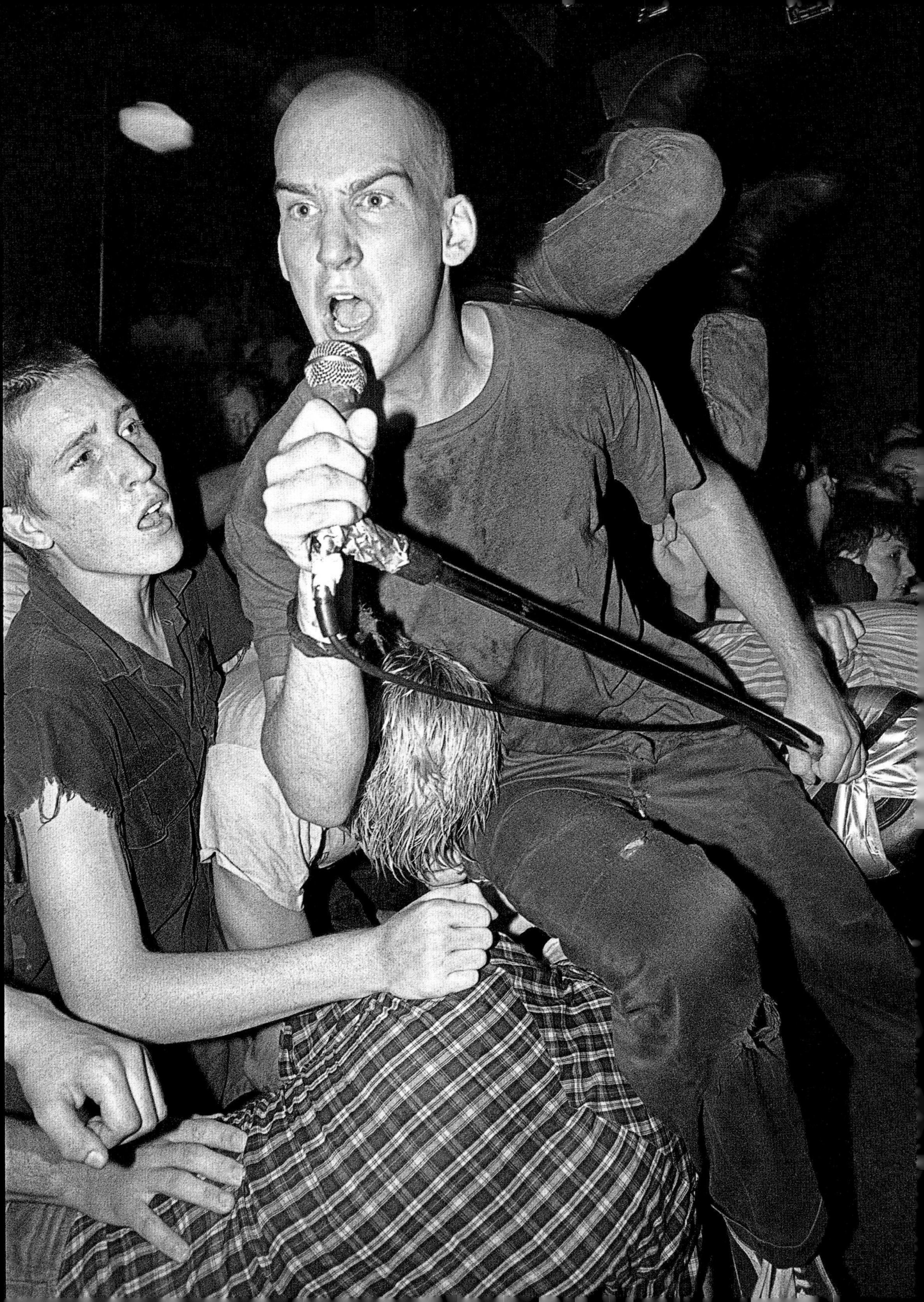

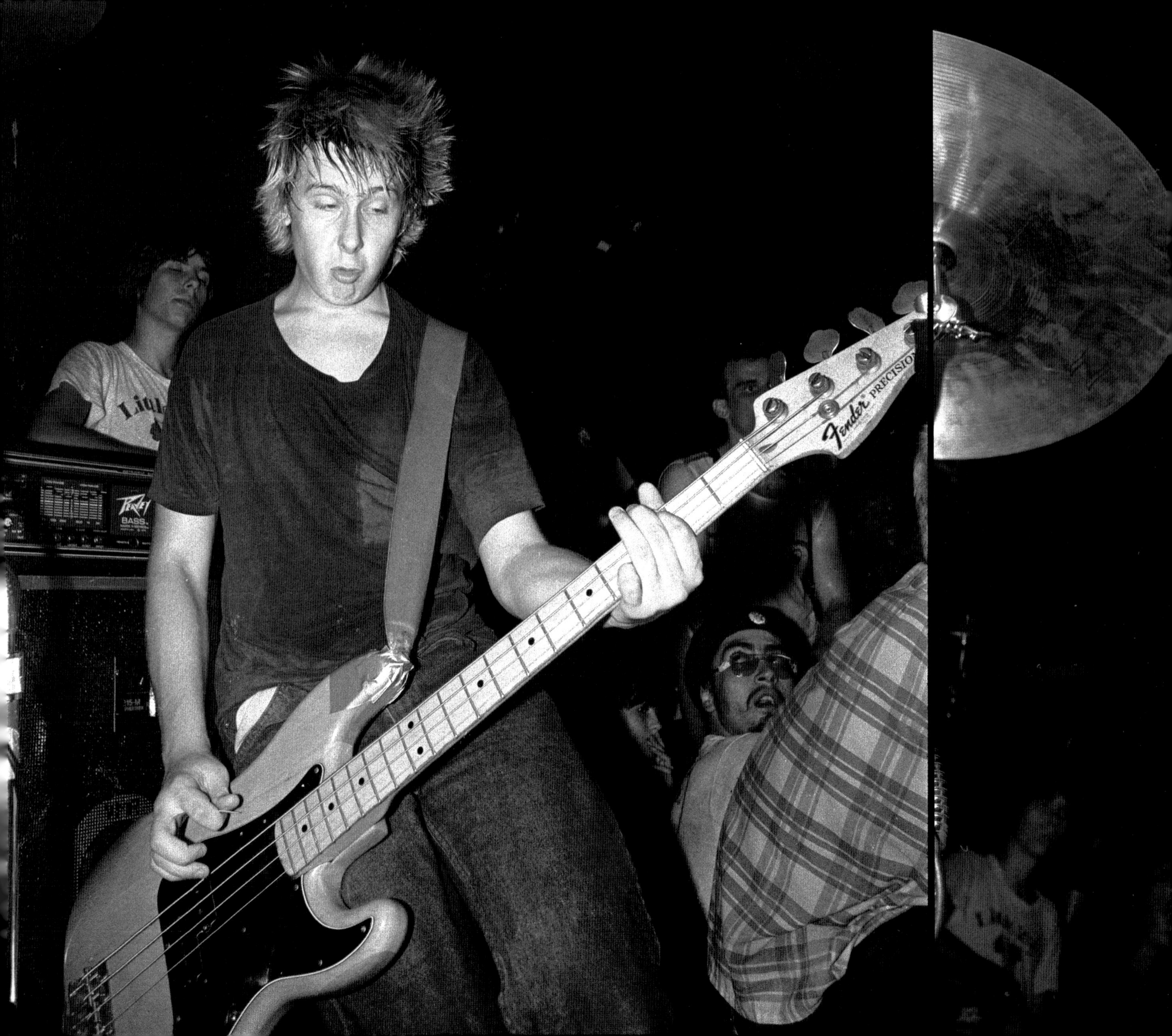
Fender PRECISION
BASS

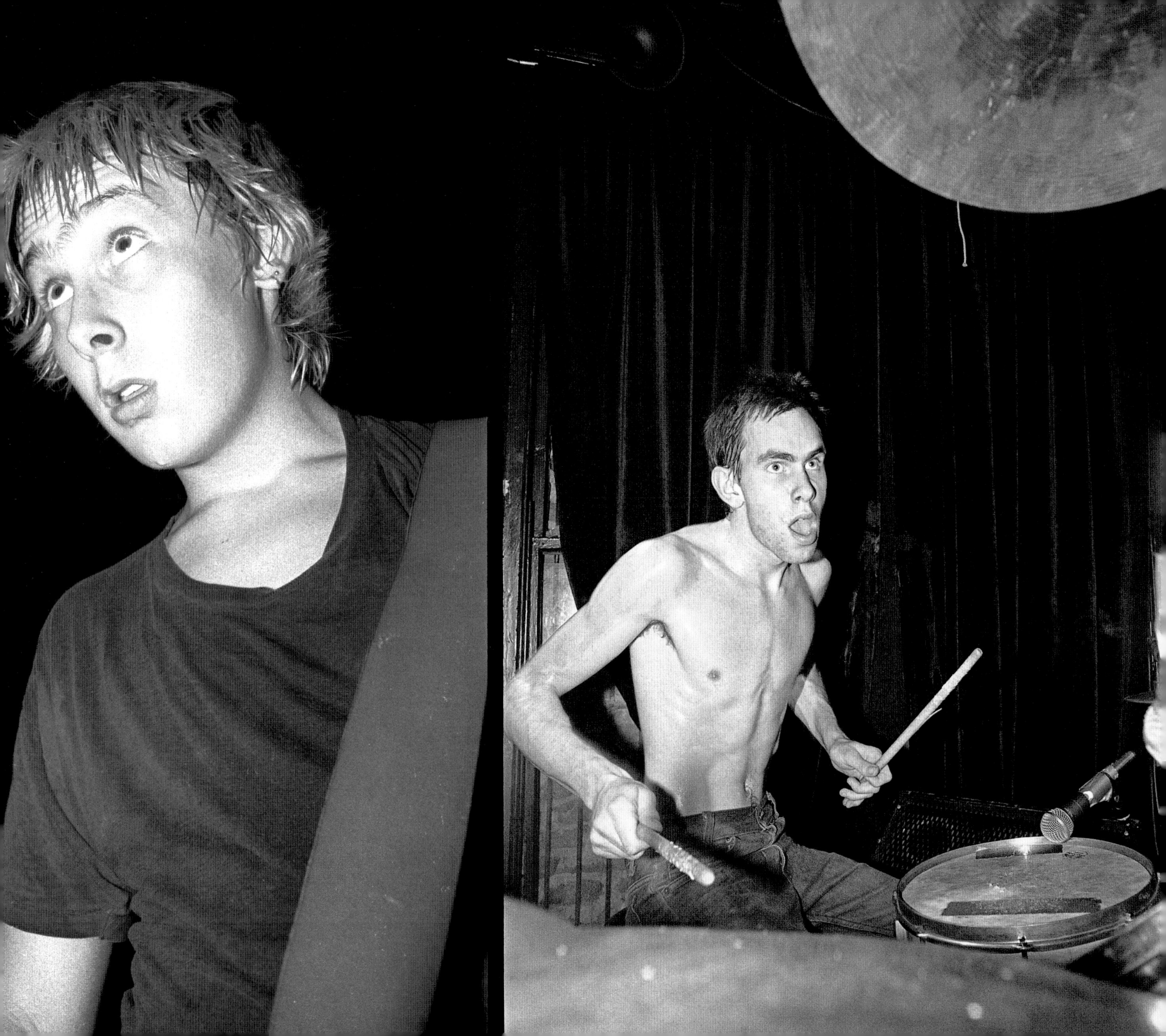

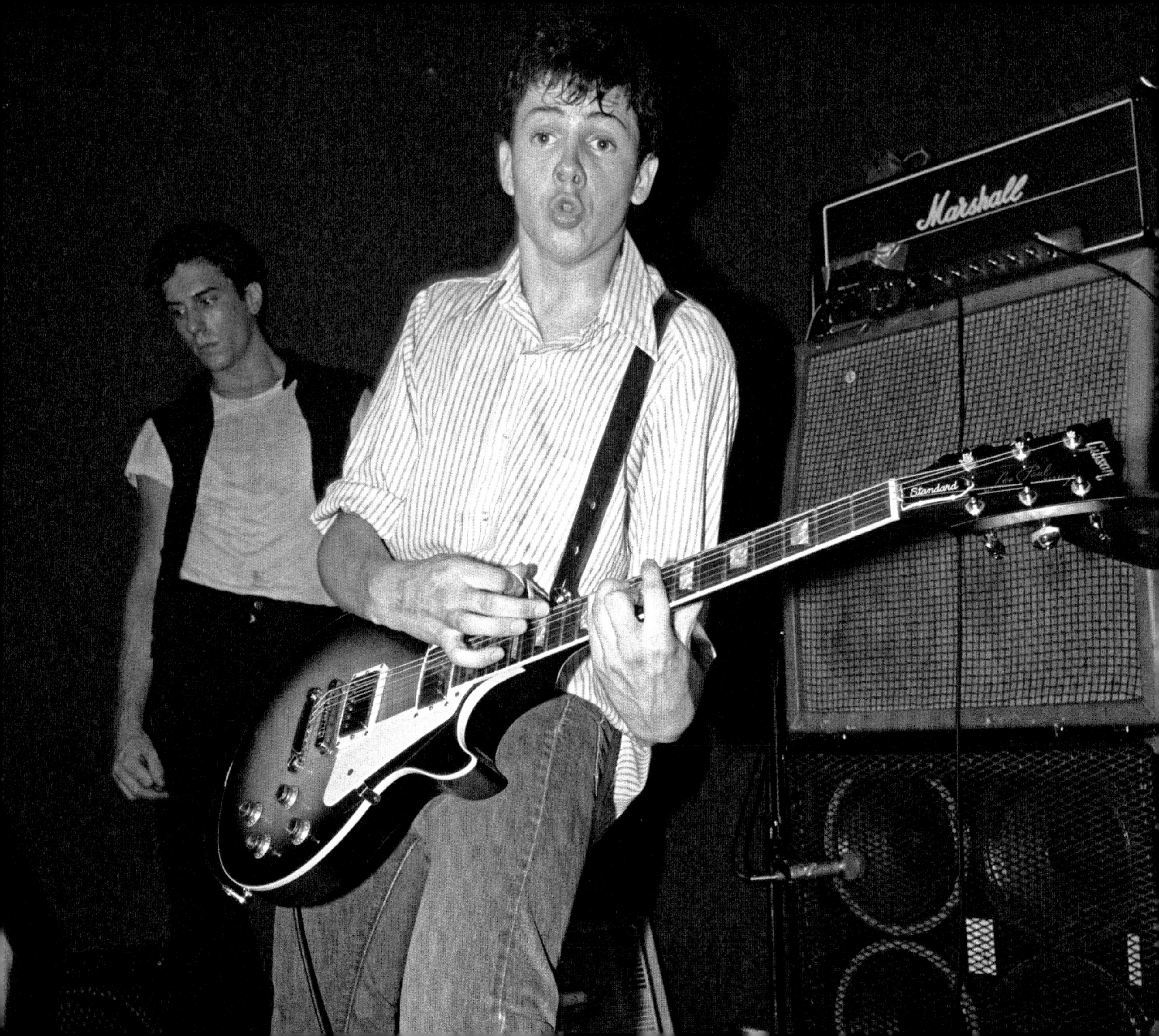

Marshall
Standard
Gibson

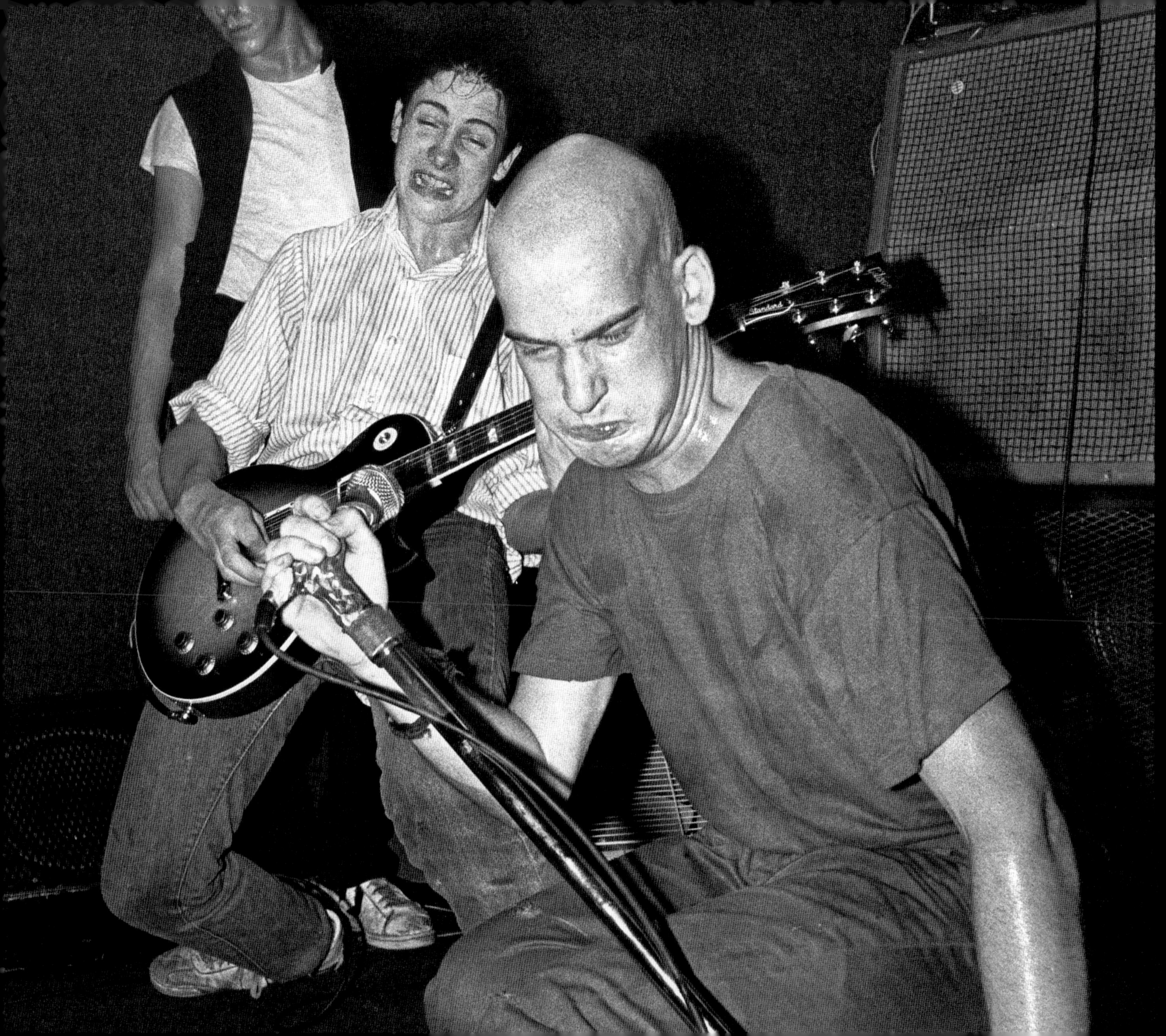

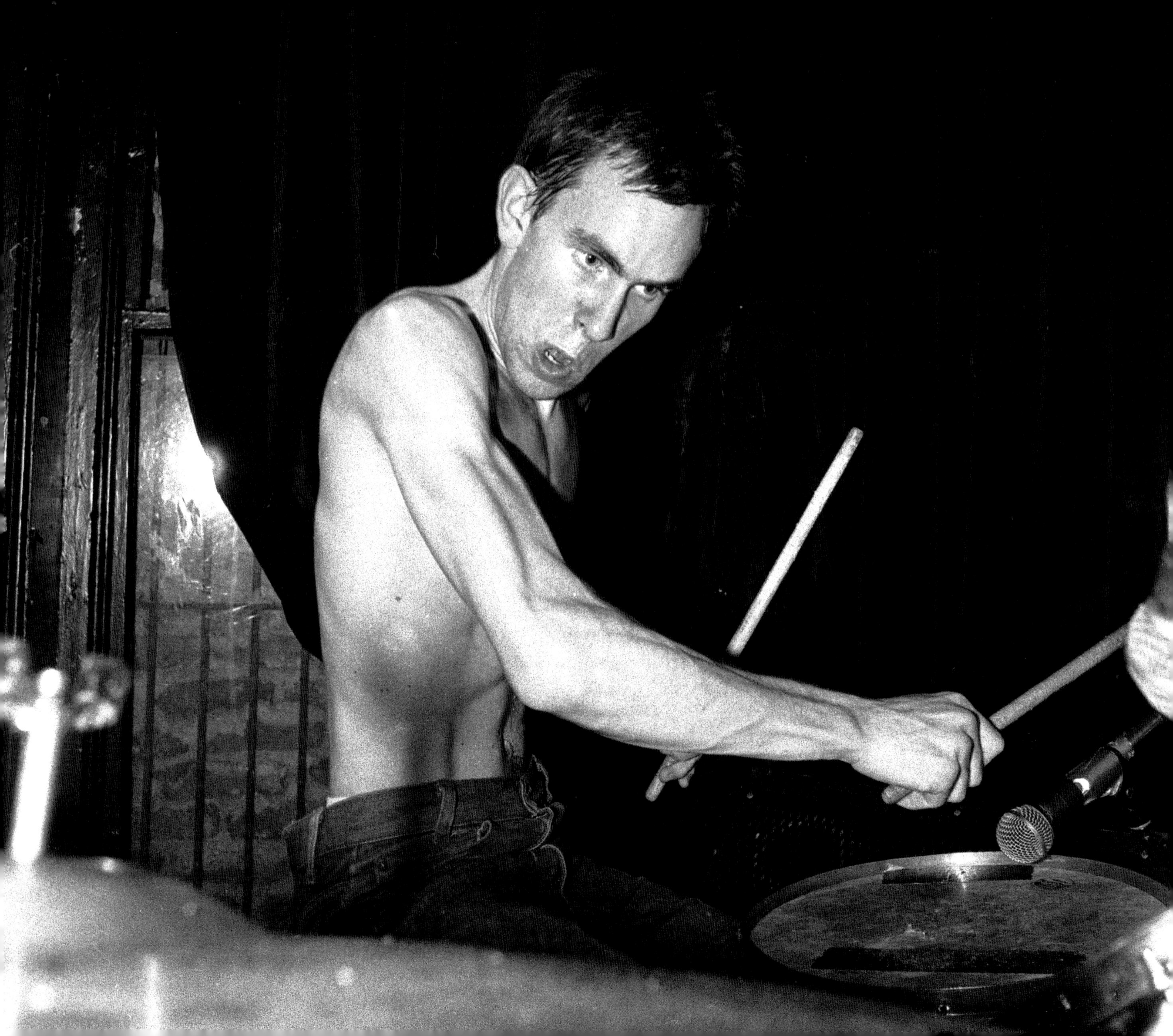

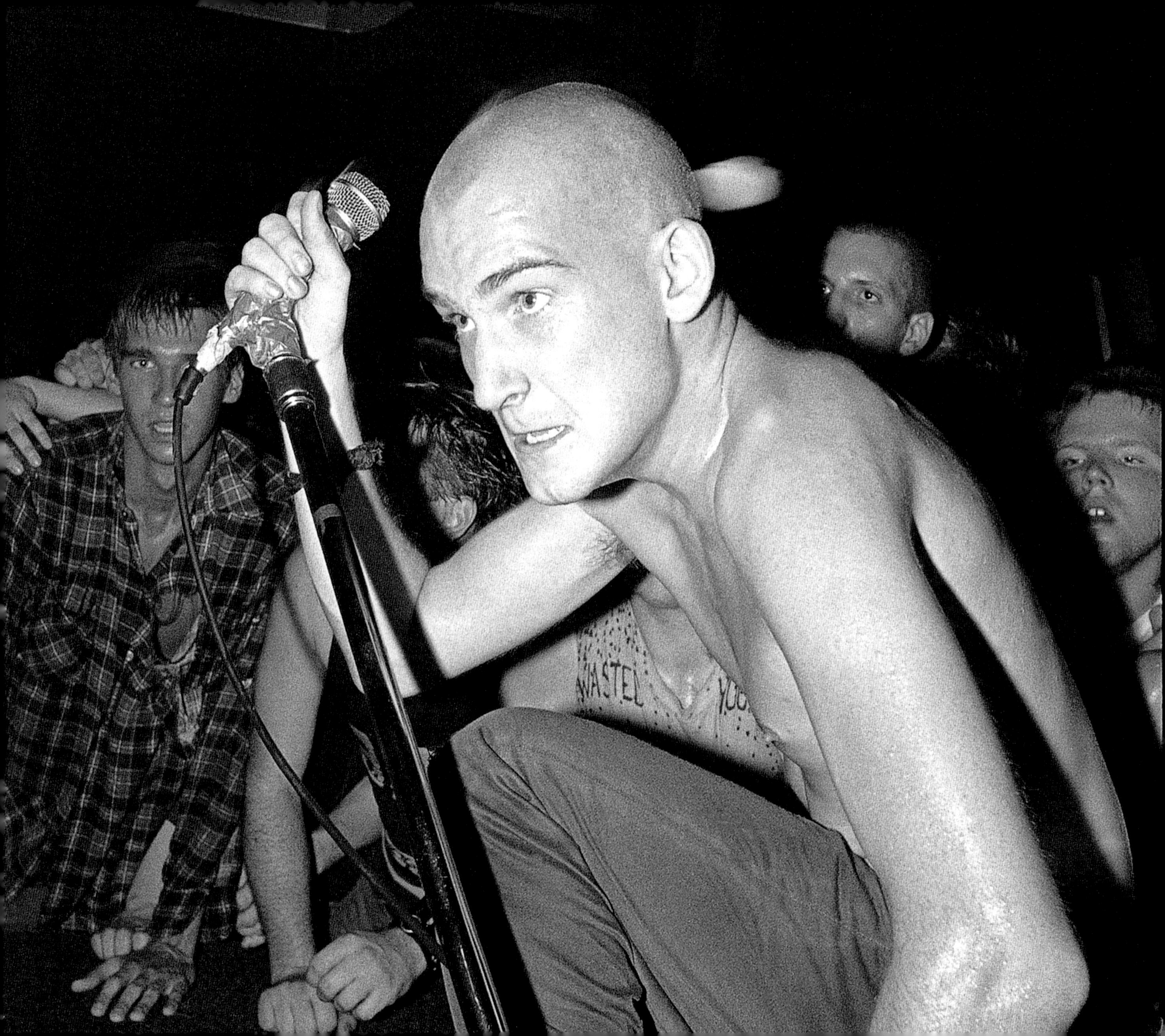
WASTED

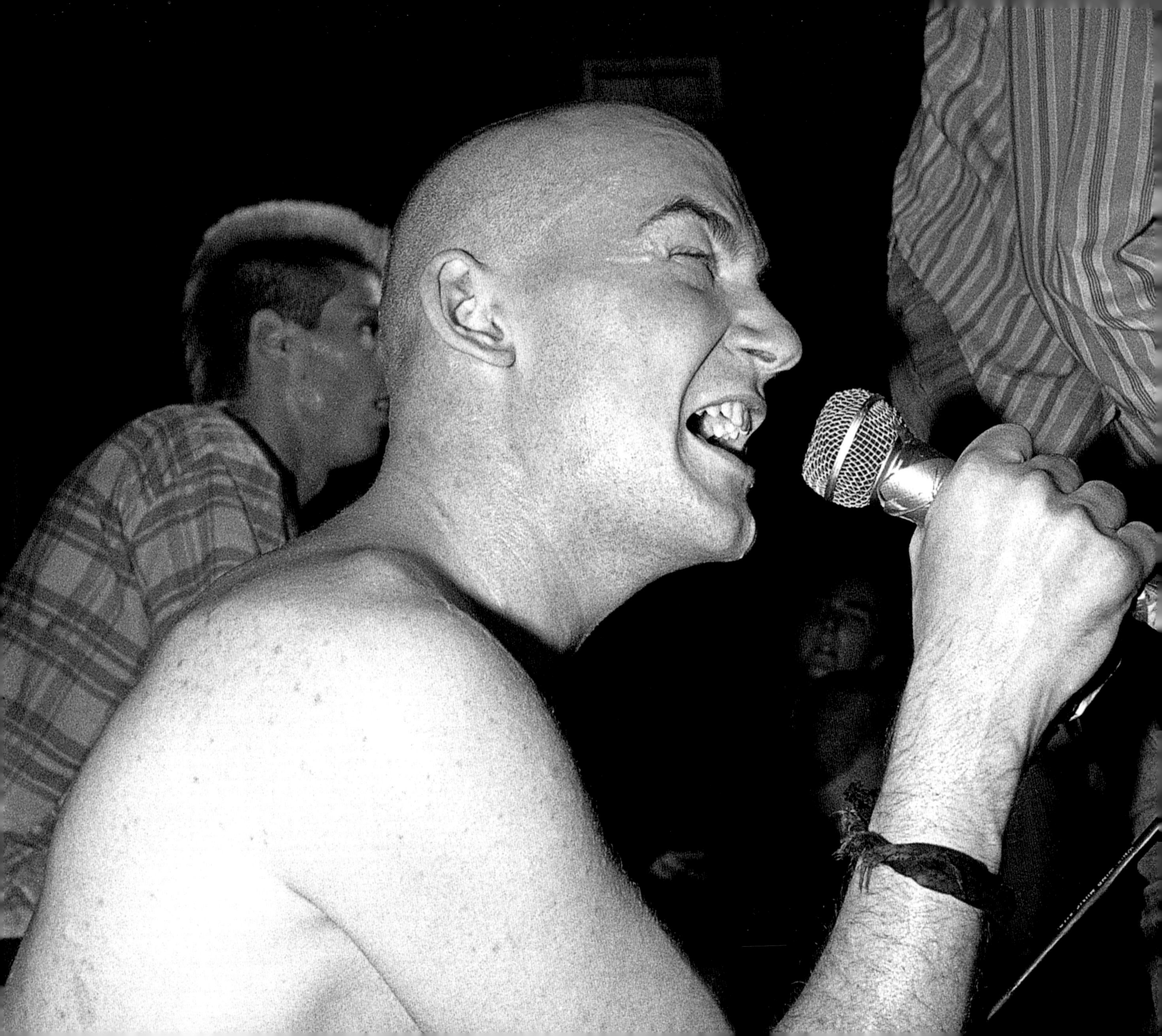

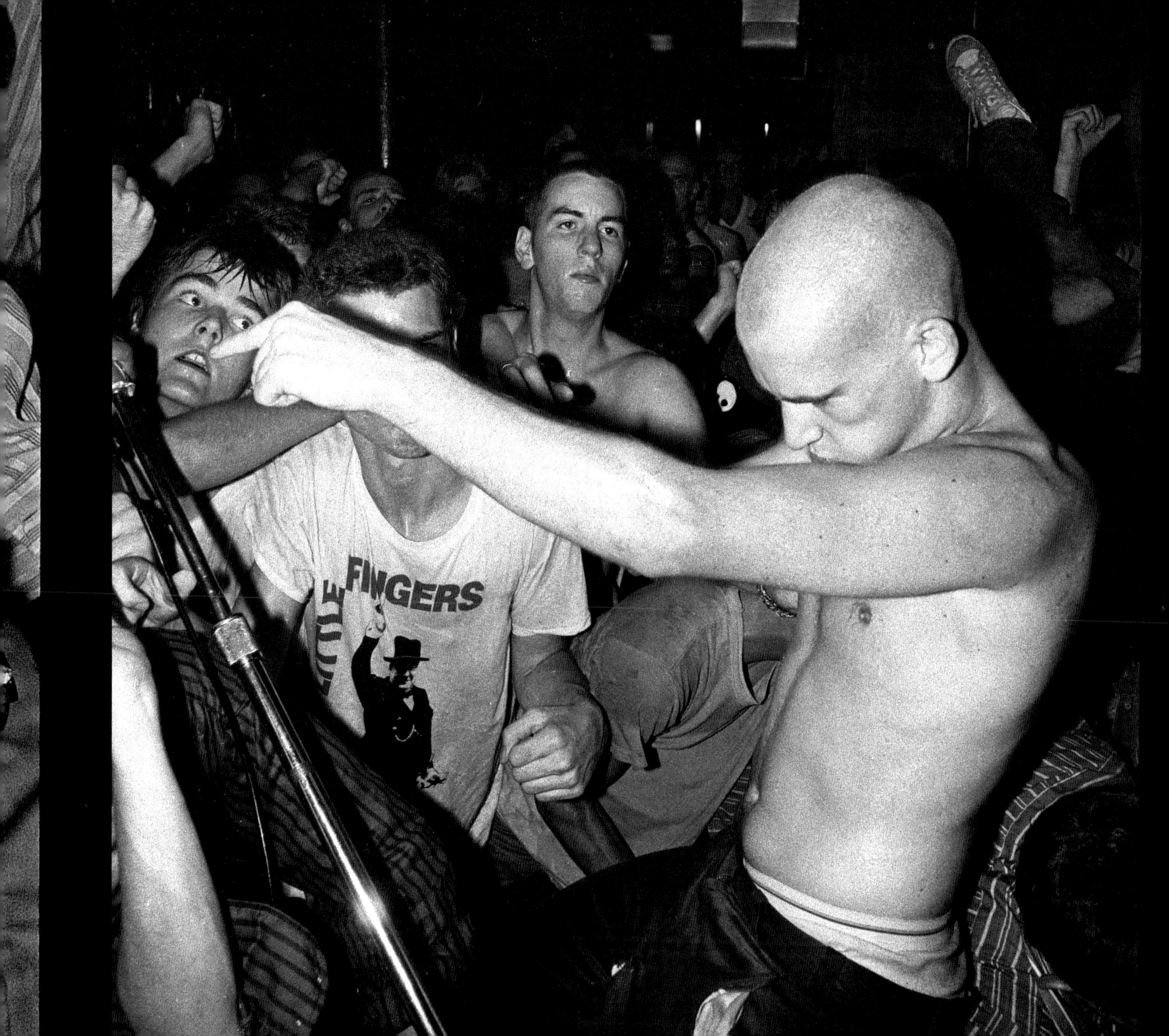
FINGERS

I have to be realistic: 1982 has become a long time ago. But it isn't hard for me to recollect in a general way what happened at this show. I know the forms of how and who. I know, and the evidence shows, it was very hot and very close. It was loud, and spontaneous energy was bursting out of people—traveling like instant contagion through the air, in just the same way that heat and sound move—invisibly charging the whole room and each person in it. There were many more people at this show than had been expected, so there was the sensation of potentiating power, as the "scene" seemed to suddenly lurch into a higher gear—which added even more energy to the event.

Minor Threat had been different from the very start. They managed to convene several essential elements that made them the perfect punk band for the time, and they leaned steeper into their songs than those around them. The early 1980s qualifier "hardcore," which had been used as an adjective to describe faster, more concisely brutal punk rock erupting in the USA, suddenly became a stand-alone noun. Minor Threat crystalized not just the speed that we were all going for, but the attack. It was something about the bass and guitar slightly ahead of the beat that made Minor Threat sound like a freight train running flat out down a hill, its engine trying to keep up with its wheels. More than just quick—they were exhilarating, the way you feel when you get going too fast on your skateboard to be able to jump off, so you just let yourself go with it, outpacing gravity.

When someone achieves this state of mind—the letting go of self and the complete surrender to sound—they will feel like they can attempt anything, and the audience at a Minor Threat gig would spend as much time in the air as they would on the floor, as these images attest.

There were others on the bill that got the ball rolling:

My band, Faith, was on the same tip musically, but we hadn't pushed through into that same Mach-speed regime. We did, however, throw ourselves into it as hard as we could, with the physicality of our performance.

Void—well, they were as much a pyro-chemistry experiment gone rogue as they were a band. They dispensed with any concept of "controlled" chaos completely and went for unrelenting and unfettered explosions of songs onstage. Their sets sounded like a truckload of steel office desks being thrown down a long flight of stairs, with a howling guitar chasing.

Scream played fast and clean, kept it together. They drew from some non-punk sources that offered solid ground to stand on and had mighty sing-along choruses that reminded each one of us that we were also all of us. They proved that the feeling of uninstructed unity, naturally formed by attraction, rather than compulsion, cannot be realized by the mere discussion of unity.

Picture if you will, then—when the headliners Minor Threat hit the stage. More than 400 people were pressed into a club that had a legal capacity of 199. The way the place was laid out, the band was semi-trapped; backed into a corner of the room with the audience surrounding them. They delivered music that drove into—and through—the crowd, with exactly the rhythm and force of the sturdiest quarter horse you have ever seen or heard. The people, experiencing some sort of internal conversion (as previously described), felt like they needed to test the limits of club rules, bouncers' patience, and physical science as they surged around in front of the band, or ran up on stage left and lofted themselves over, into, and onto one another. The band and the crowd, in mutually assured propulsion, each driving the other.

Sometimes, when people are looking at pictures from this era, they say, "I wish I had a time machine!" The thing is, you don't need to invent a time machine when you have pictures like these—because they are proper portals. Look into them and you are there.

—Alec MacKaye

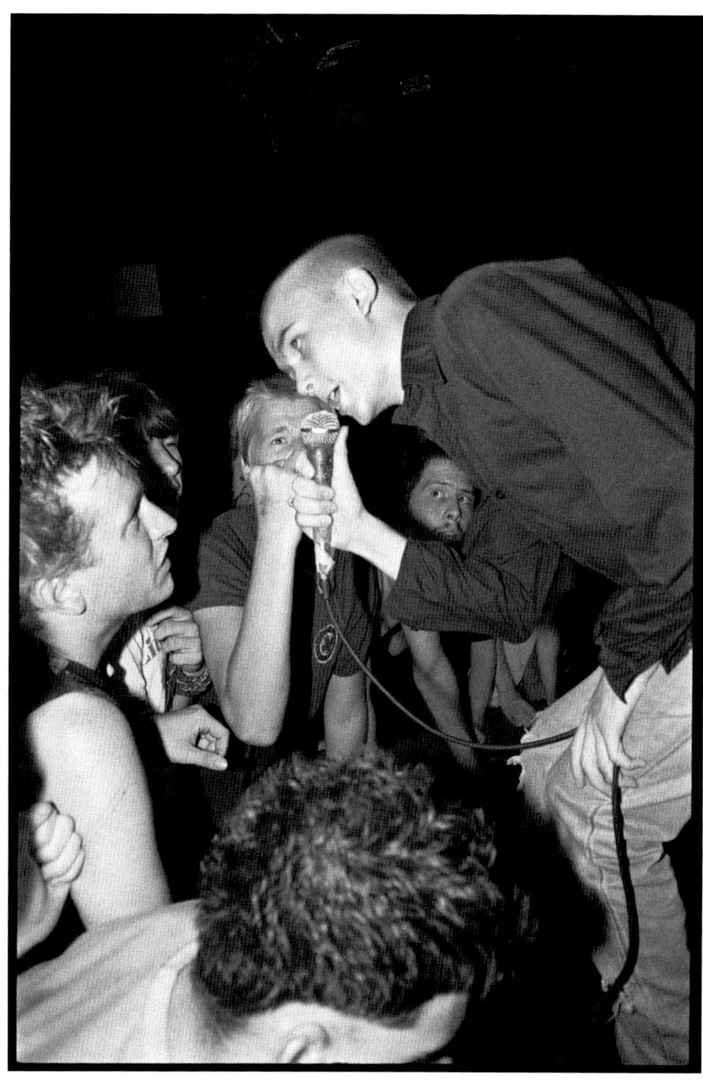

Alec, that very night.

December 18, 1982
CBGB
New York, NY

Ian MacKaye – vocals
Lyle Preslar – guitar
Brian Baker – guitar
Steve Hansgen – bass
Jeff Nelson – drums

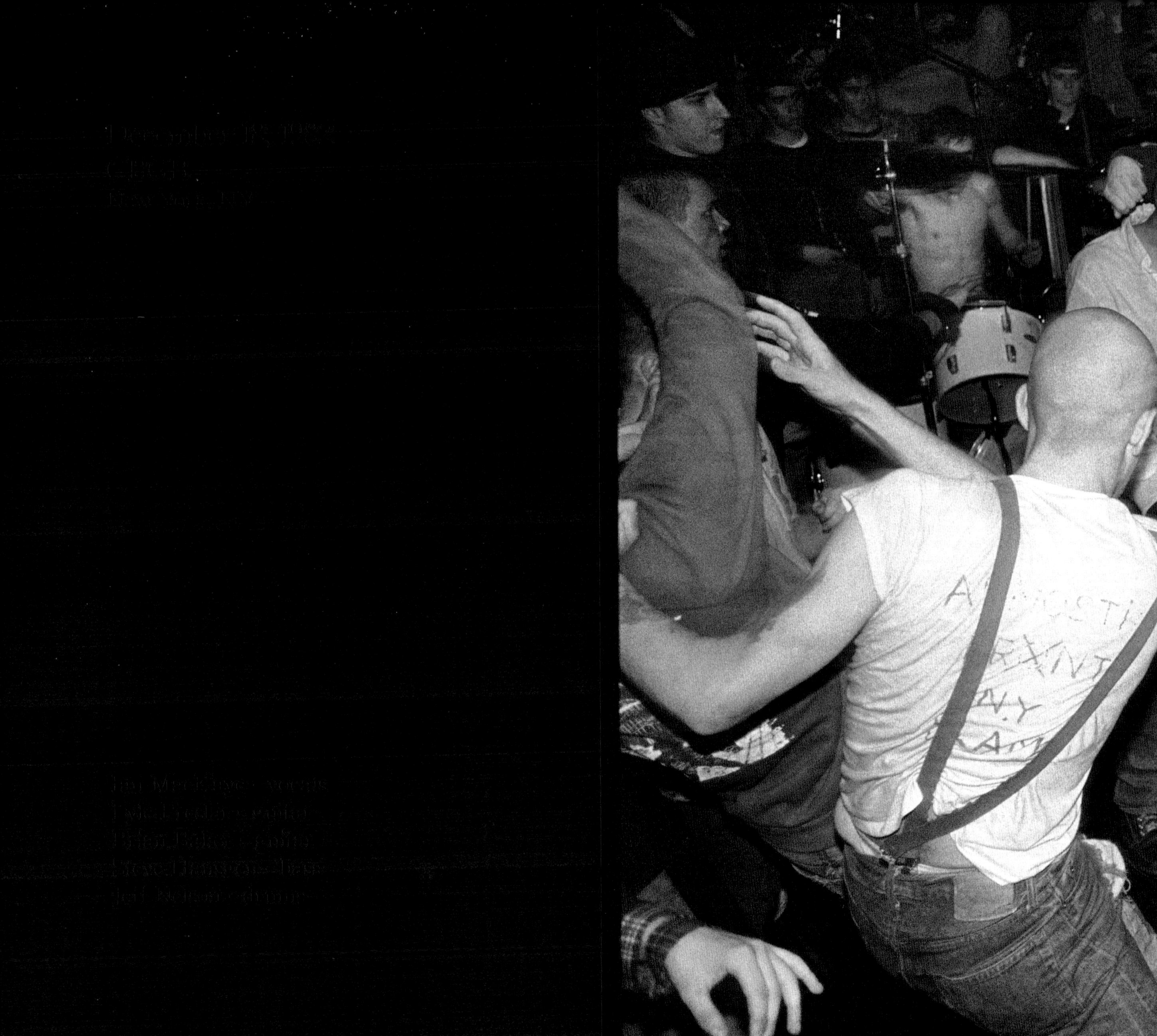

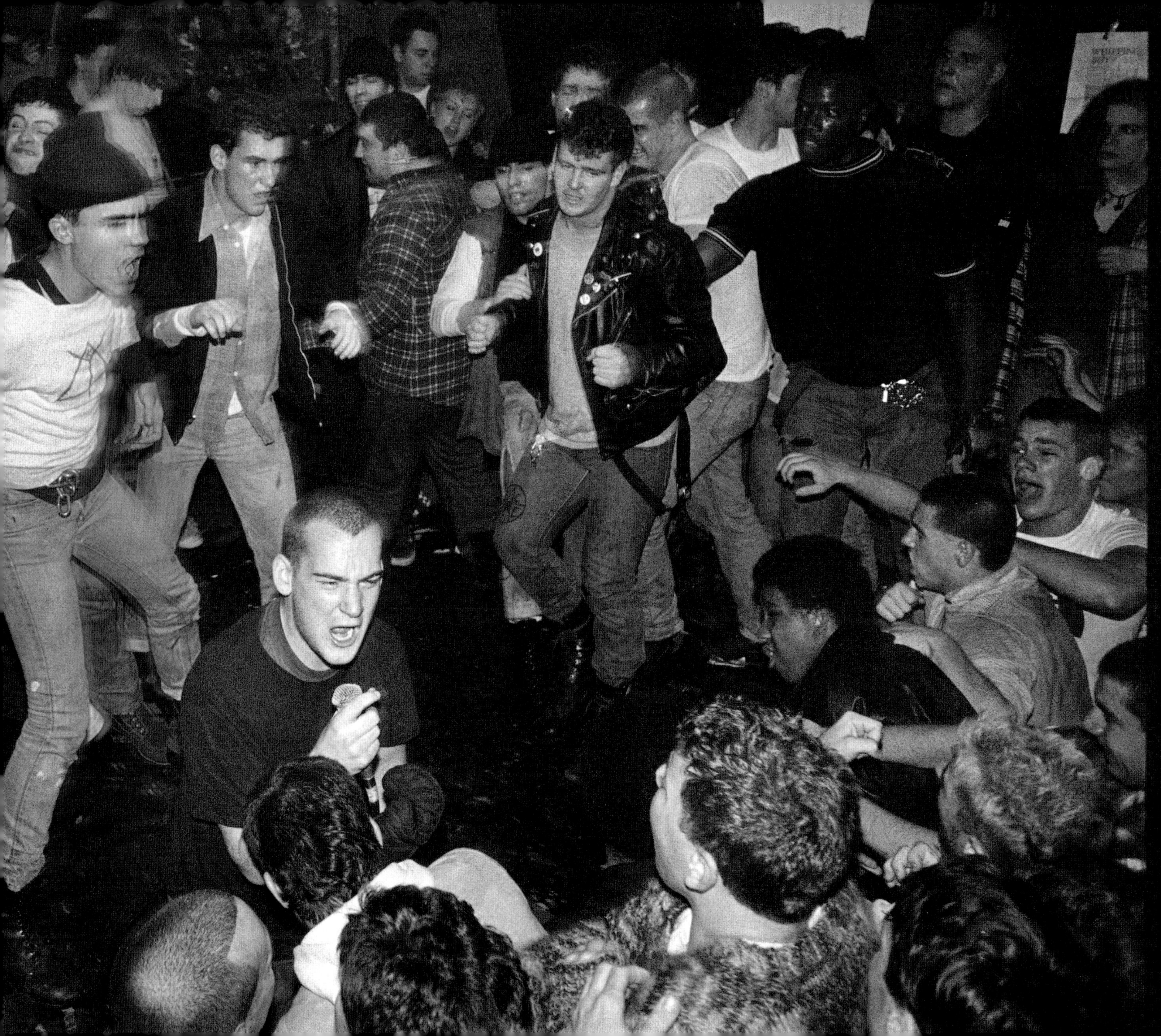

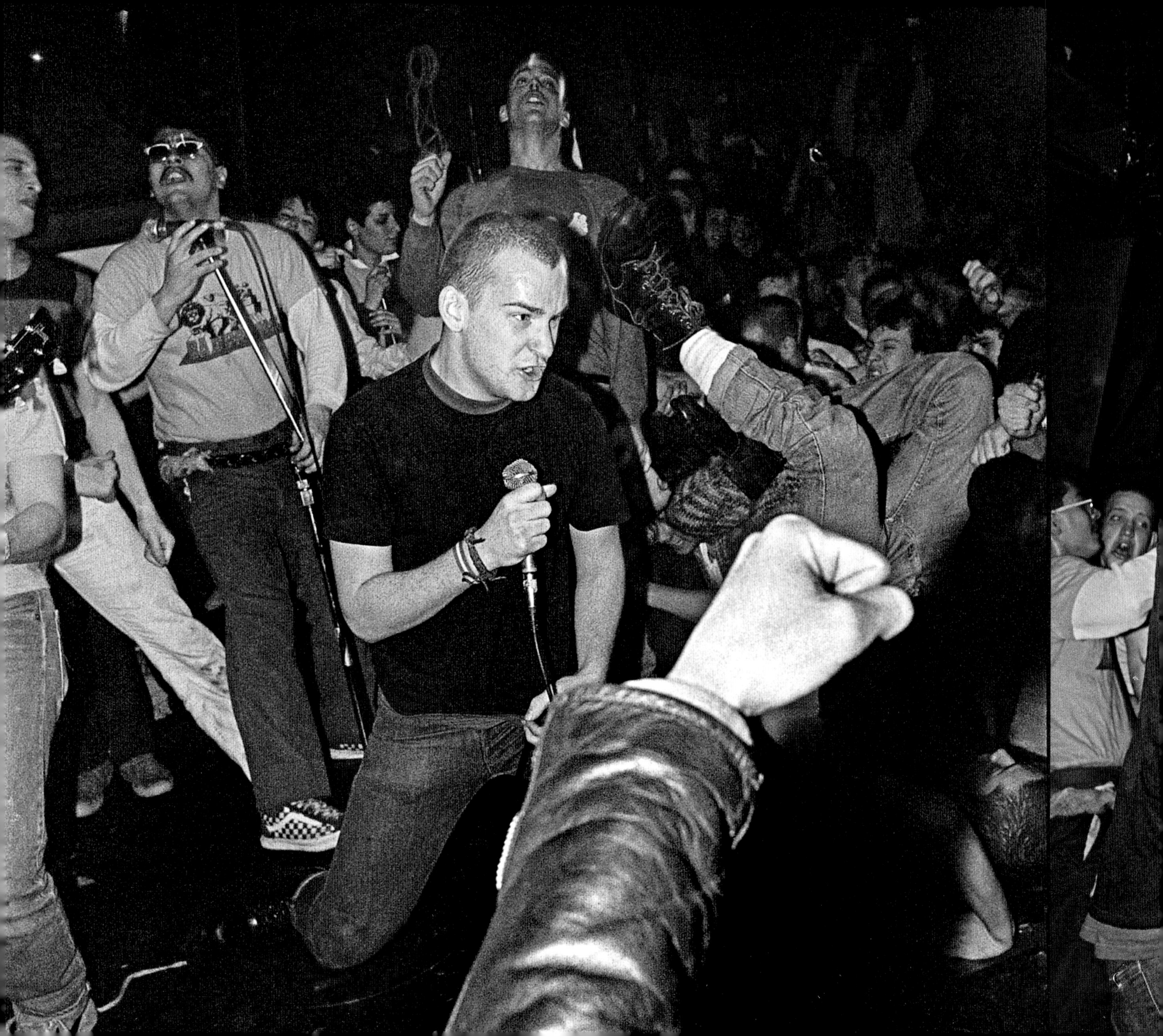

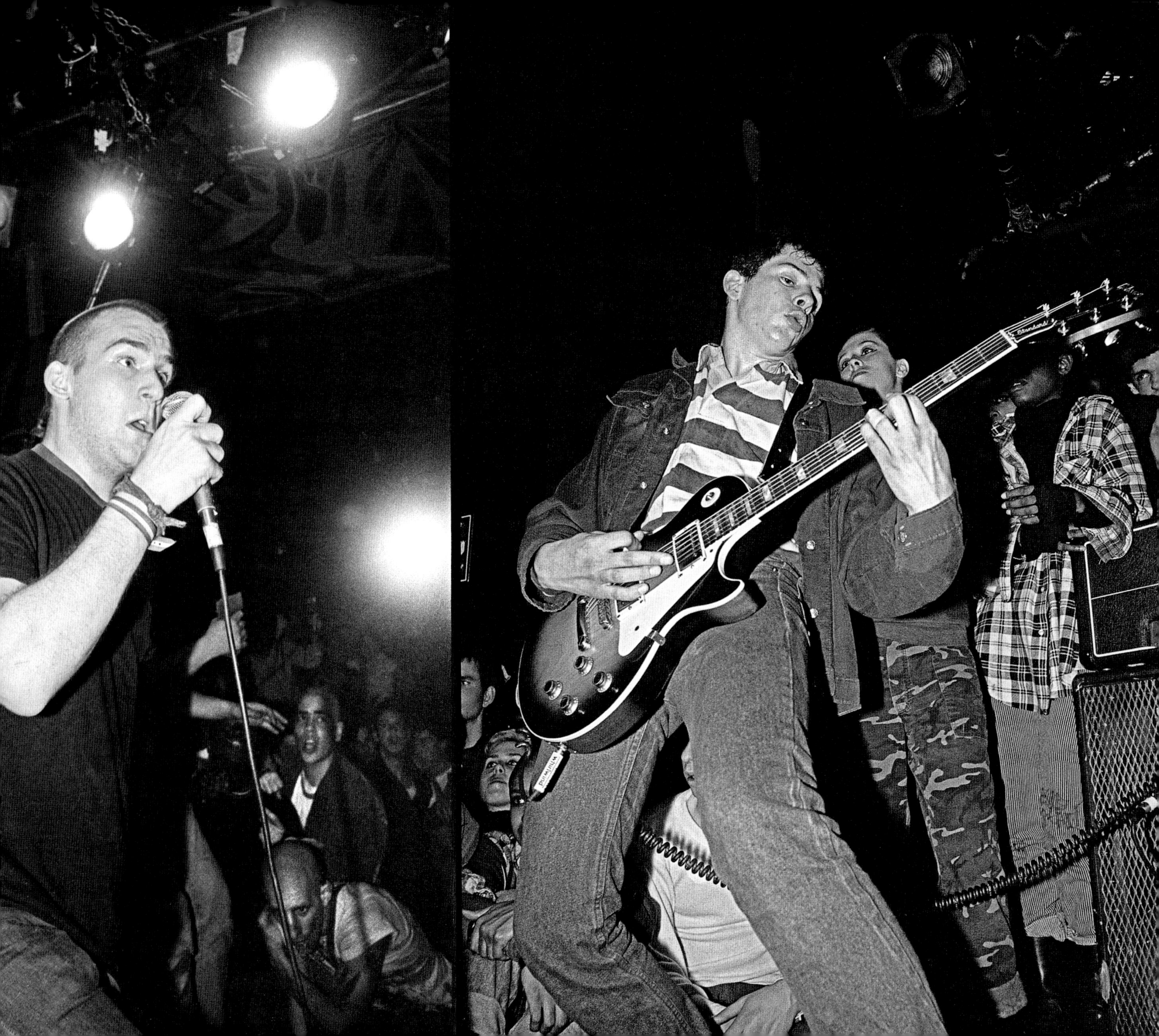

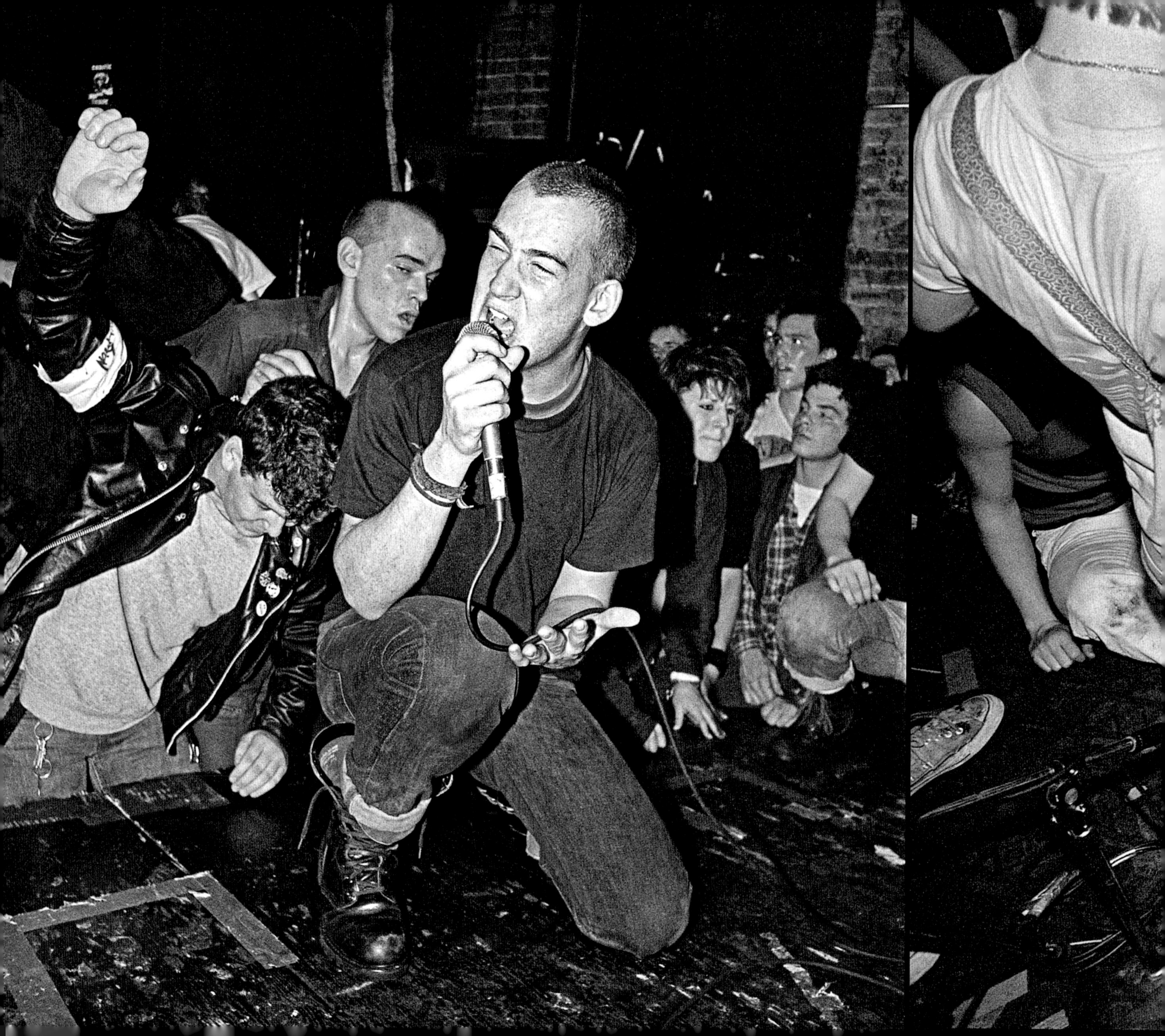

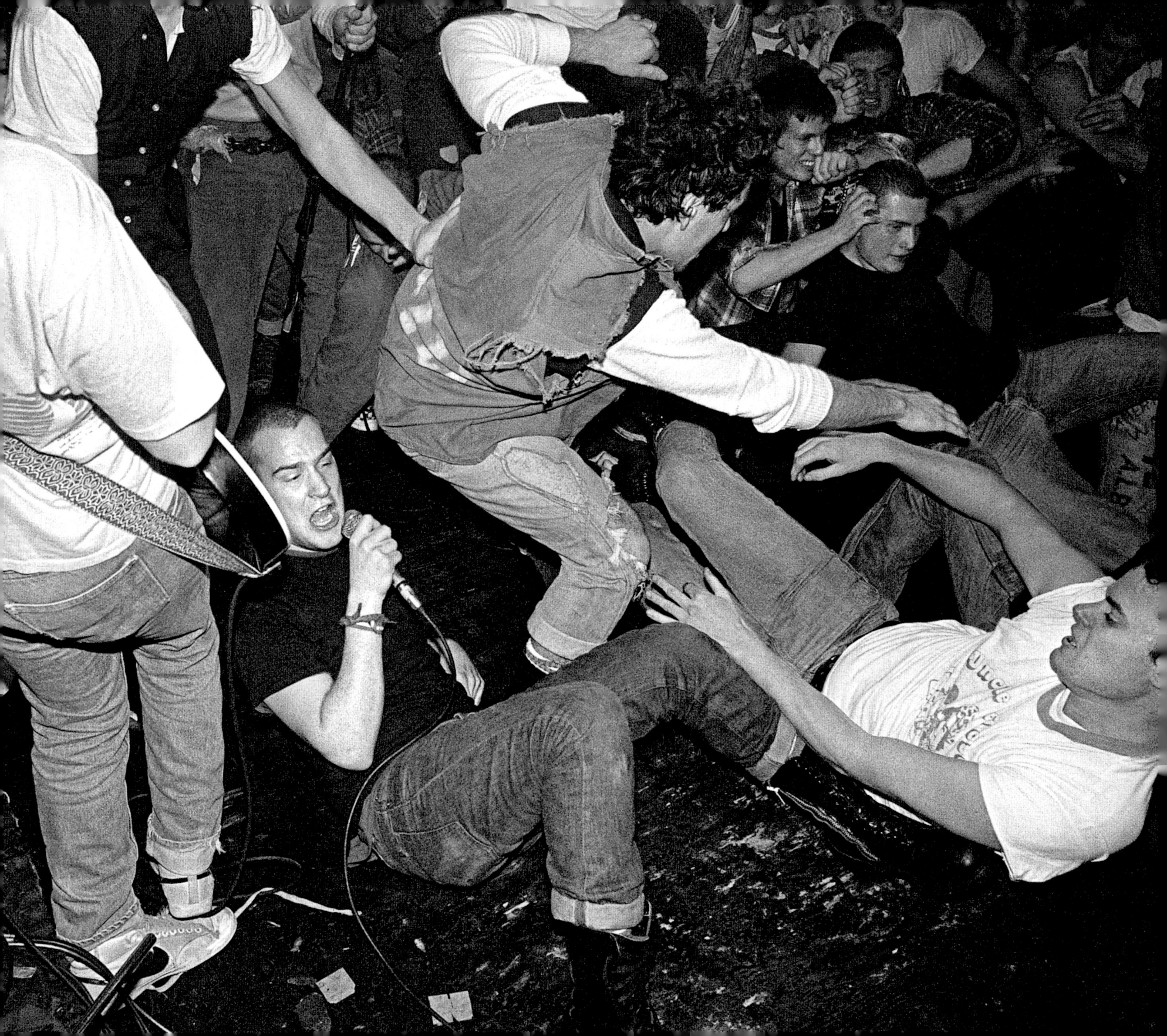

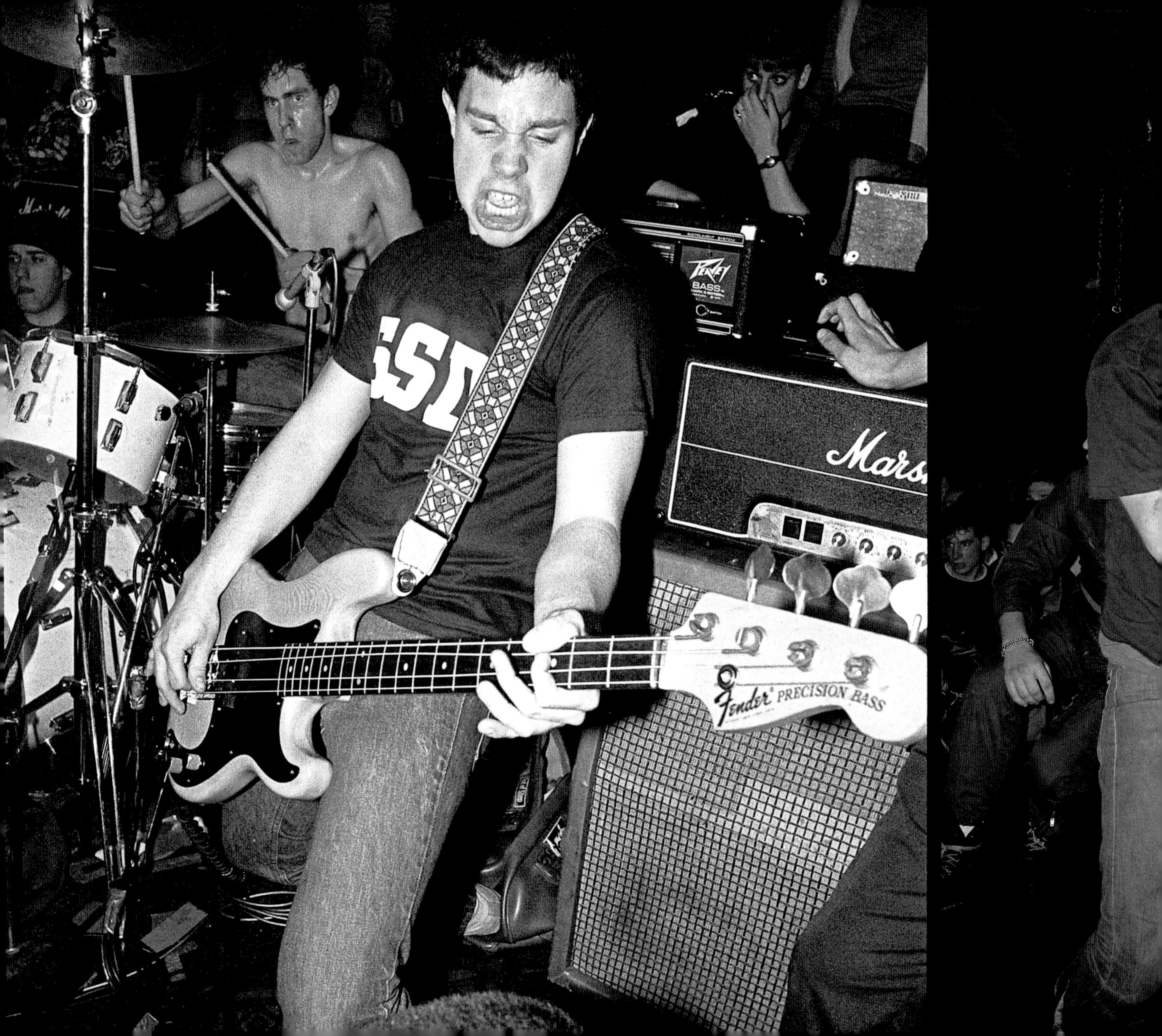
Peavey
BASS
Fender PRECISION BASS

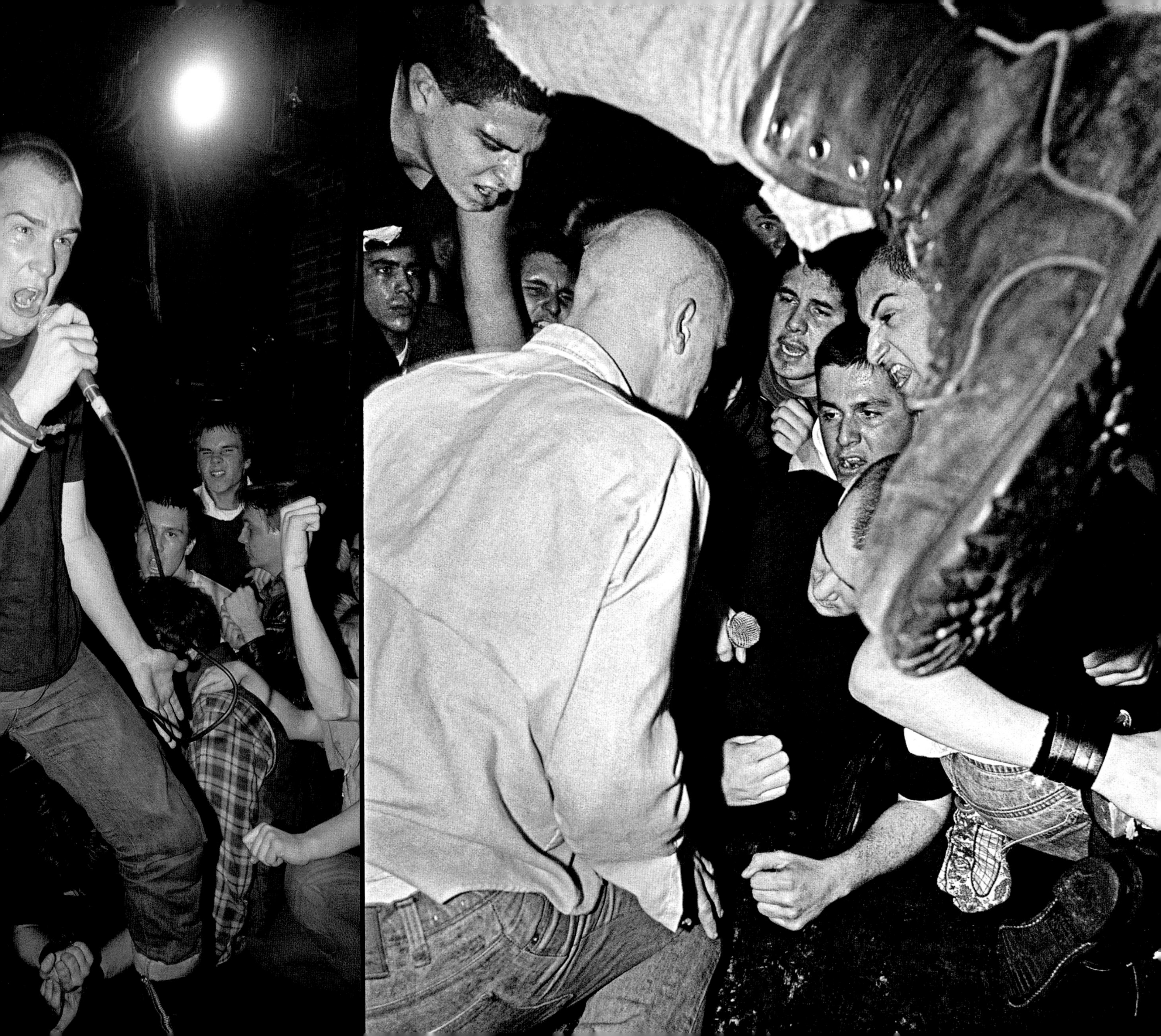

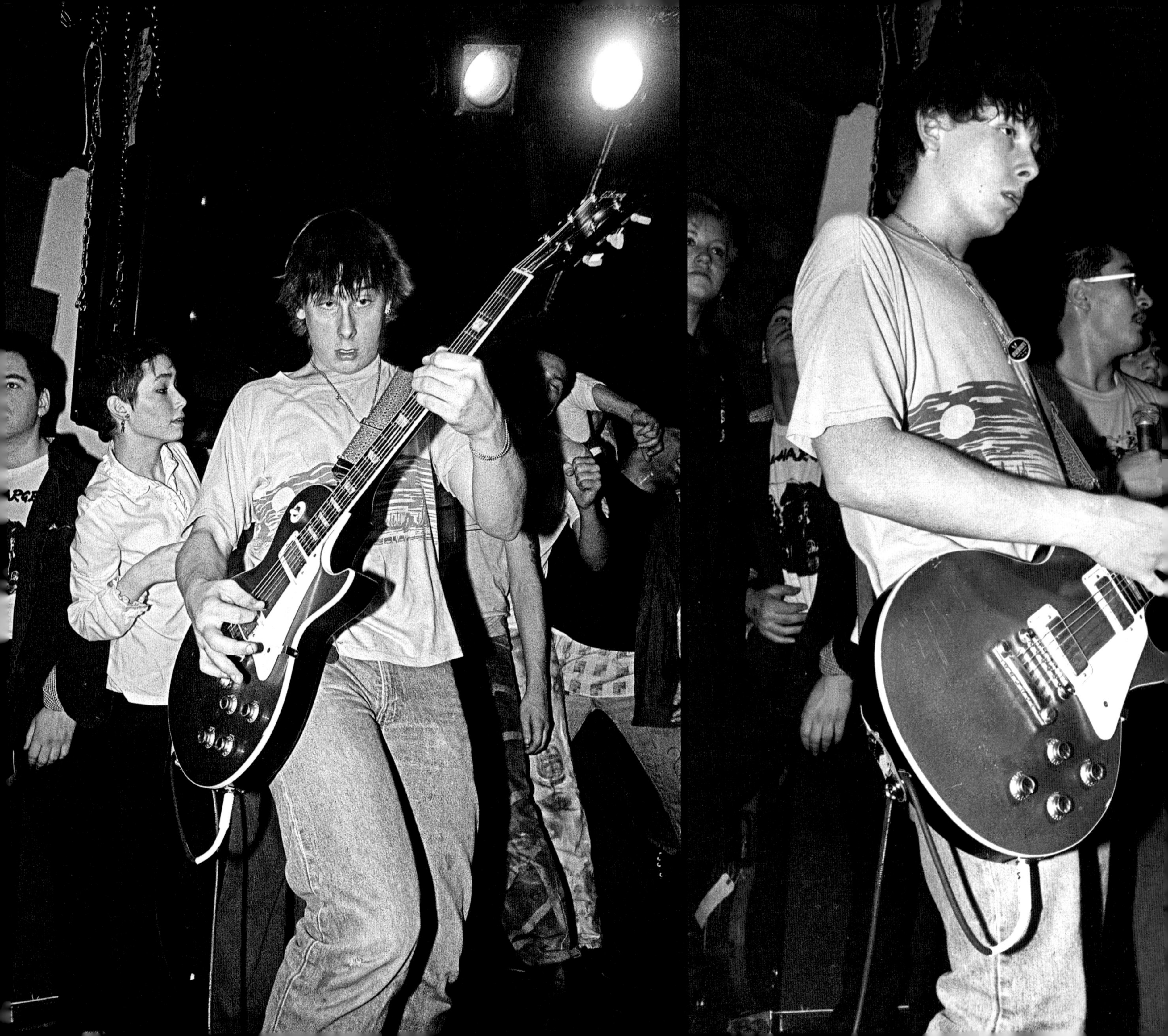

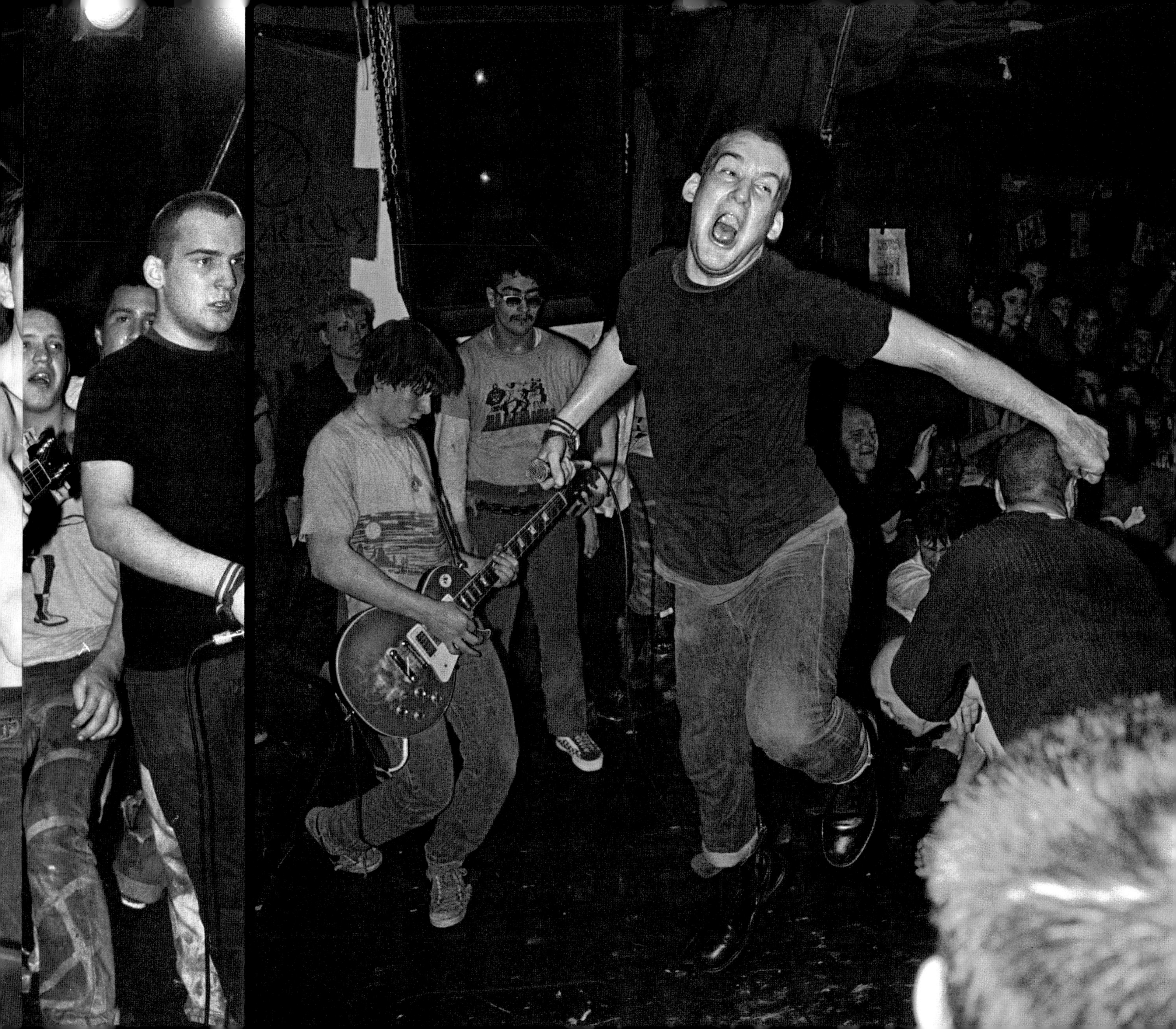

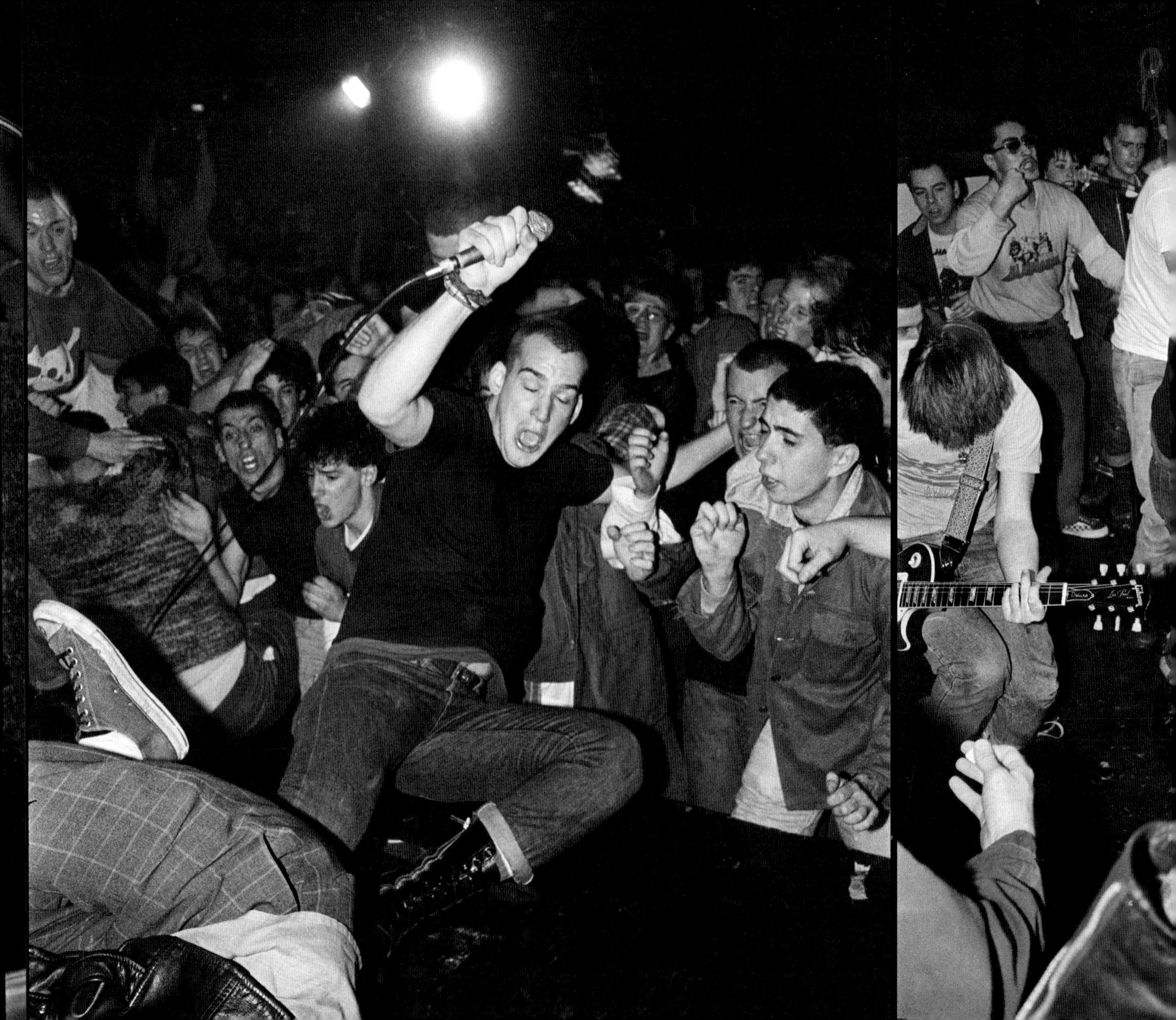

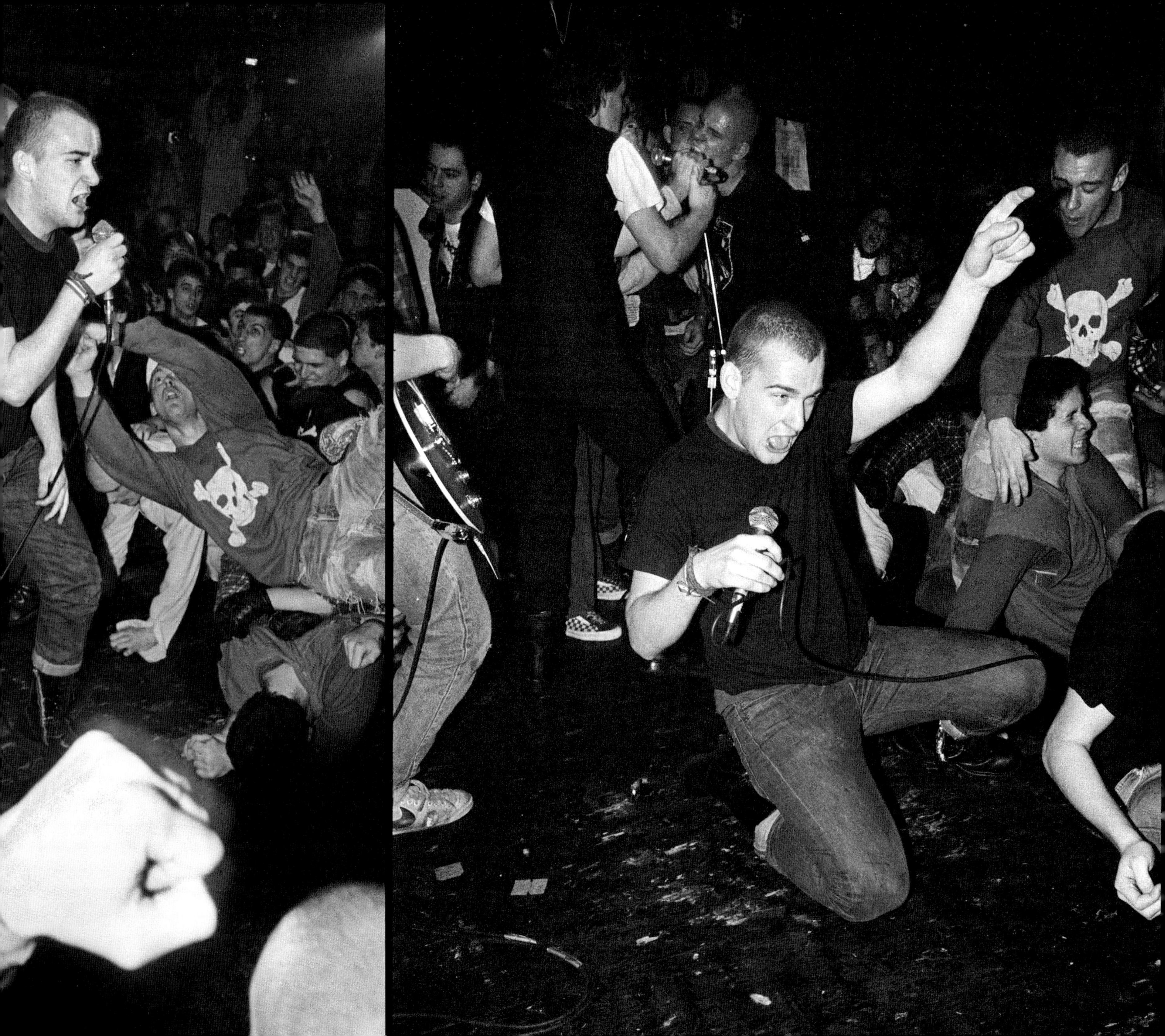

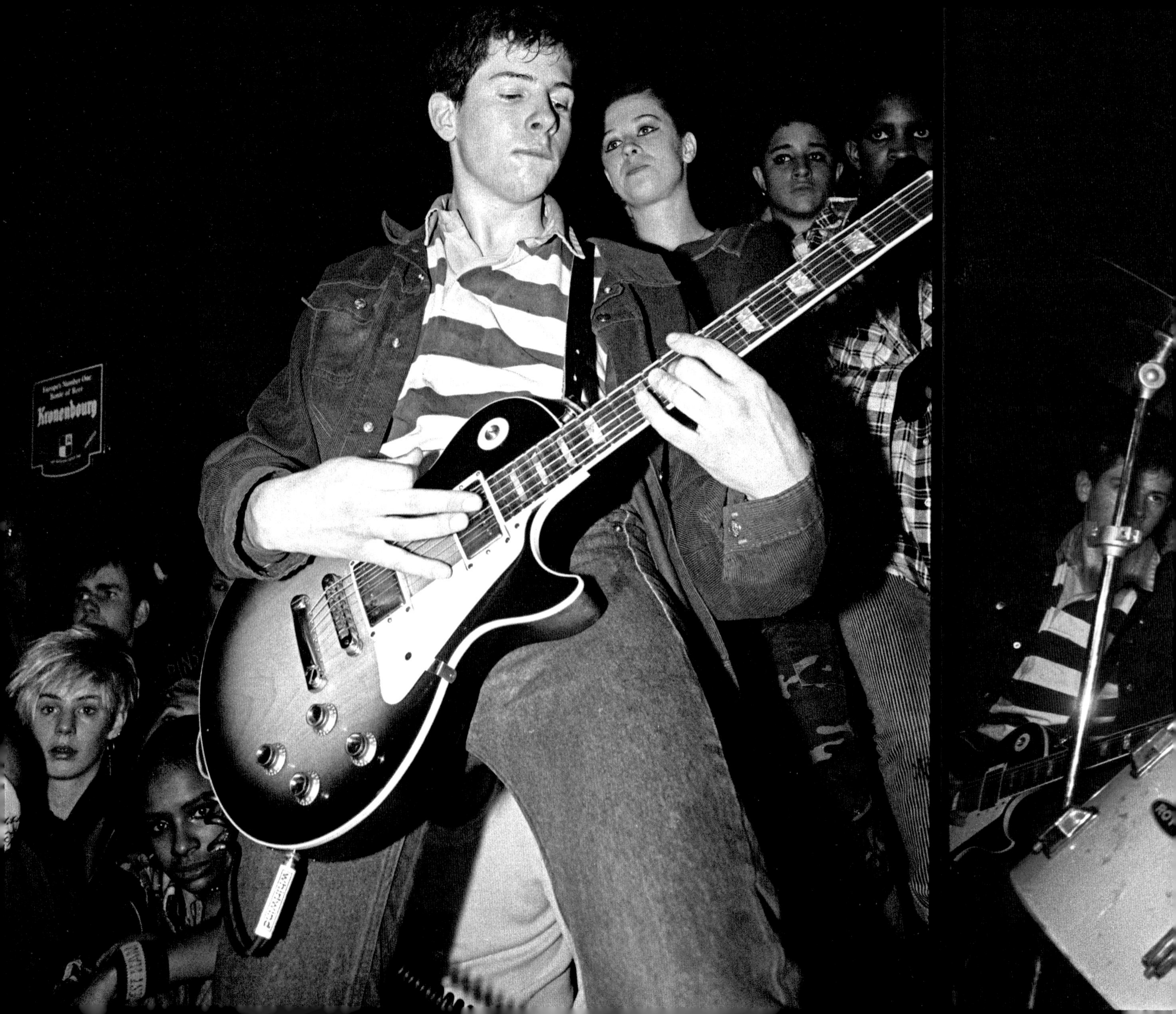
Kronenbourg

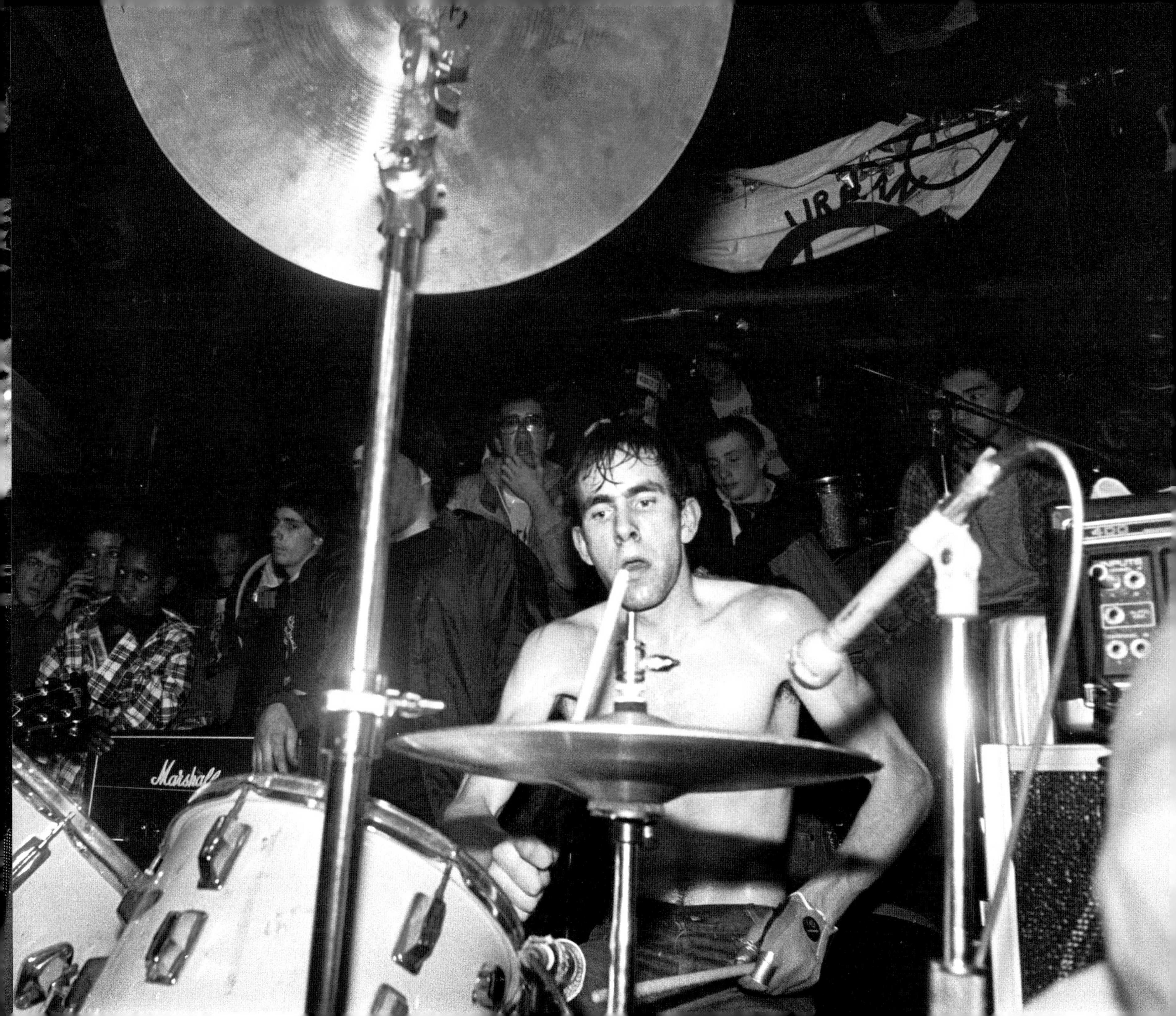

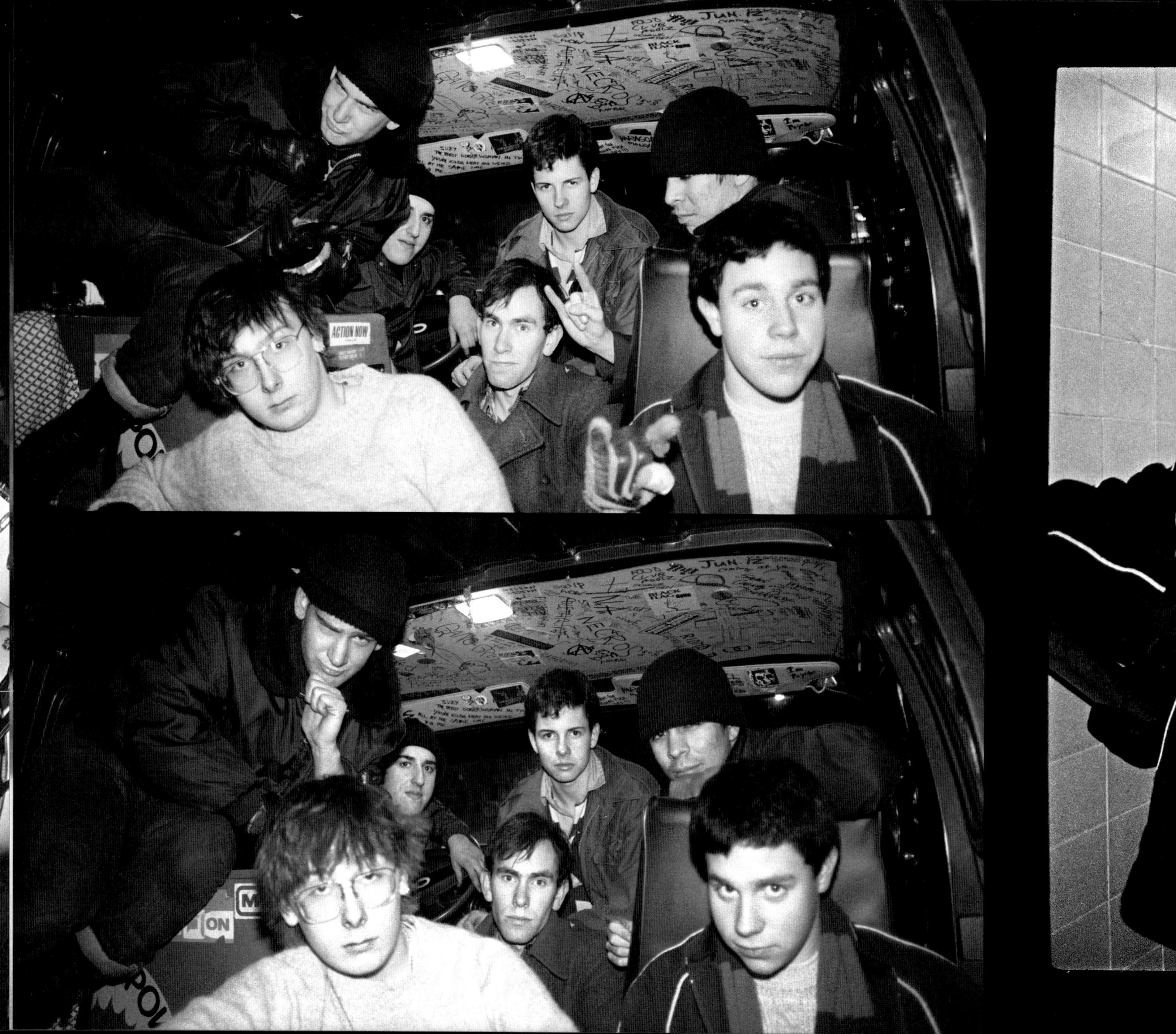
ACTION NOW
NECROS

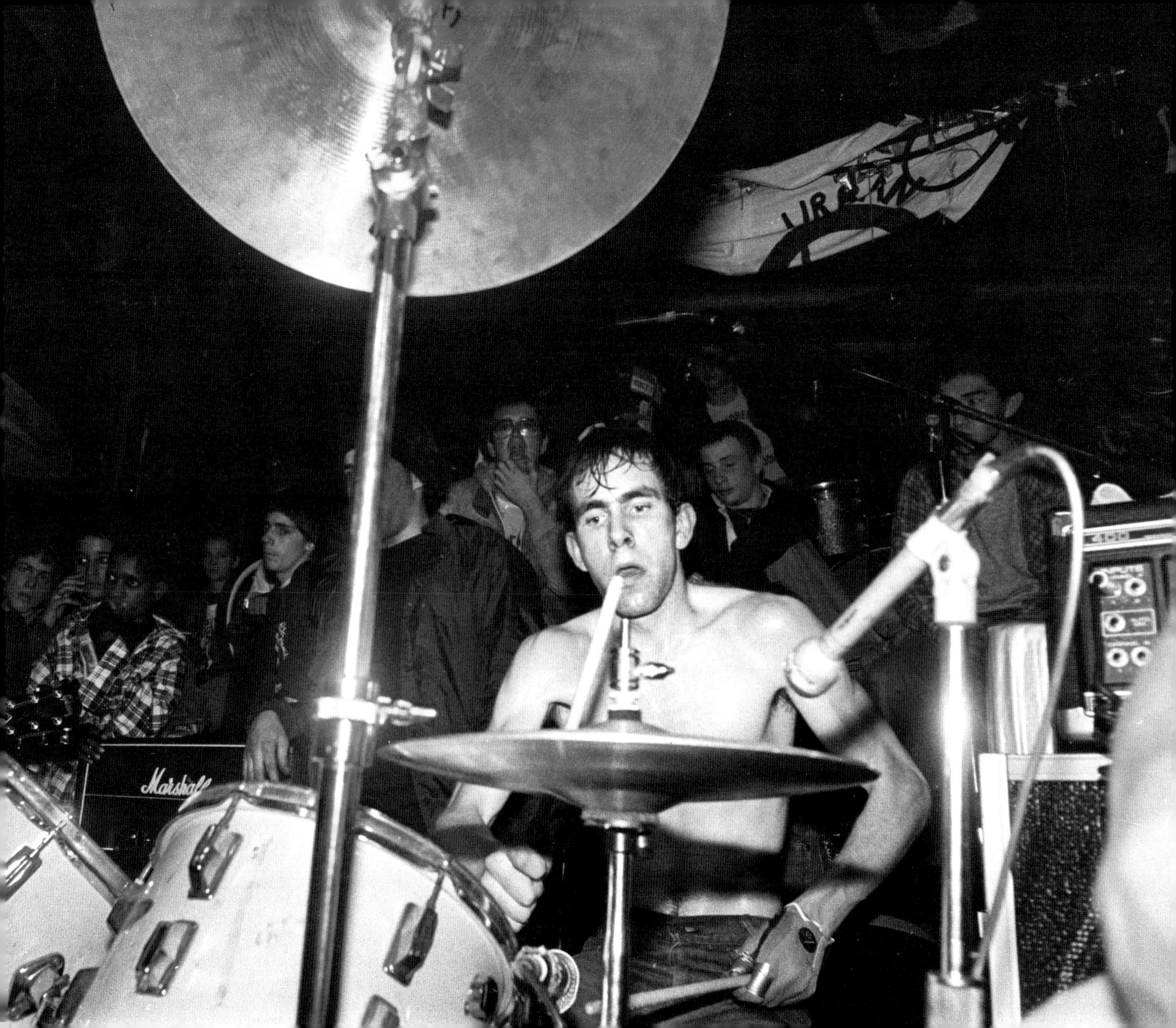
Marshall

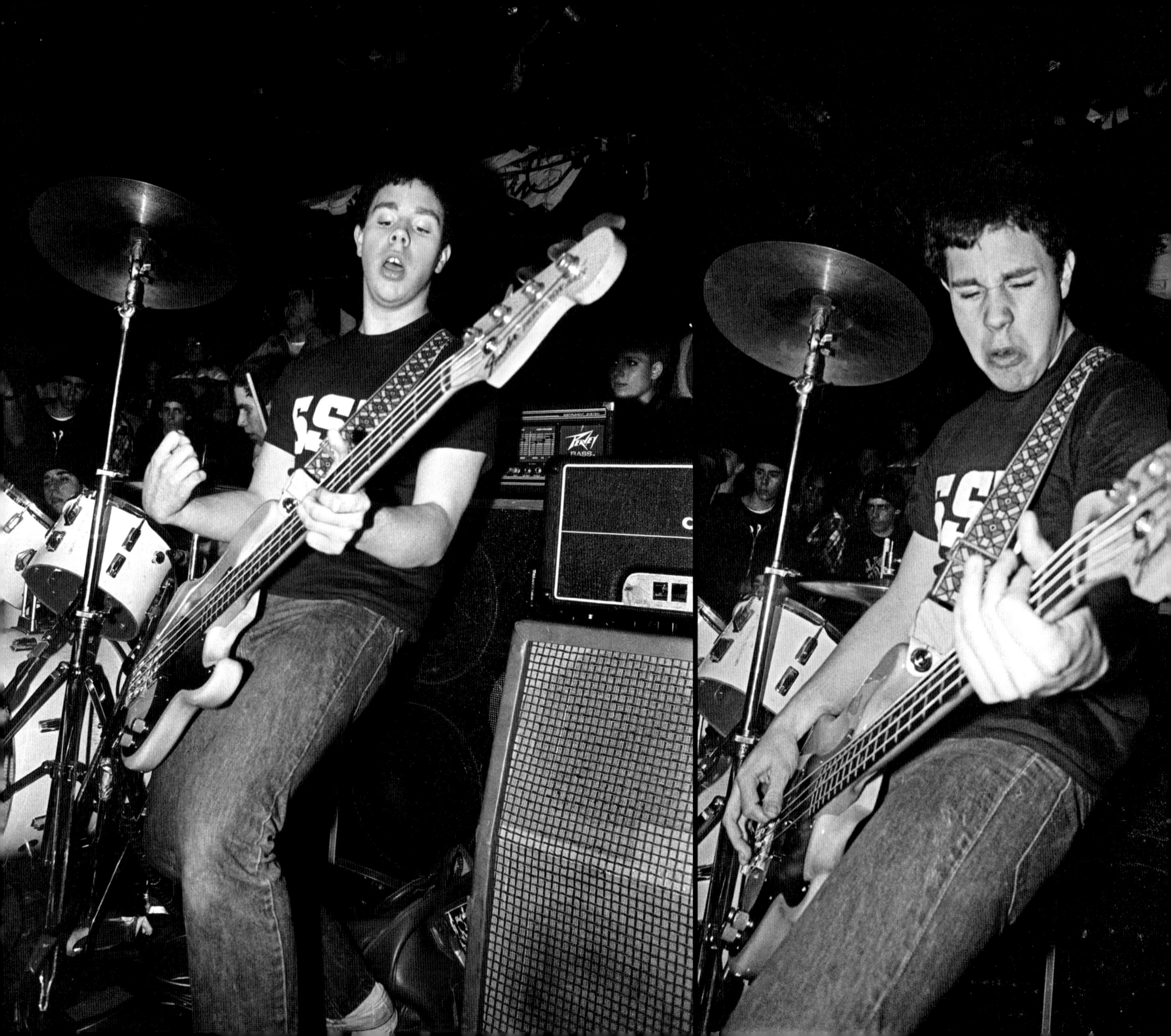
Peavey
BASS

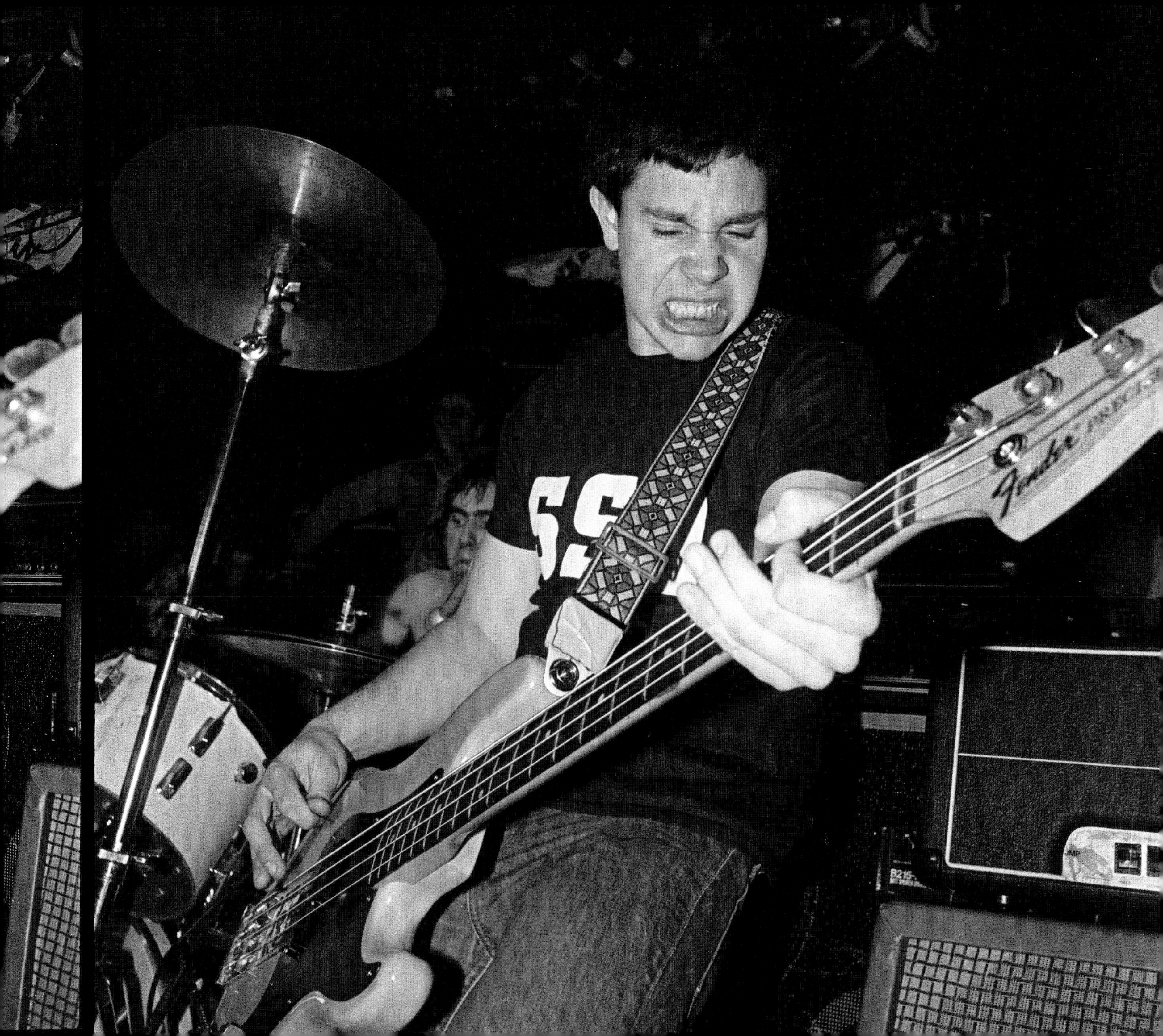
Fender

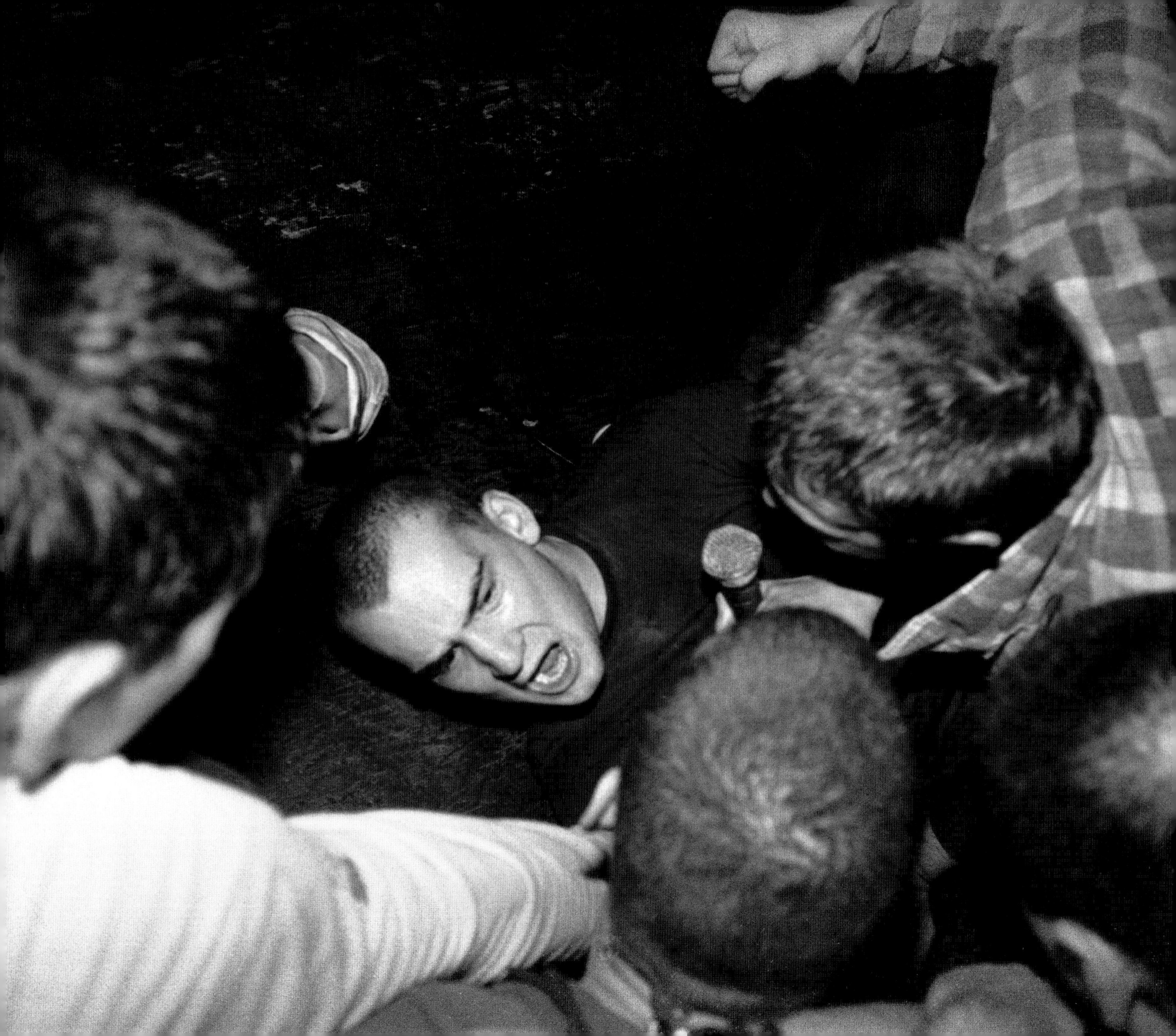

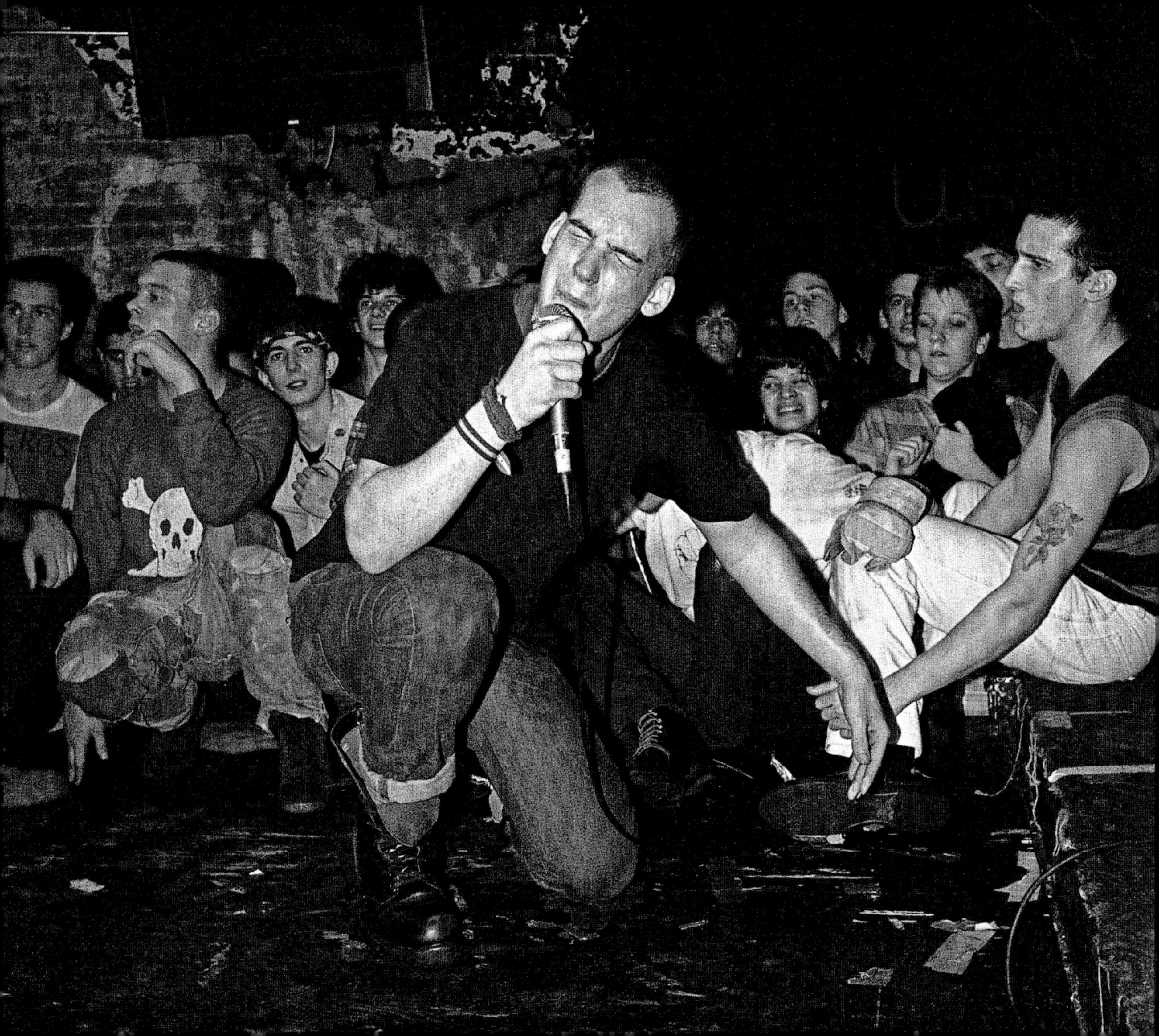

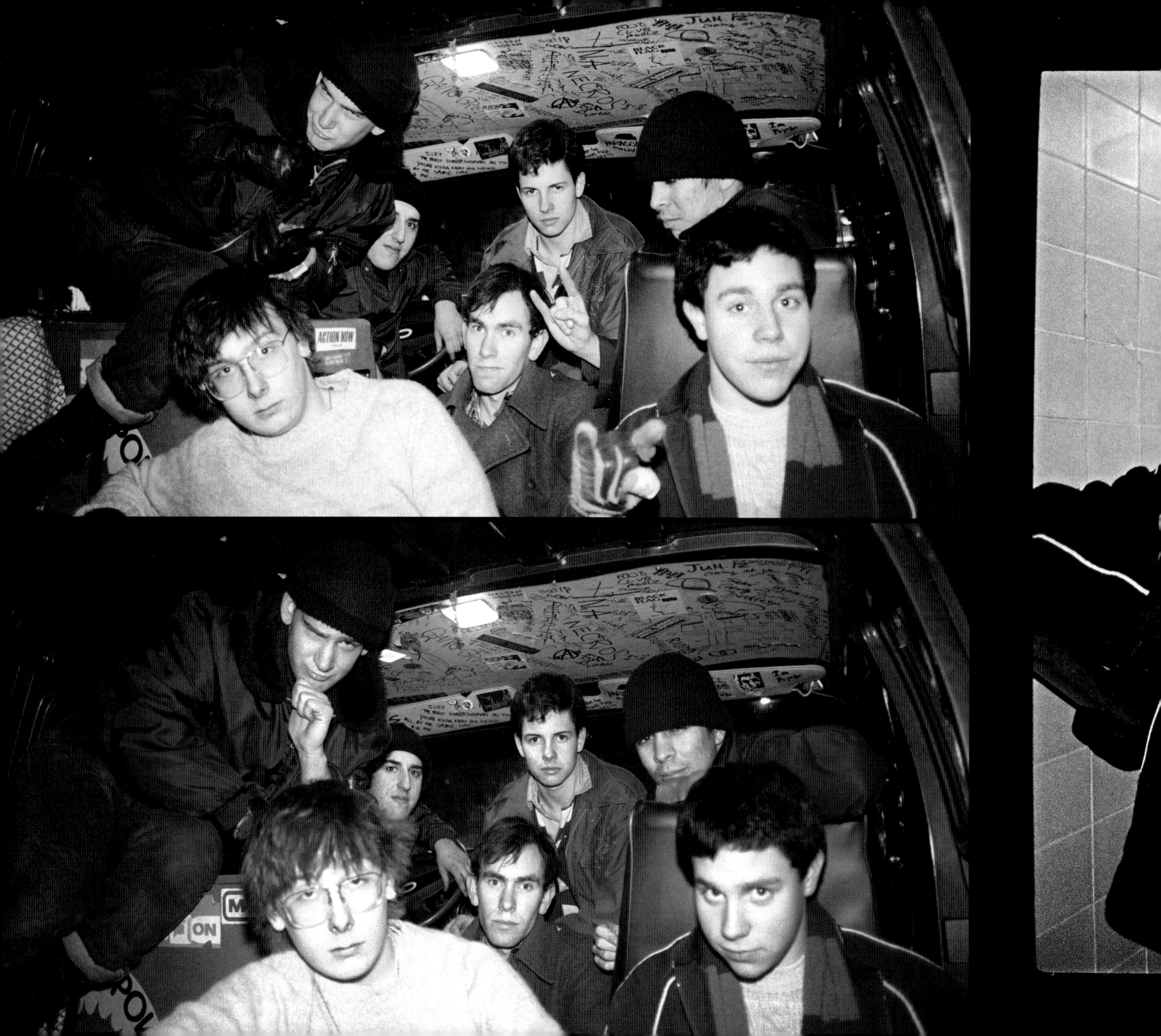
JUN 12
NECROS
ACTION NOW

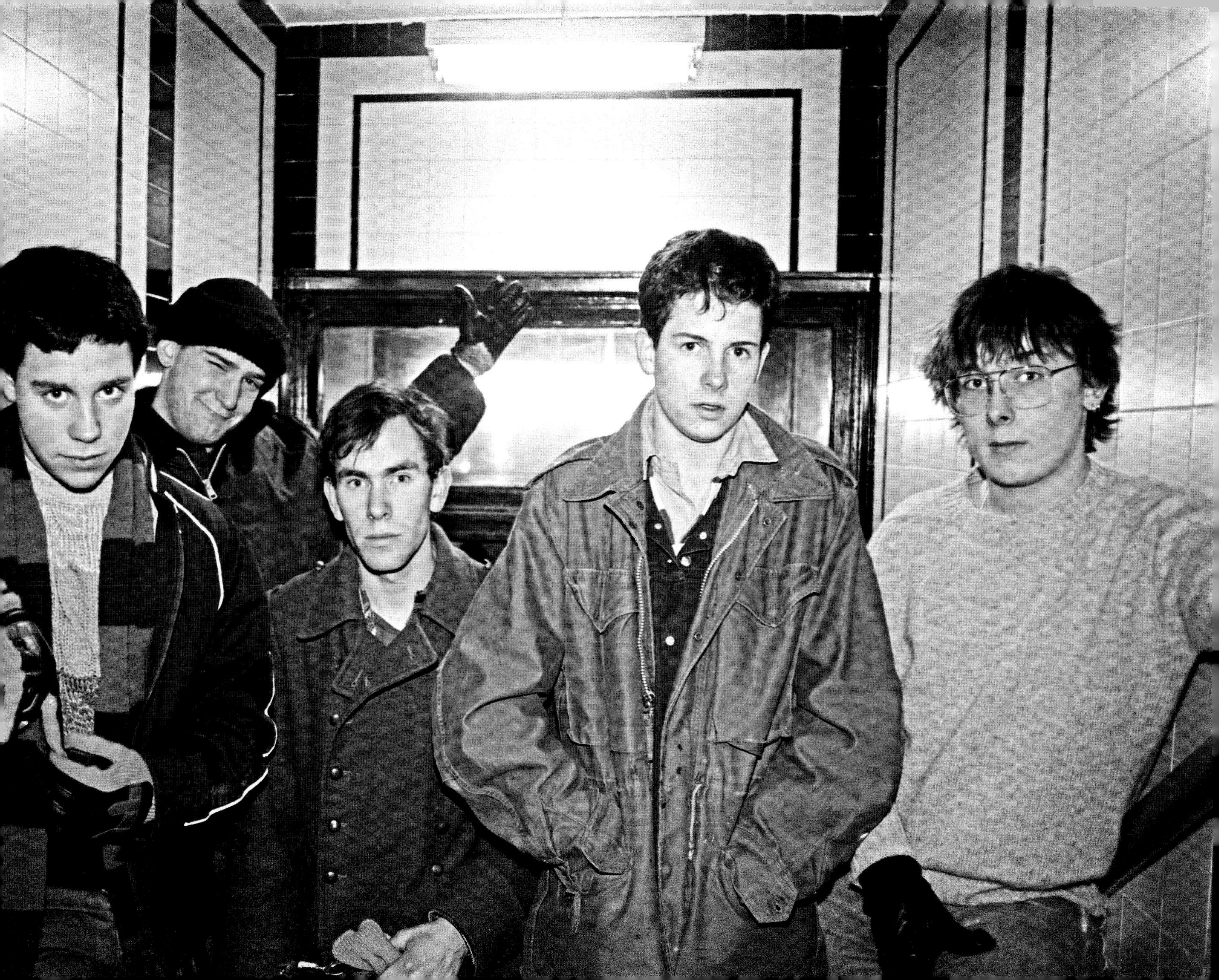

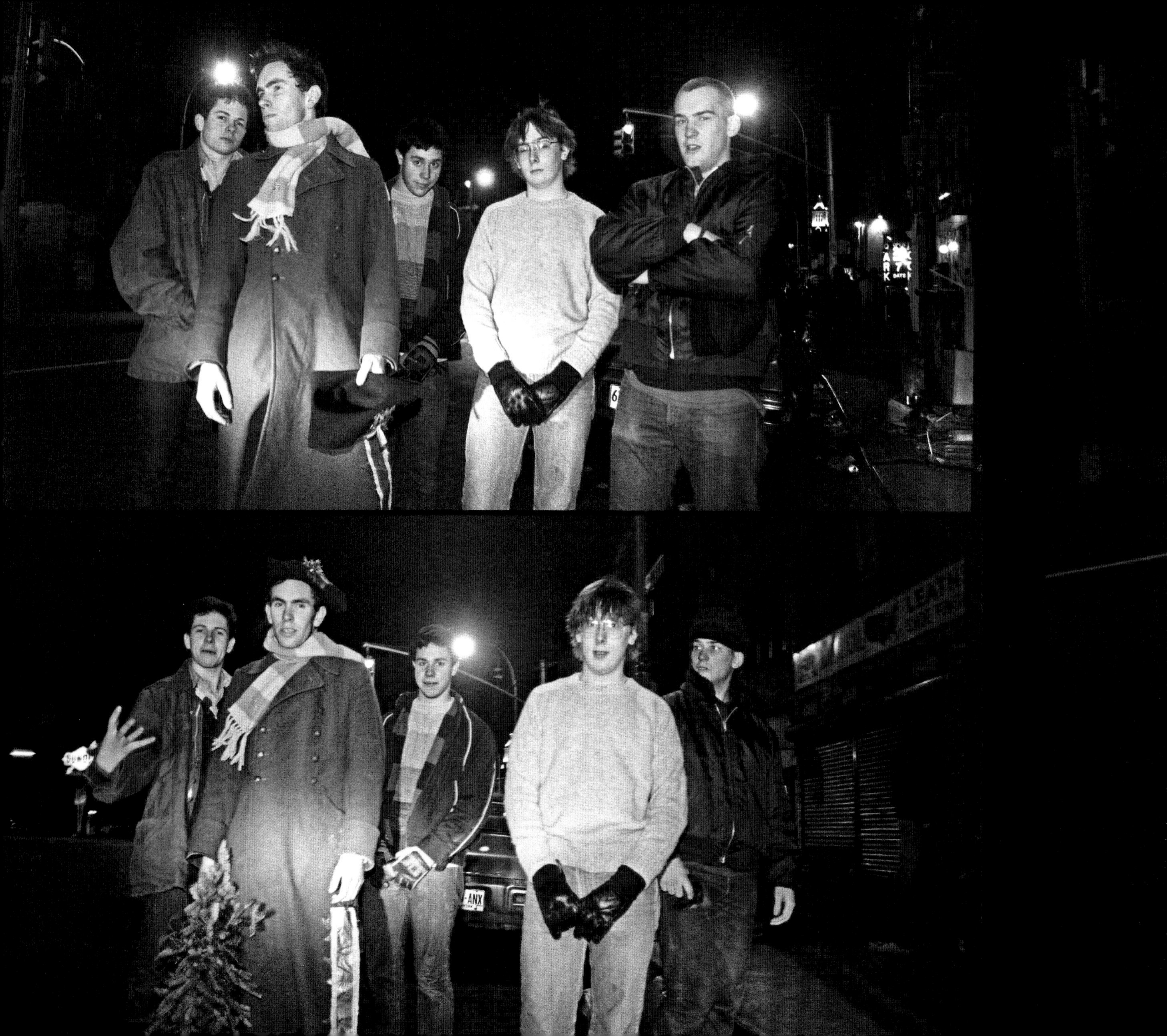

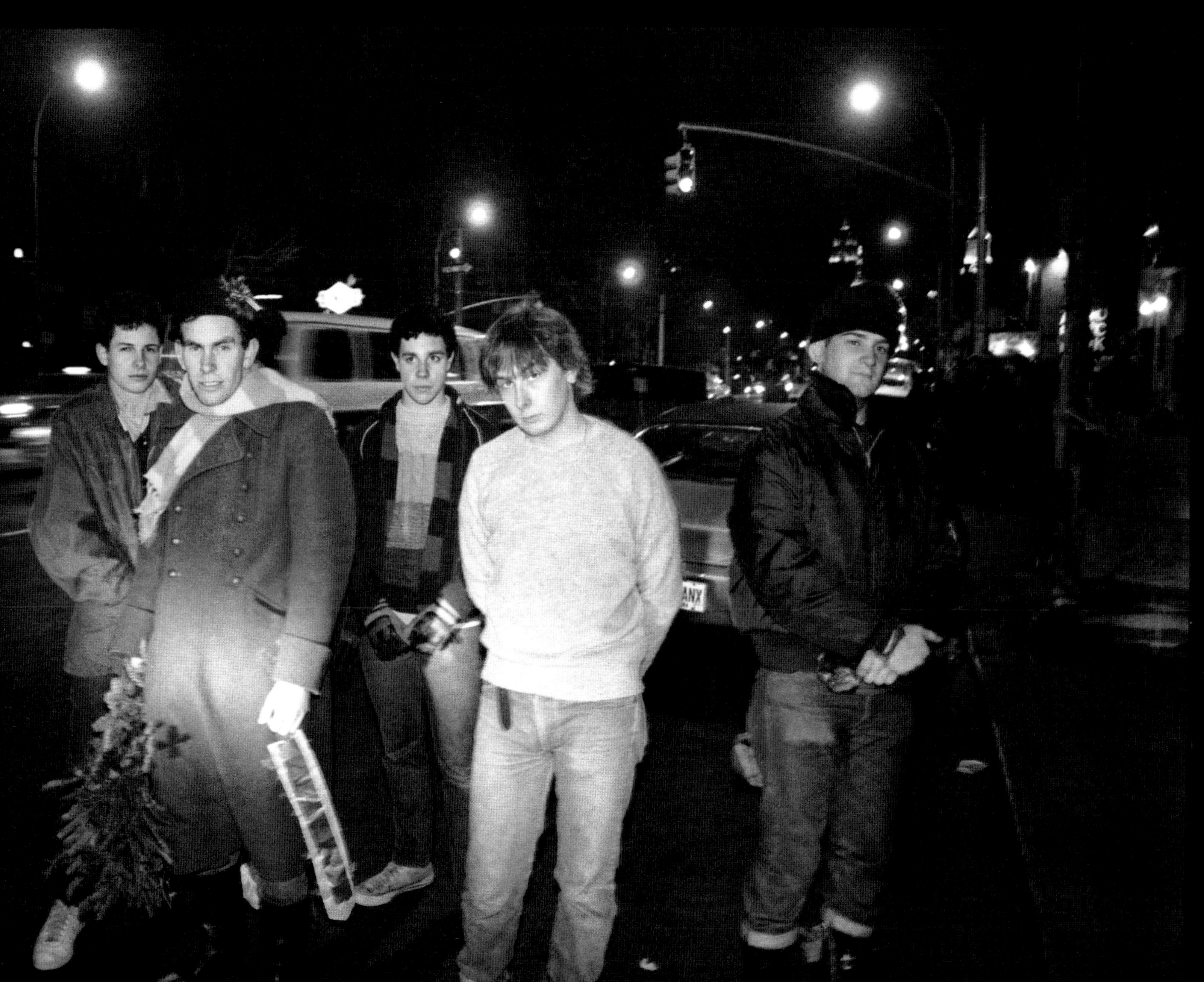

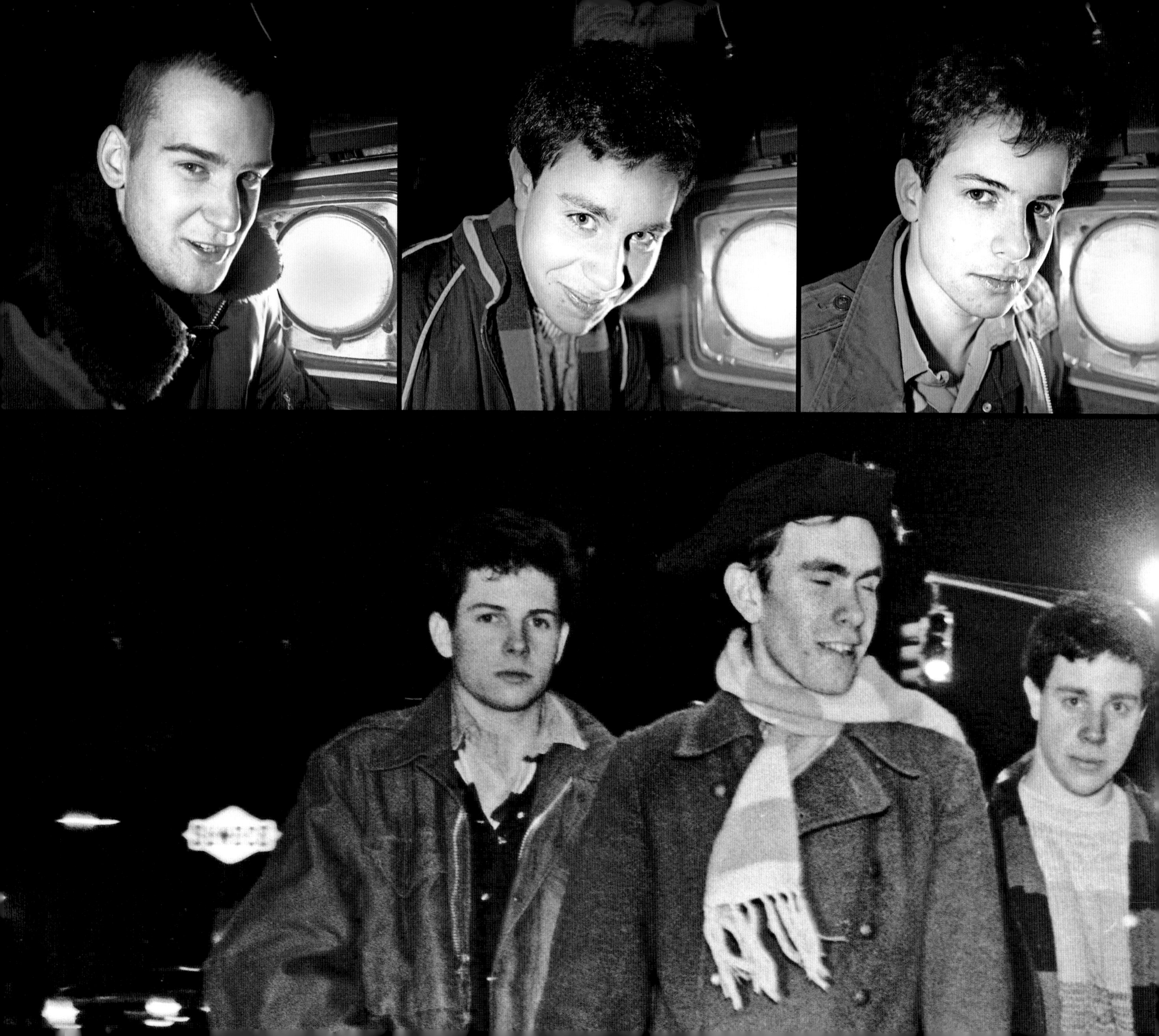

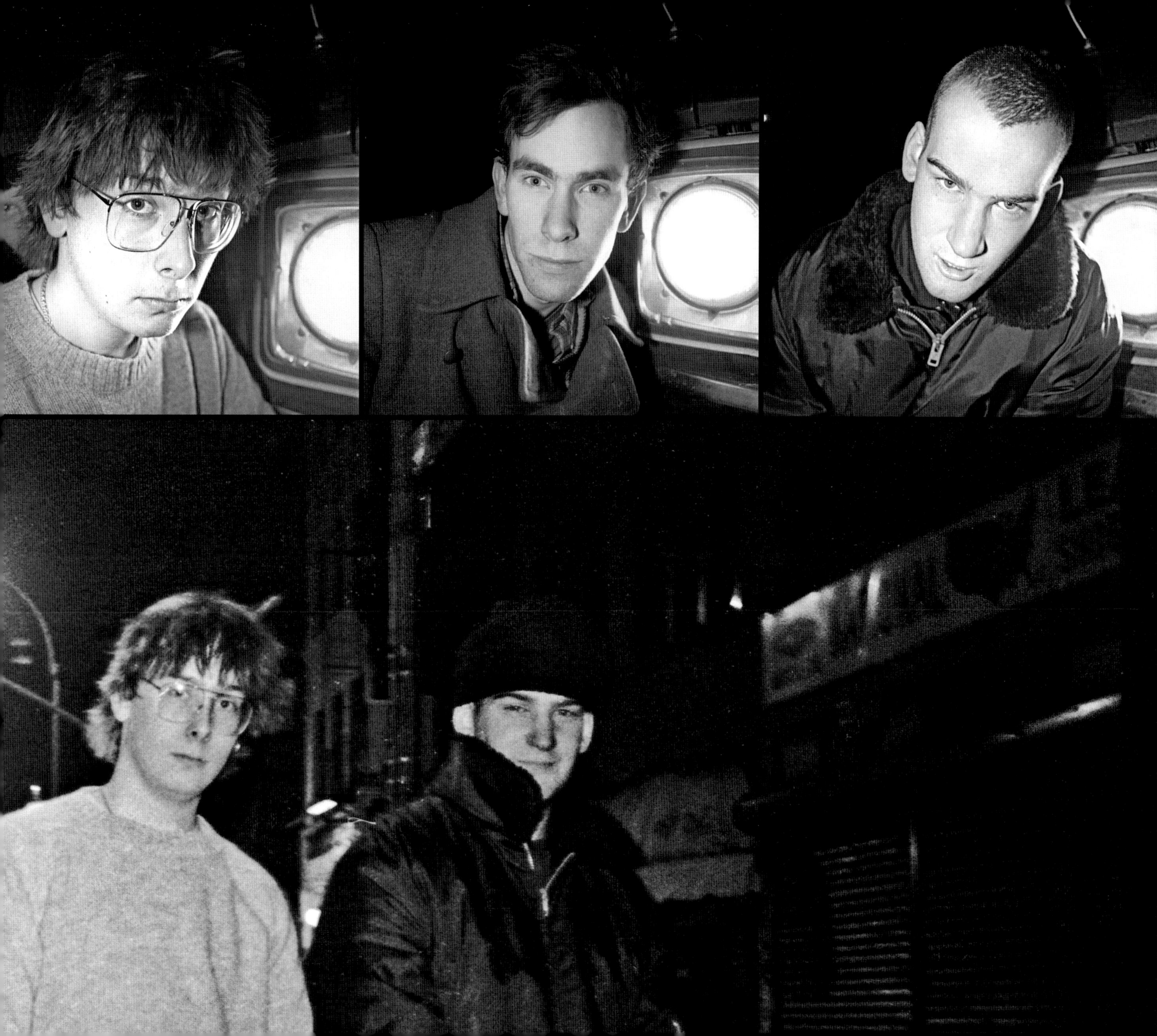

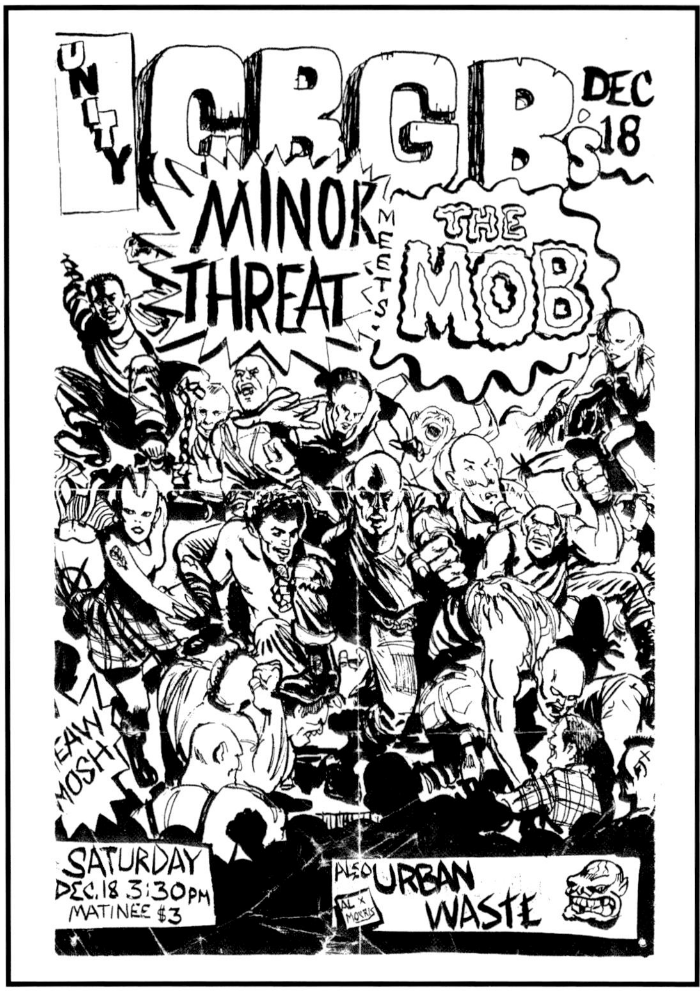

Minor Threat had supposedly reformed after a short breakup. They had played a couple of shows in New York recently and my band, the Mob, really wanted to get them to a CBGB matinee and share the bill.

We were at our rehearsal spot in our guitar player's parents' basement, planning the next "big" show. We weren't completely sure if Minor Threat were still together as a band, or if they would even consider a show with us. We usually dealt with local bands, and Minor Threat were relatively established, they were from DC, and everyone knew that they were the real deal.

Our guitar player Jack also did all of our managing stuff and he was especially apprehensive, as bands back then were pretty tribal and somewhat territorial. After a measure of egging on by the rest of us, he got the phone number of Dischord House, where half of Minor Threat lived and ran their small independent record company. He made the call! Ian picked up the phone, Jack introduced himself and our idea for the gig—it was easy, Ian asked for a very reasonable $300 guarantee, no strings attached. Jack agreed. No emails back and forth or any bullshit (because there was no such thing!). We agreed to the date and that was it.

We would get our friends Urban Waste to open the bill—they were crushing the NYC scene at the time.

Day of the show, CBGB was packed, it was like a steam bath. Urban Waste played especially great and we threw down one of our best sets ever. The energy in the room was palpable. It was blood, sweat, and slamming. The crowd energy was revving up more and more as the afternoon continued; everyone wanted to see Minor Threat. Just one thing—they were nowhere to be seen.

They missed load-in, missed sound check, and no one really knew when or if they would arrive. Since we had put the show together, our rep was on the line too. We were playing an intense set, and if they didn't arrive soon there was the real threat by CBGB's management that they would not be allowed to play, and this show would be a bust. All the while onstage we would break at points between songs . . . "Are they here yet?" "No, keep playing . . ." We extended our set to keep the show moving and the walls sweating, wondering where they were. And then, at what seemed like the very last moment . . .

It turned out their van broke down and they'd had major trouble getting to town. But they finally made it to CBGB. *Minor Threat is here!* My brother Kevin was in the front of the club and saw them pull up . . . "Hey, are you Minor Threat?" They let him know indeed they were, and he let them know they had only minutes to get on the stage or they wouldn't be allowed to play at all.

They ran in with their equipment—my brother grabbed Ian by the arm and helped push him through the packed crowd and they were onstage in minutes.

Minor Threat went into the first tune and the place exploded. Bodies flying everywhere. Punks hanging on the mic with Ian. Chicken fights on the floor. People diving off and crushing the stage. It was pure adrenaline, pure chaos, all that pent-up energy from the "threat" of no show had to go somewhere! I never saw the pit like that before or again. I was on the edge of what I thought was the dance floor as it surged back violently; I actually got scared for the first time at a show and moved back toward the bar area. I watched as Minor Threat killed it, and the audience let them know in no uncertain terms that this was one for the books. It was mayhem, explosive out-of-control energy right out of the gate, off the charts.

This was the perfect storm of hardcore and would actually put CBGB matinees on the map. It wasn't the very first matinee but it was the biggest one to date. It's amazing that people who were there still talk about the drama of that day and the fucking amazing intensity of the show.

—Jamie Shanahan

April 1983
Between Shows
Los Angeles, CA

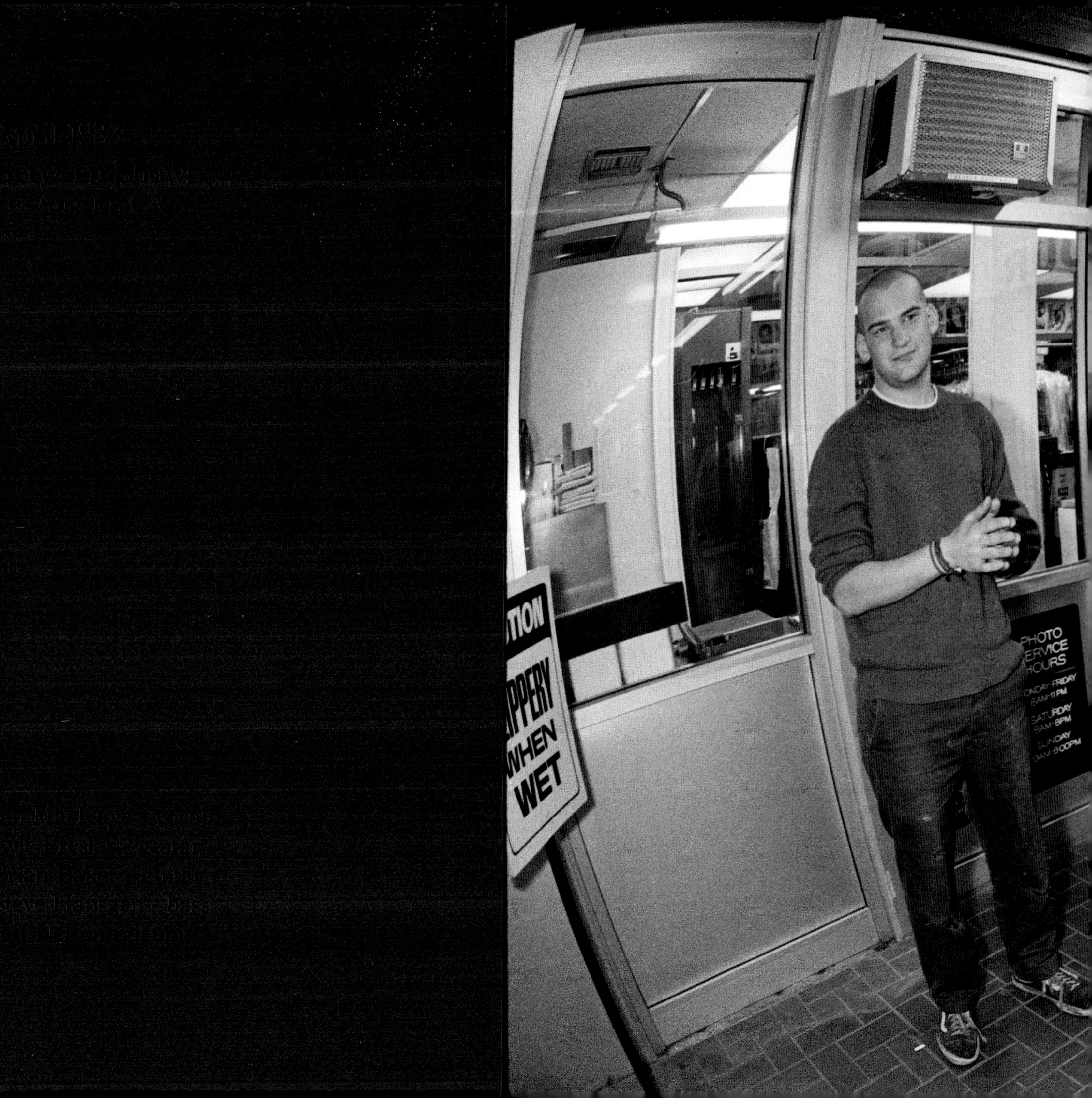

Ian MacKaye – vocals
Lyle Preslar – guitar
Brian Baker – guitar
Steve Hansgen – bass
Jeff Nelson – drums

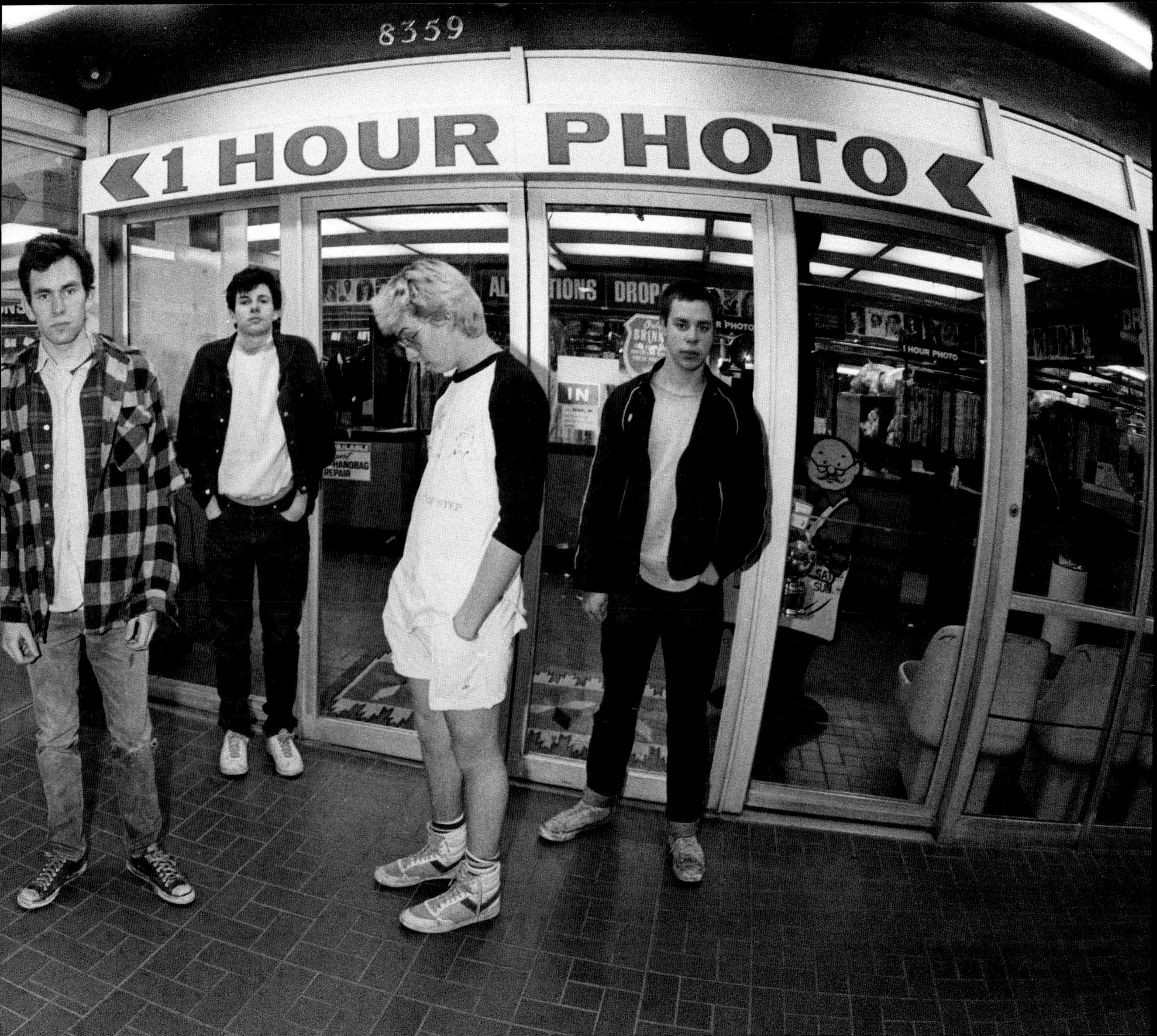

8359
1 HOUR PHOTO

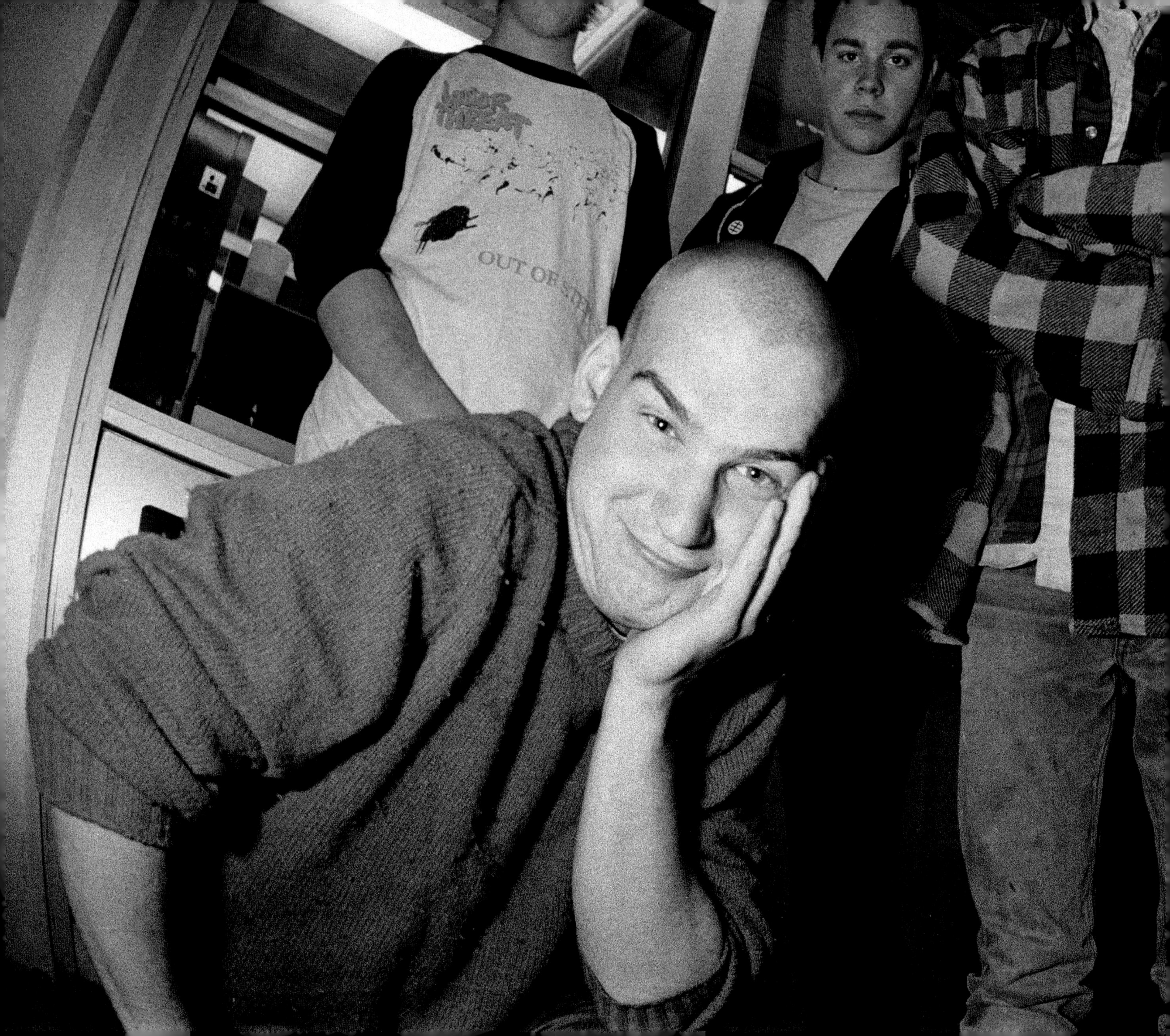
OUT OF

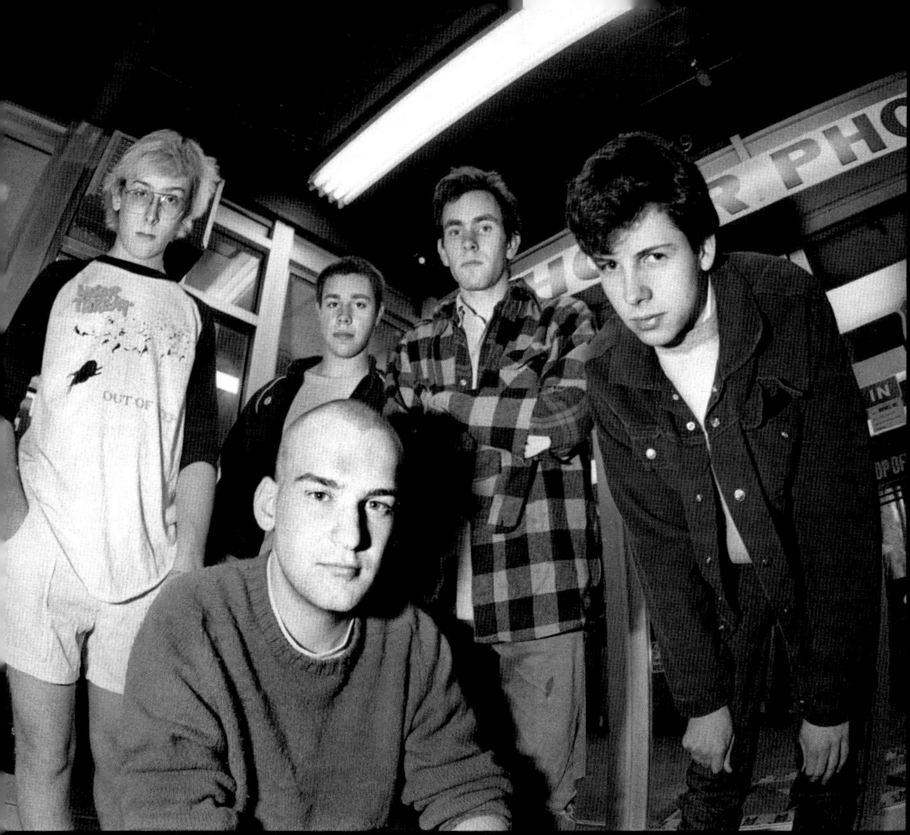

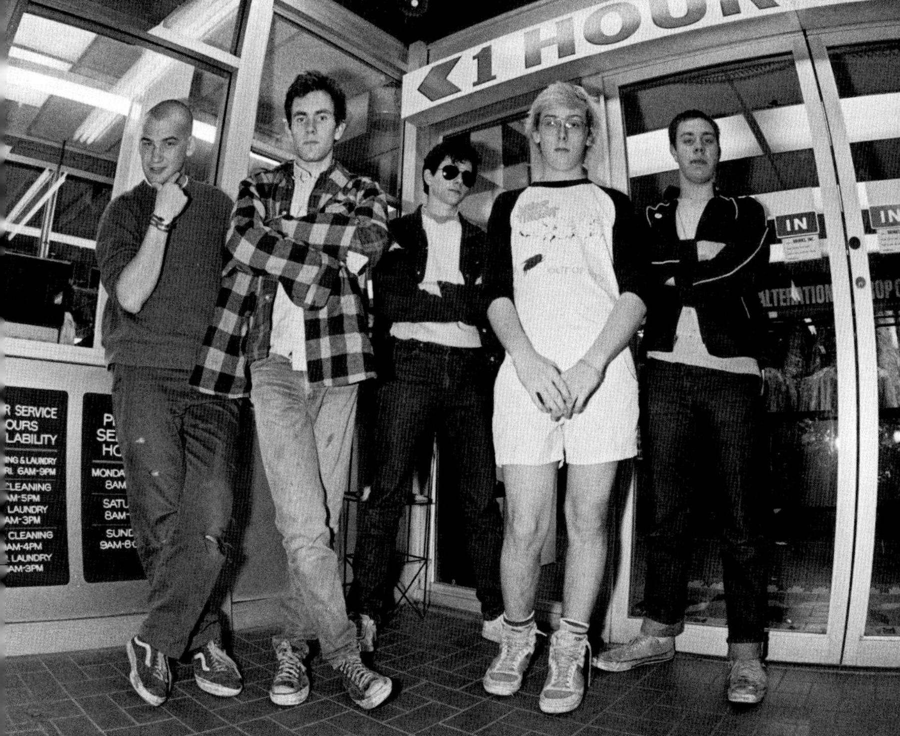
8359
1 HOUR
IN
IN

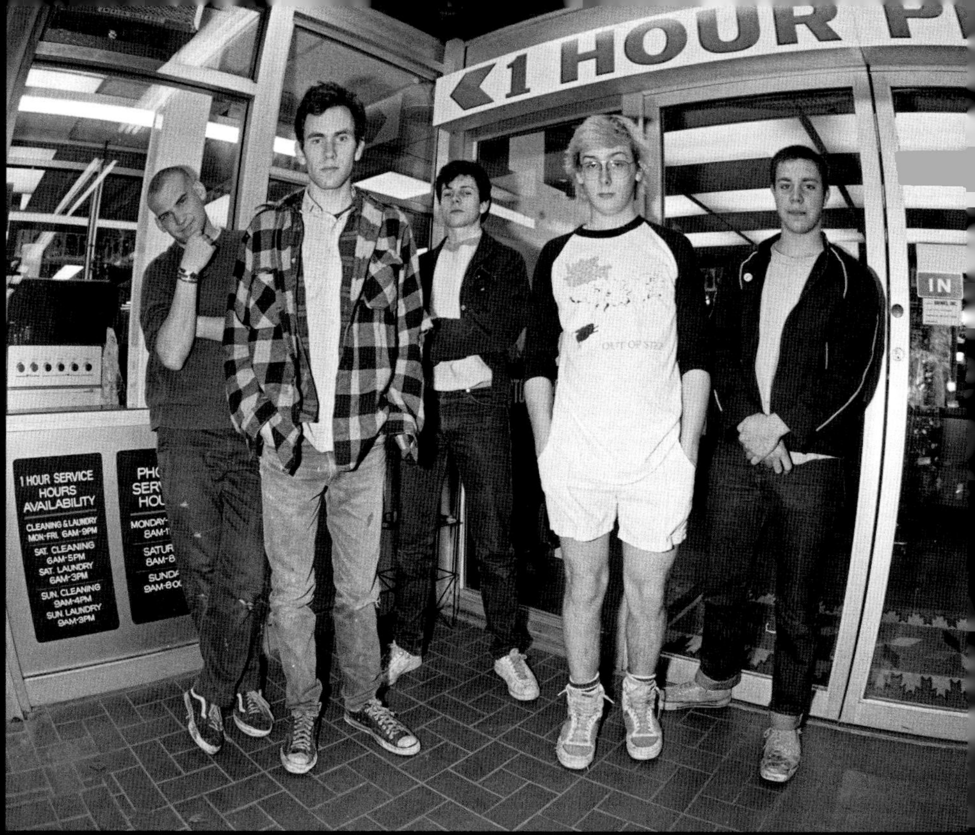

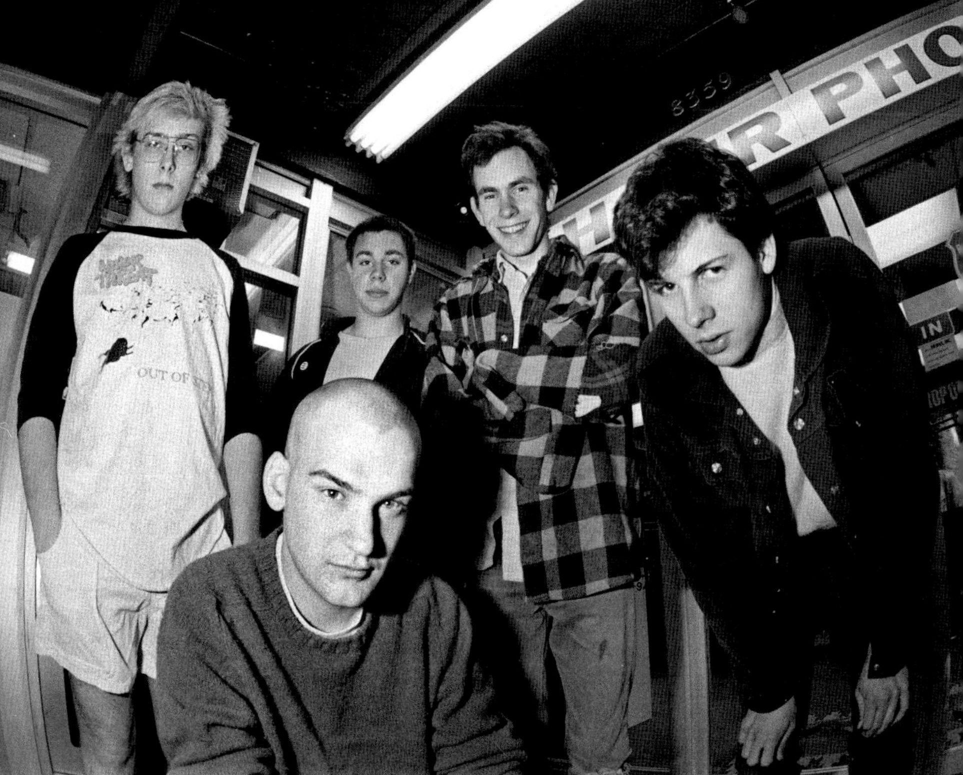
8359

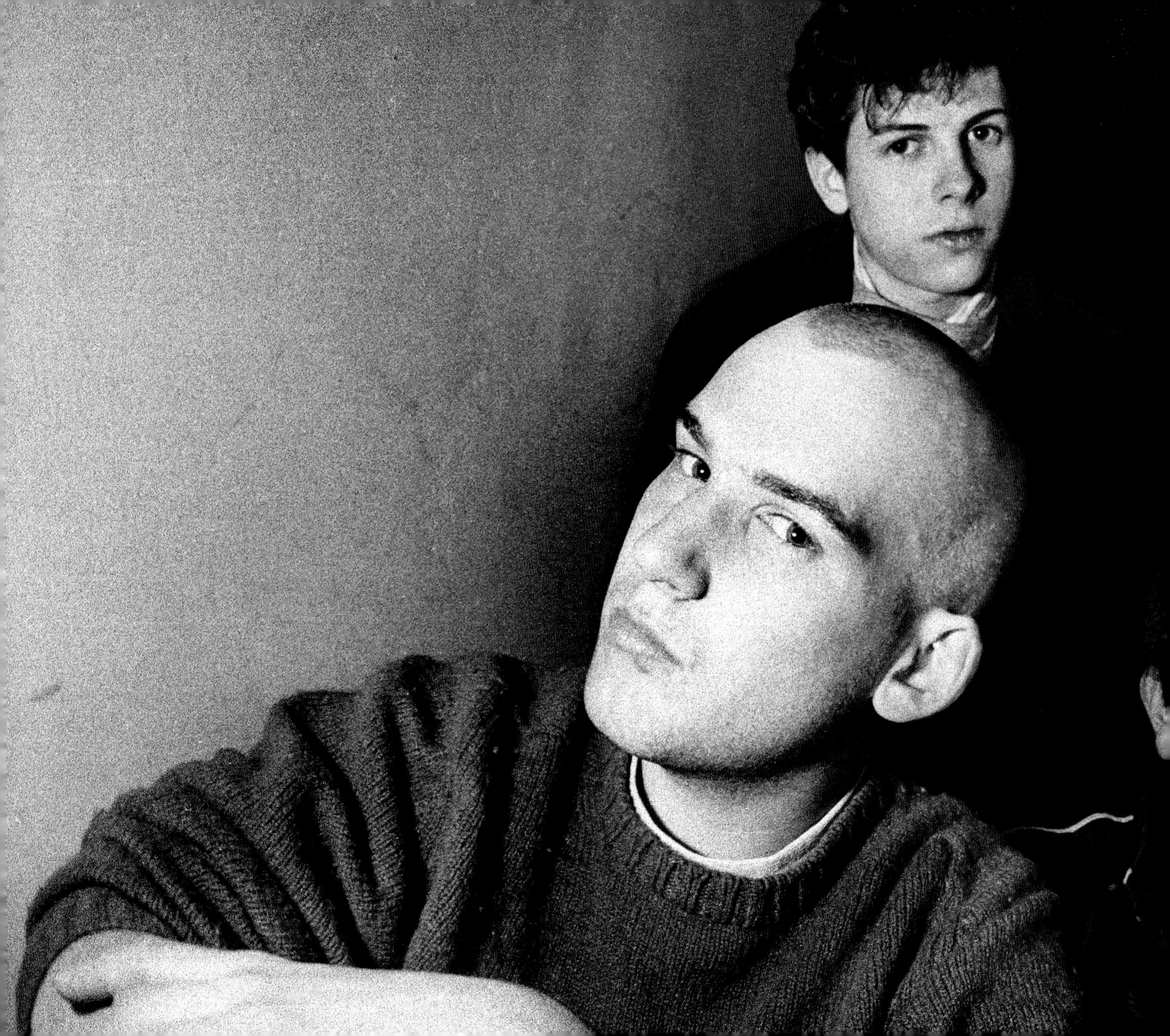

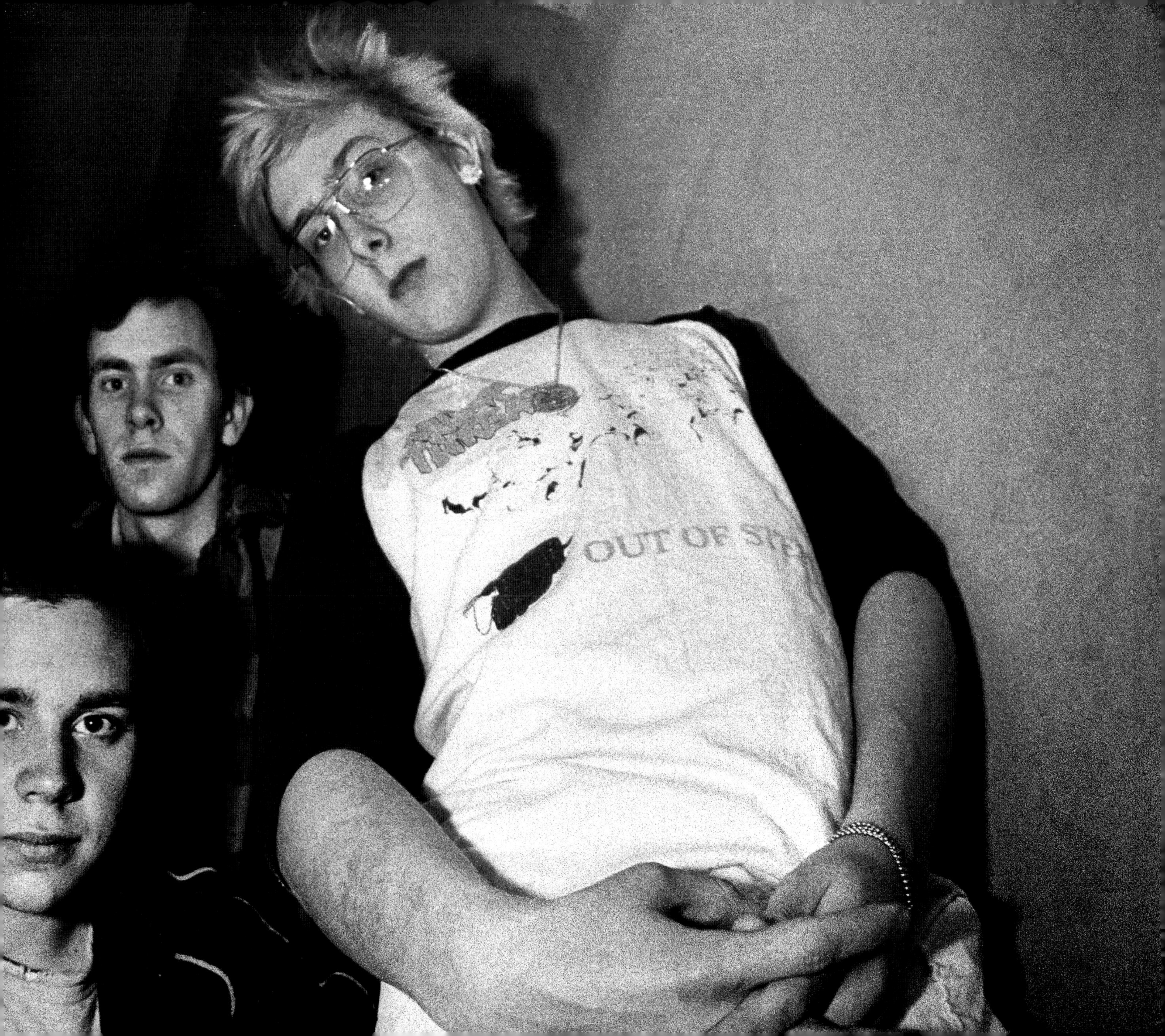
OUT OF

August 2, 1983
Dischord House
Arlington, Virginia

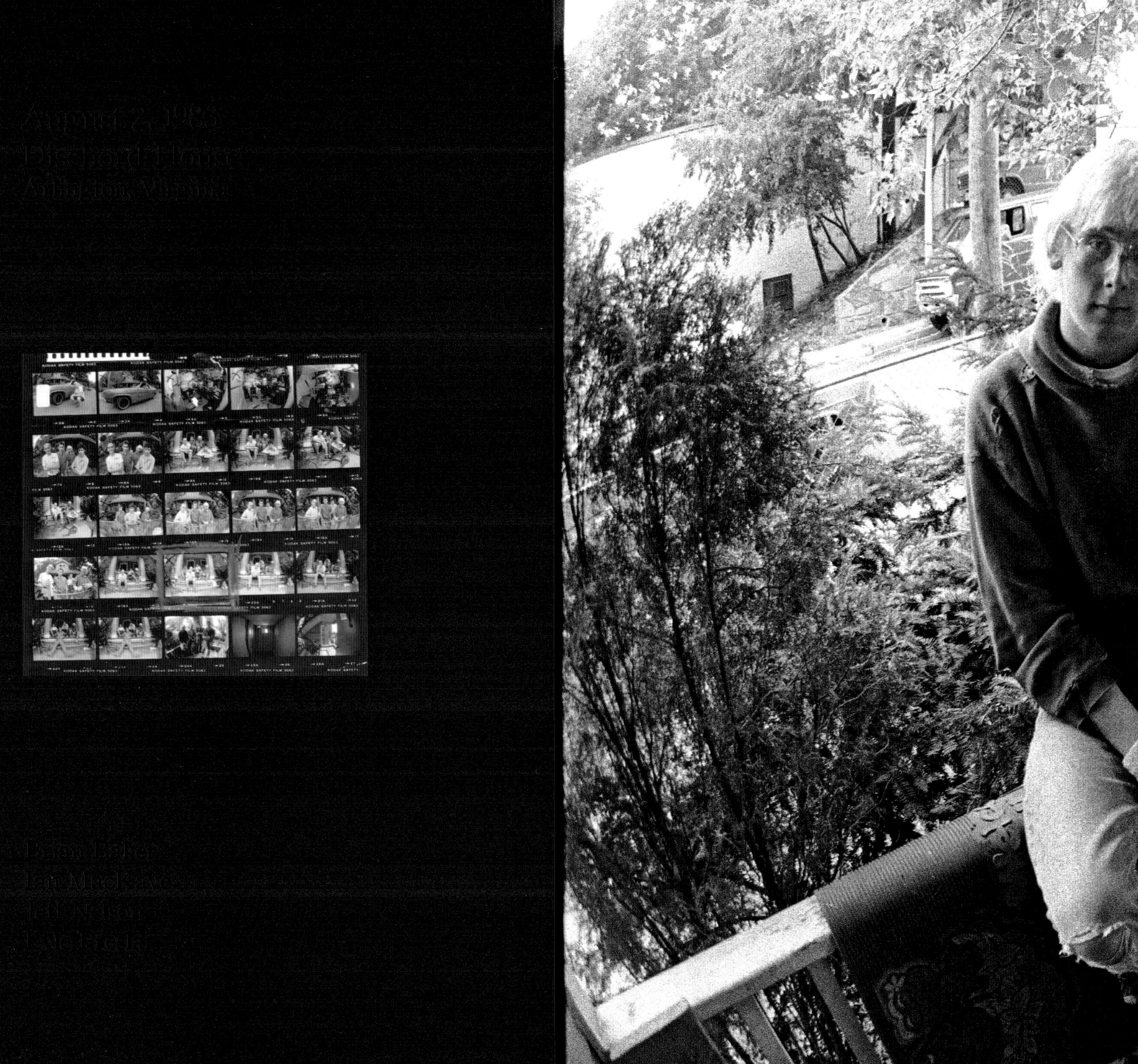

Brian Baker
Ian MacKaye
Jeff Nelson
Lyle Preslar

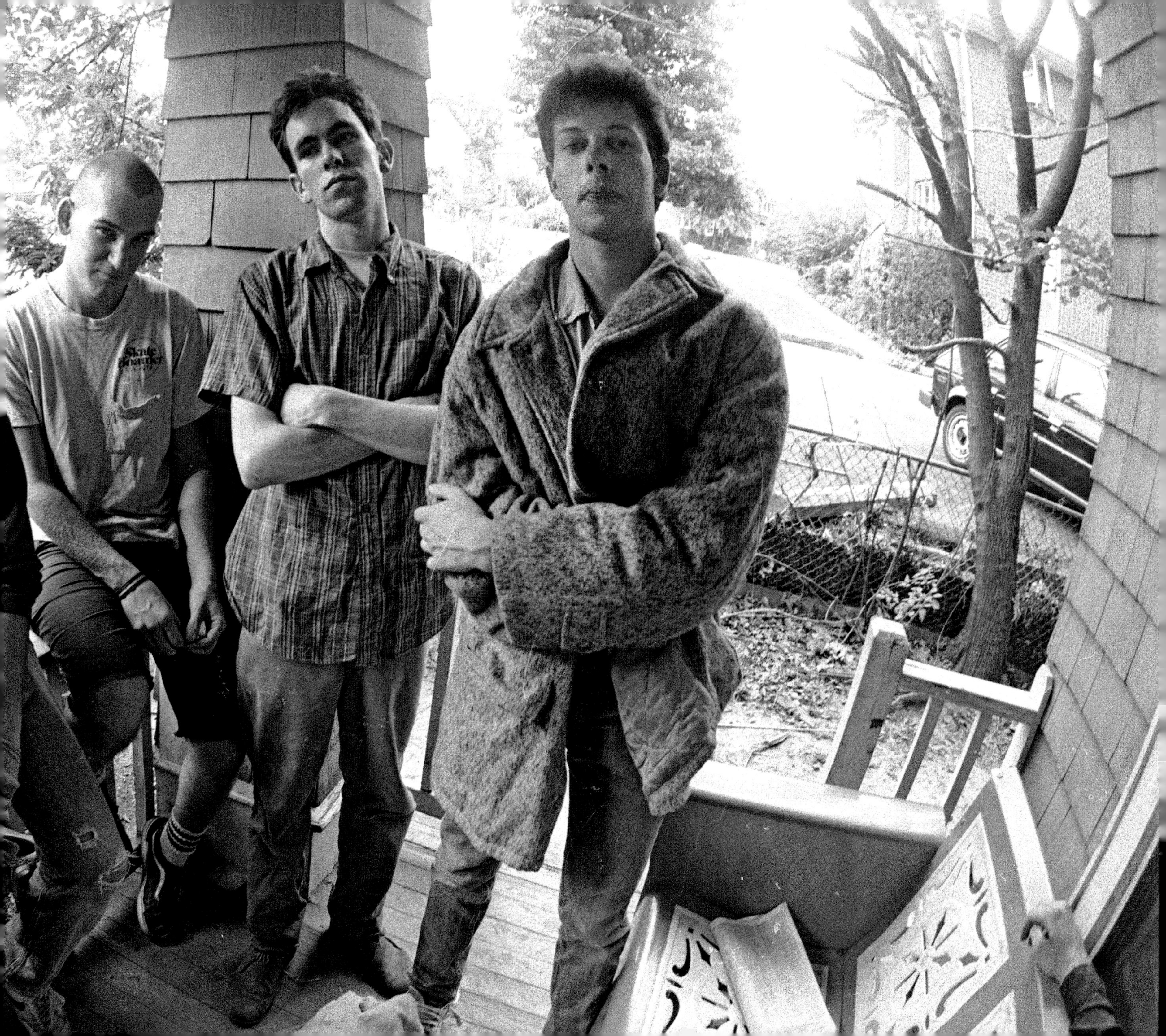

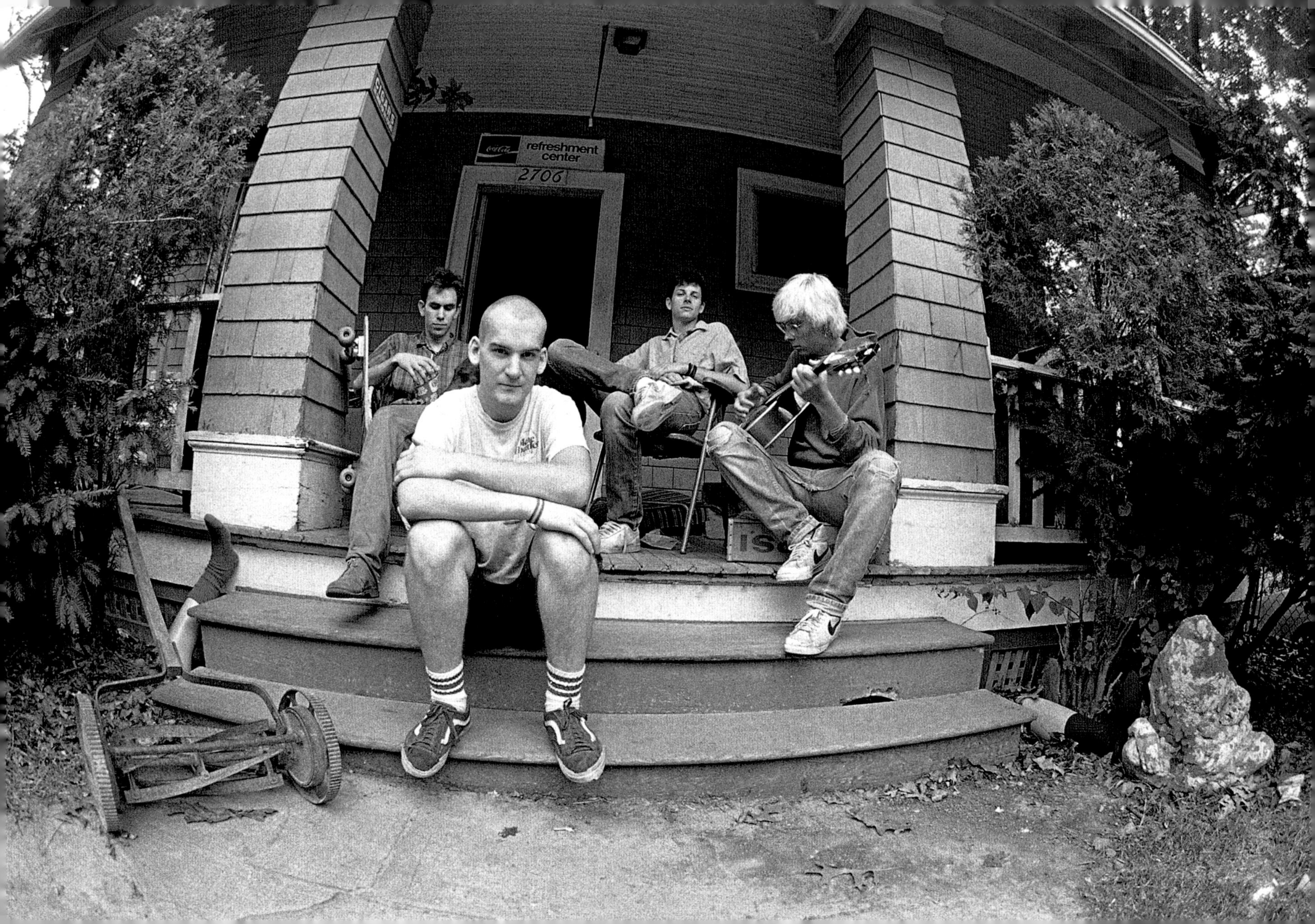
refreshment
center
2706

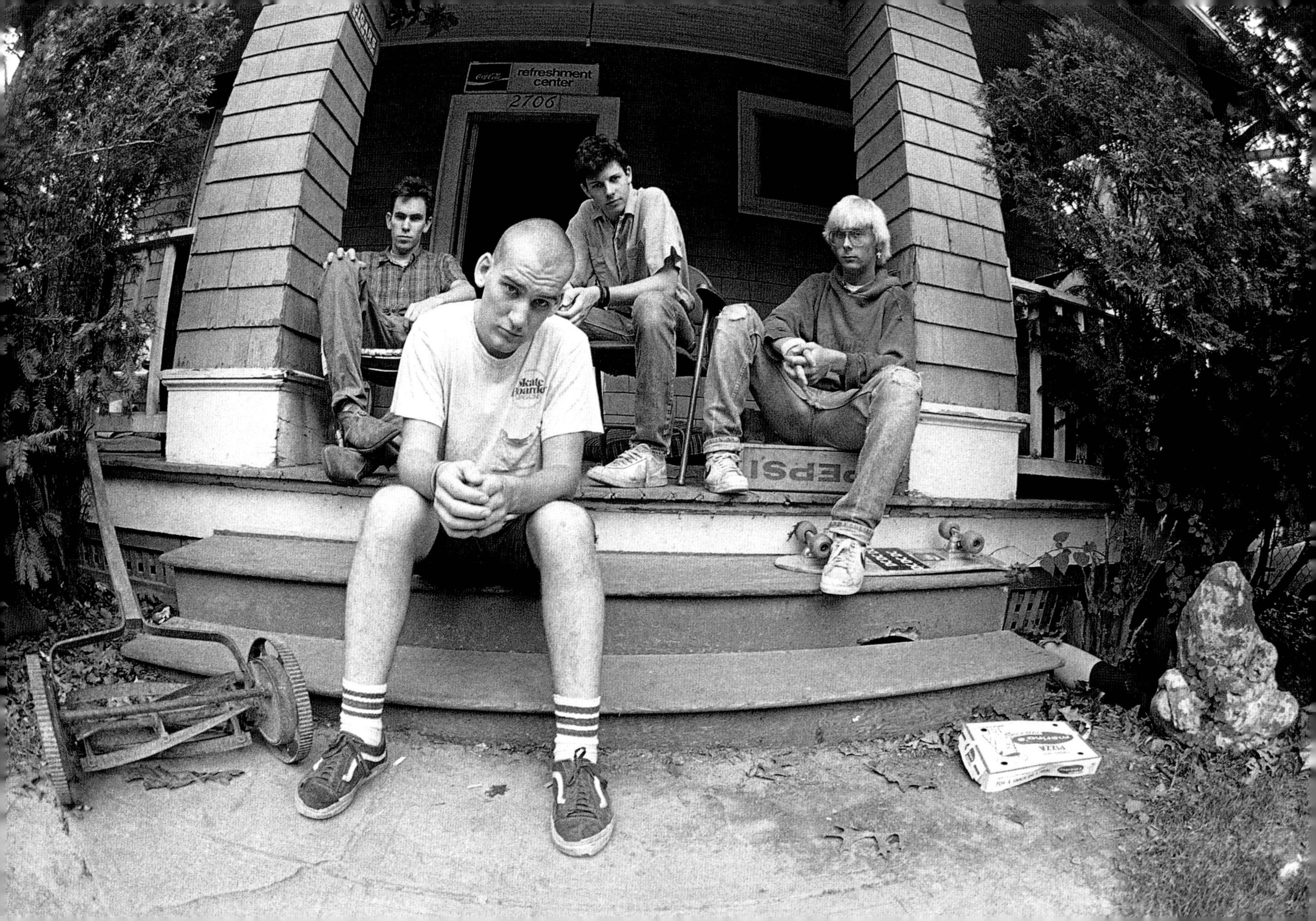
refreshment
center
2706

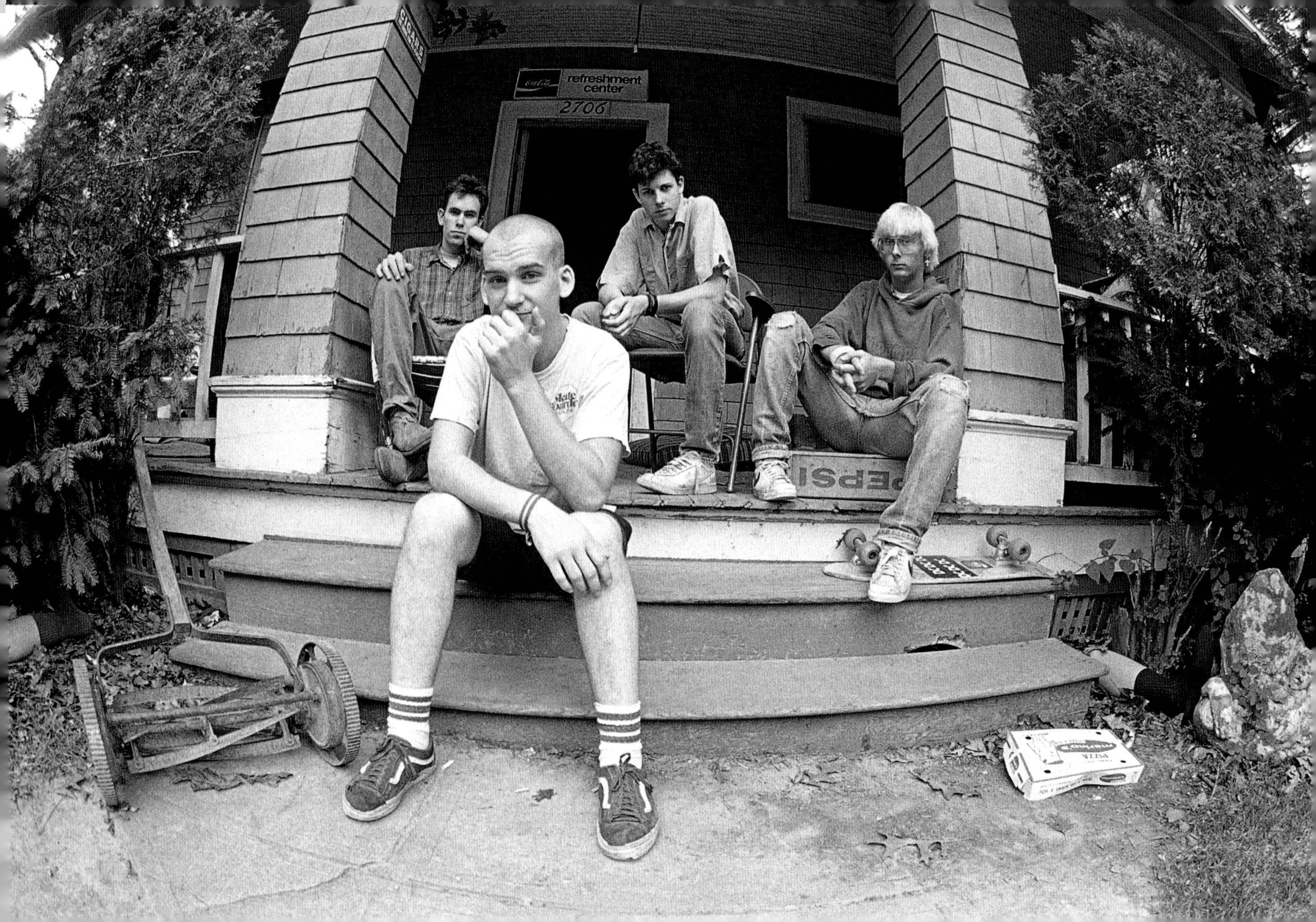
CIGARS
refreshment center
2706

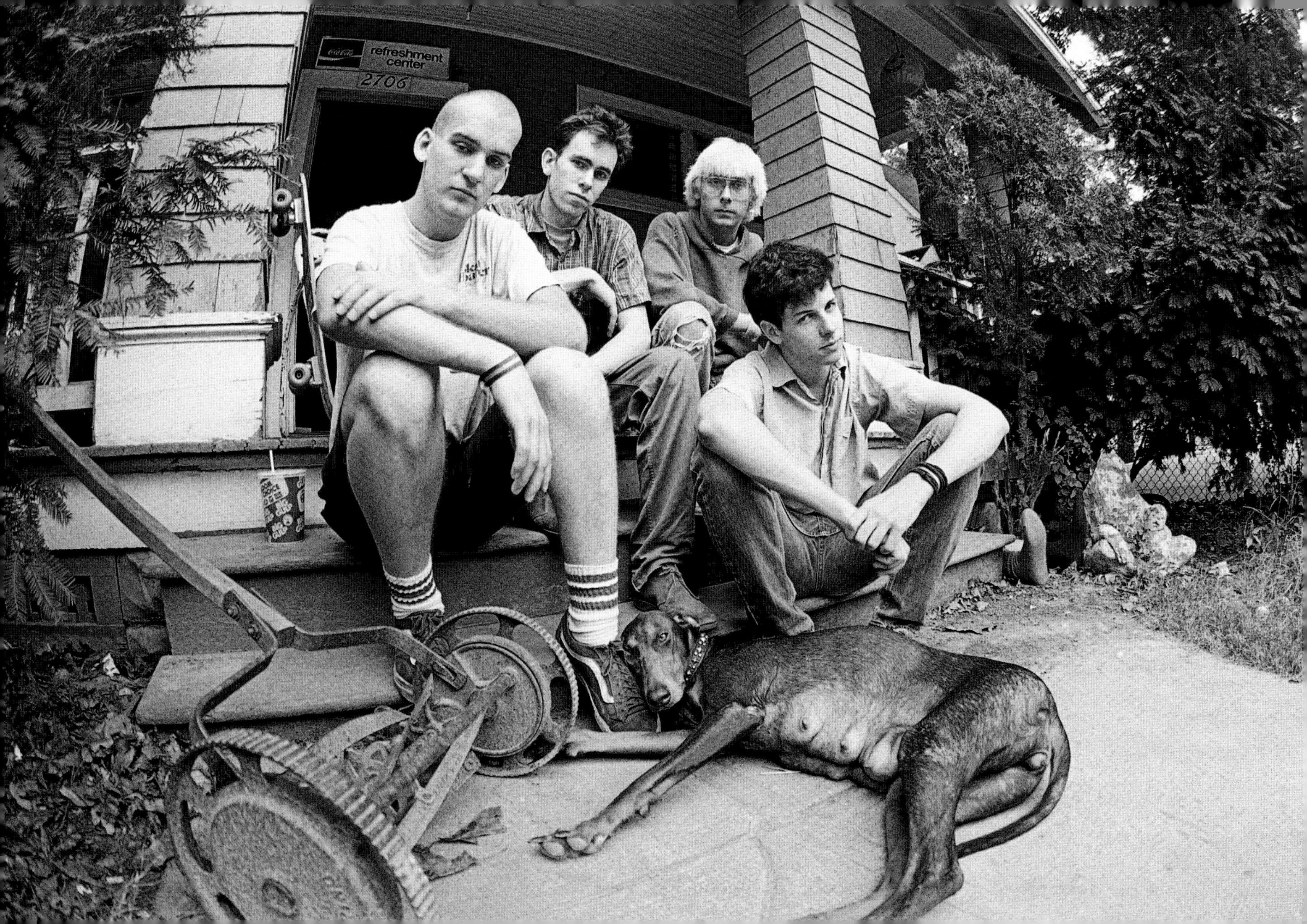
refreshment center
2706
BIG GULP

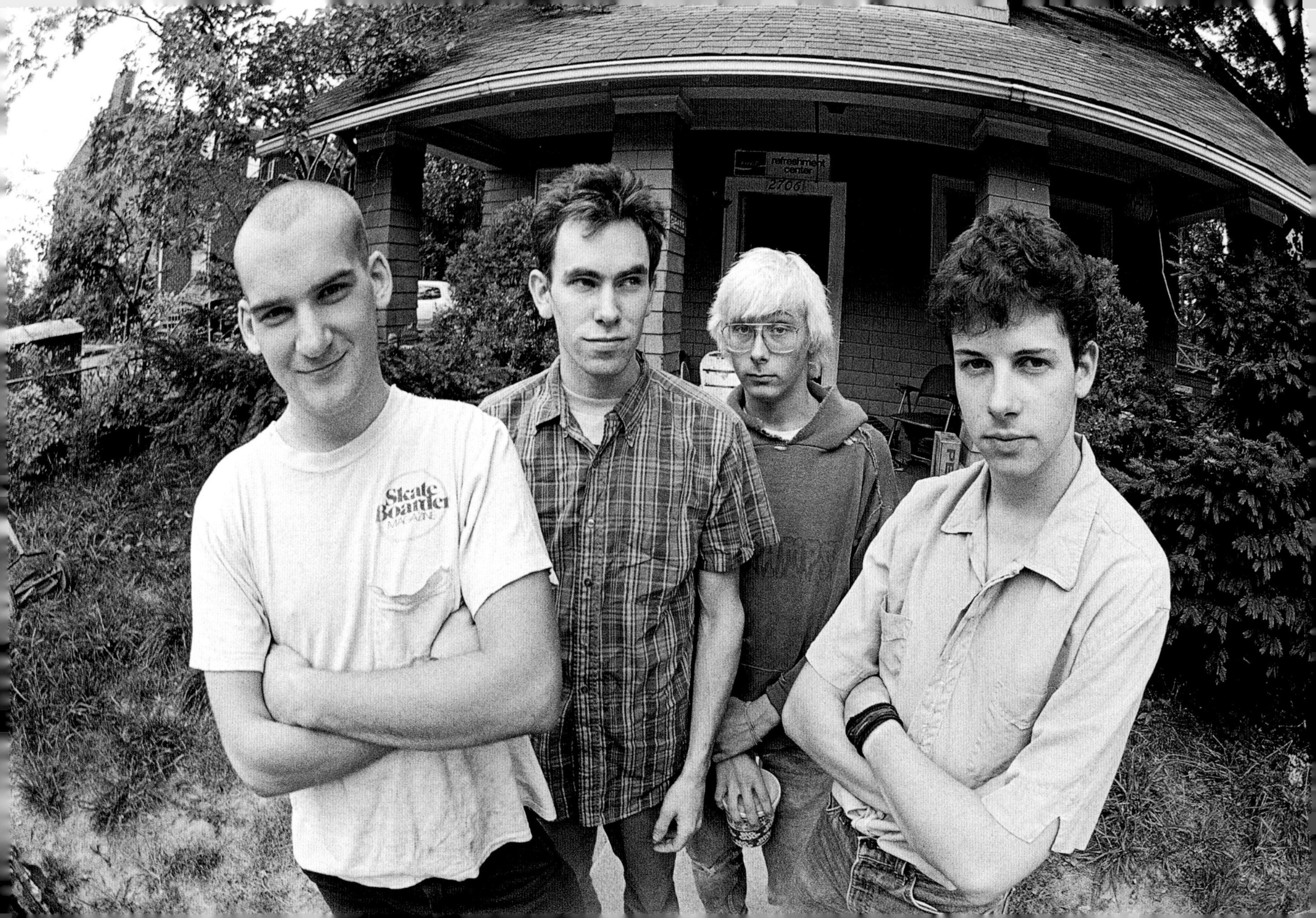
refreshment
center
2706
Skate
Boarder
MAGAZINE

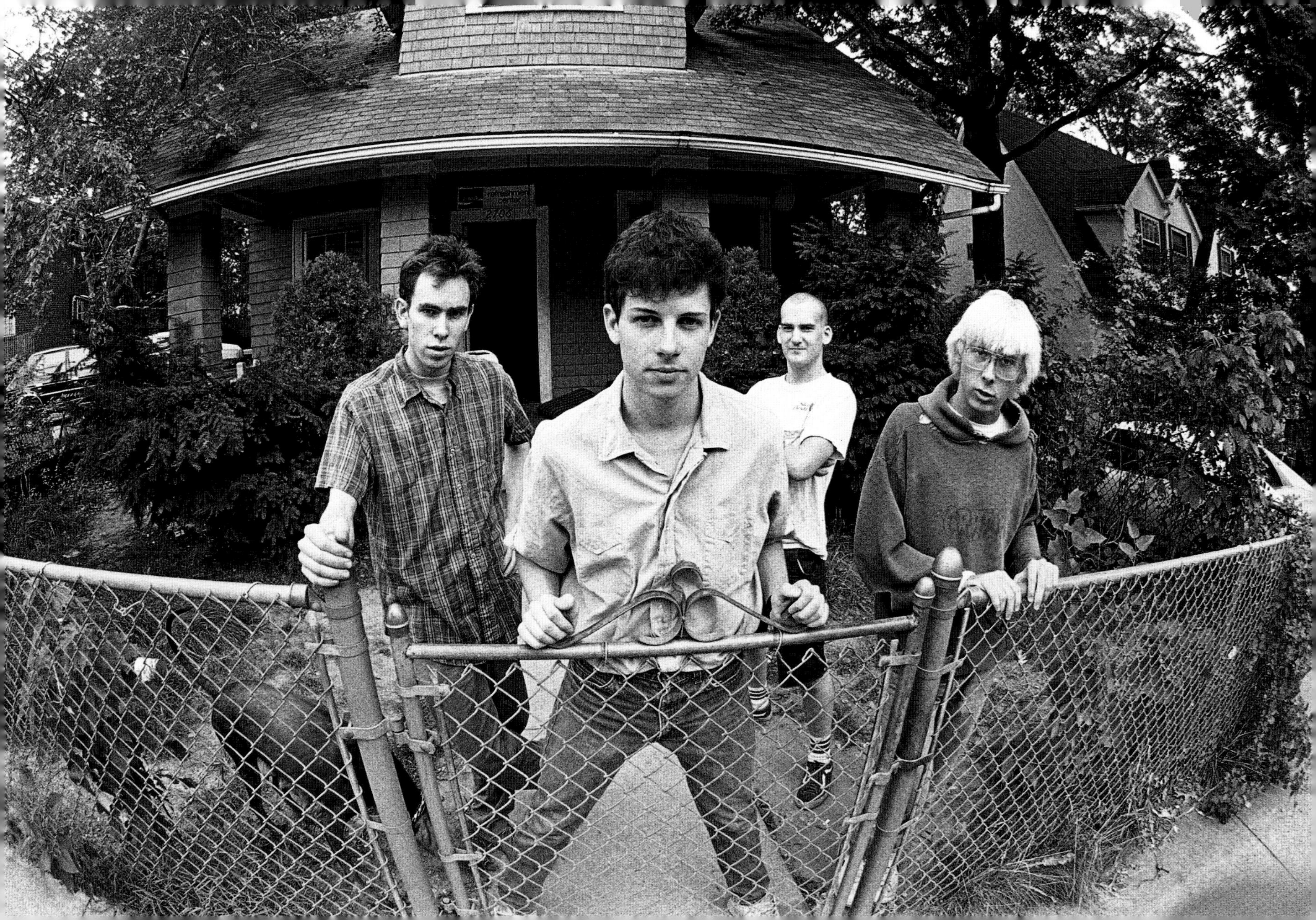
2706

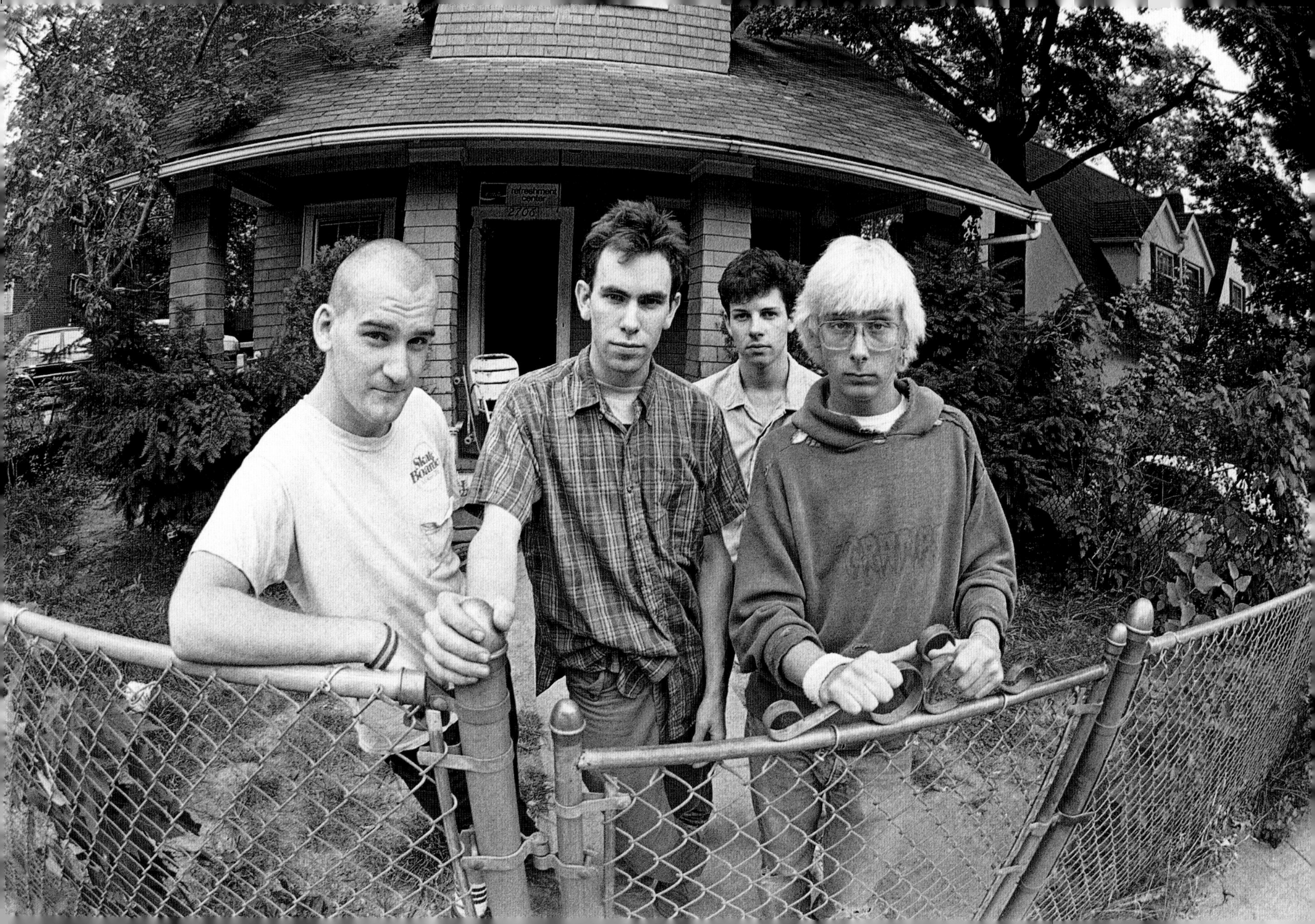
refreshment center
2708

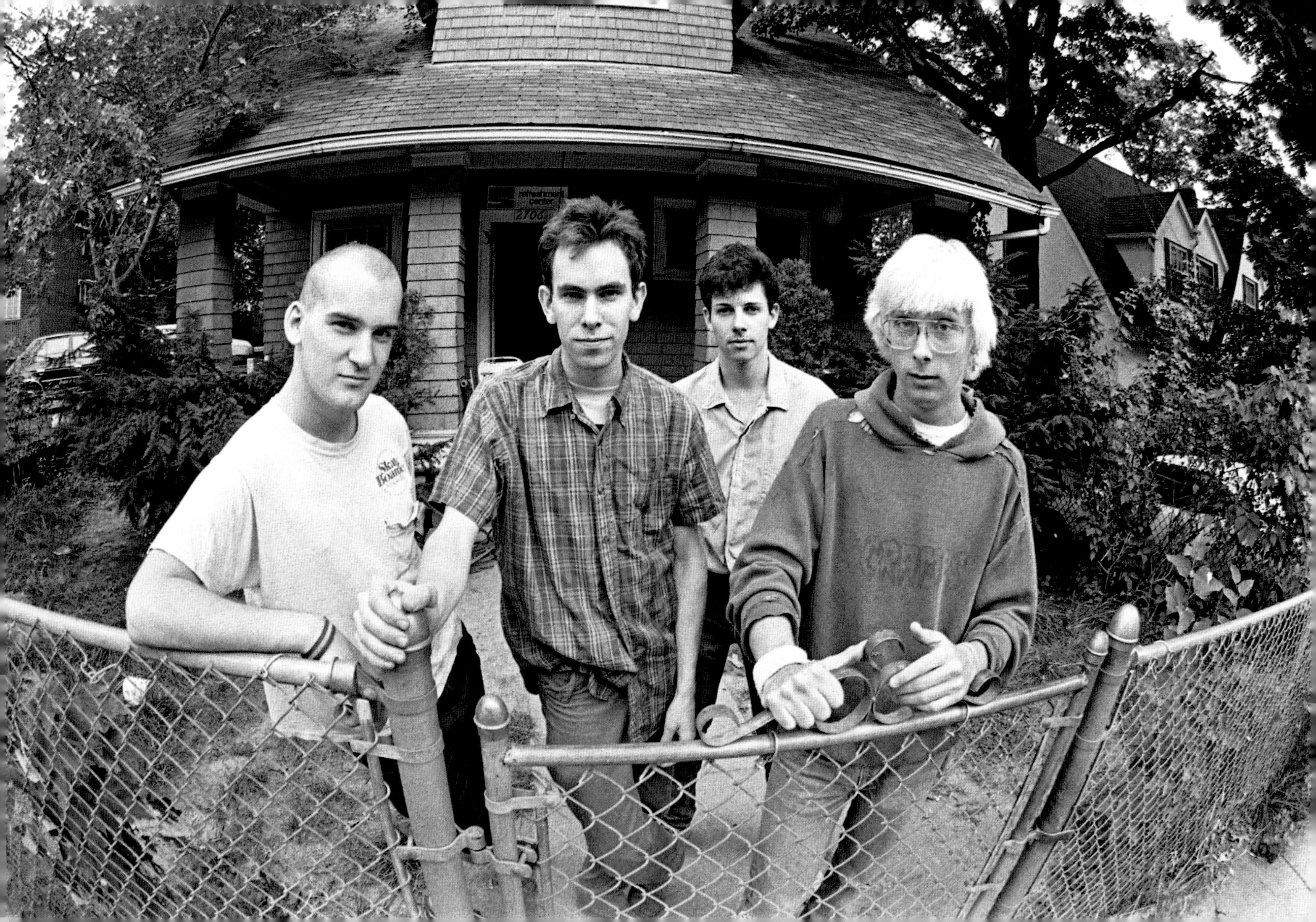
refreshment center
2706

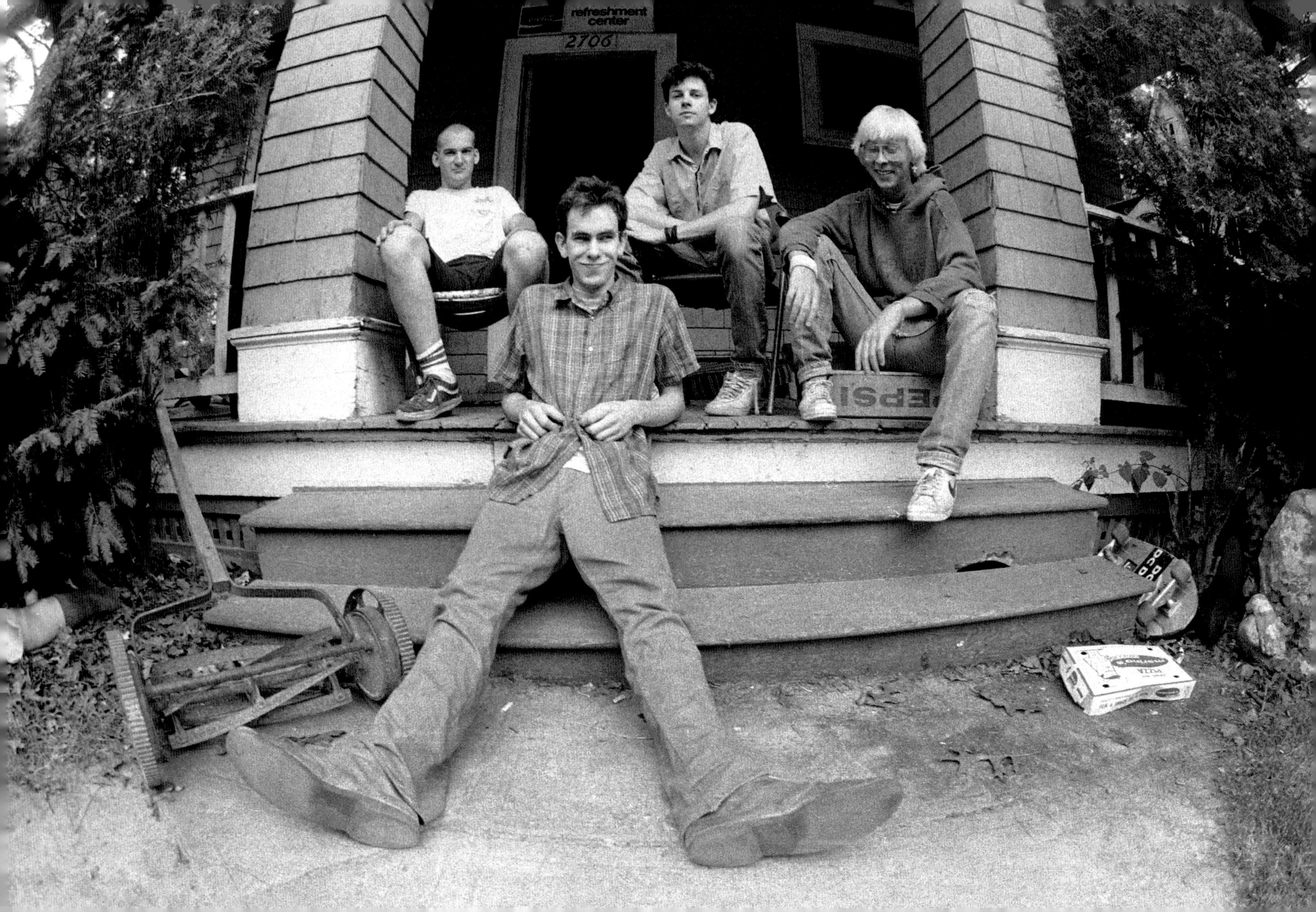
refreshment center
2706

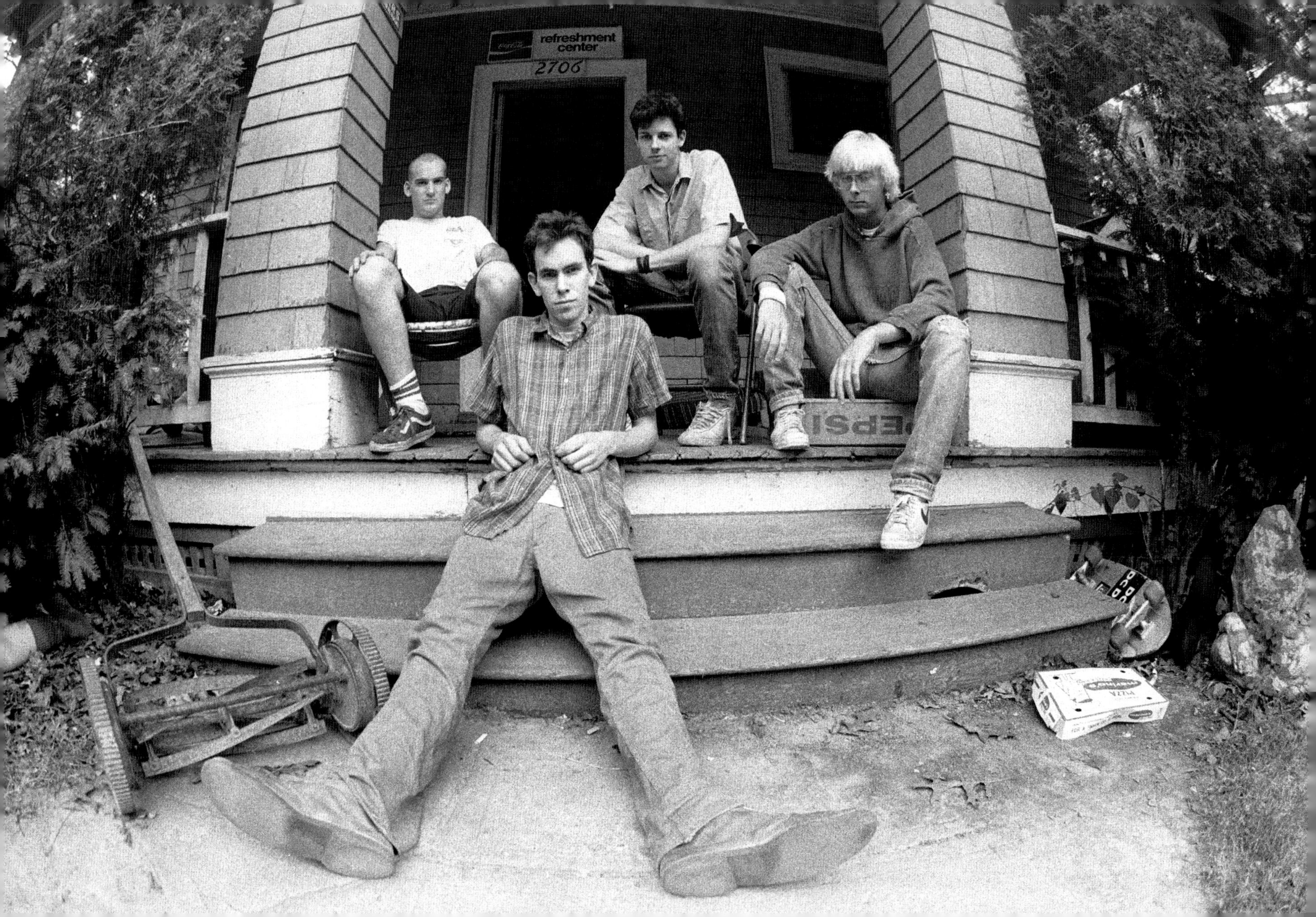
refreshment
center
2706

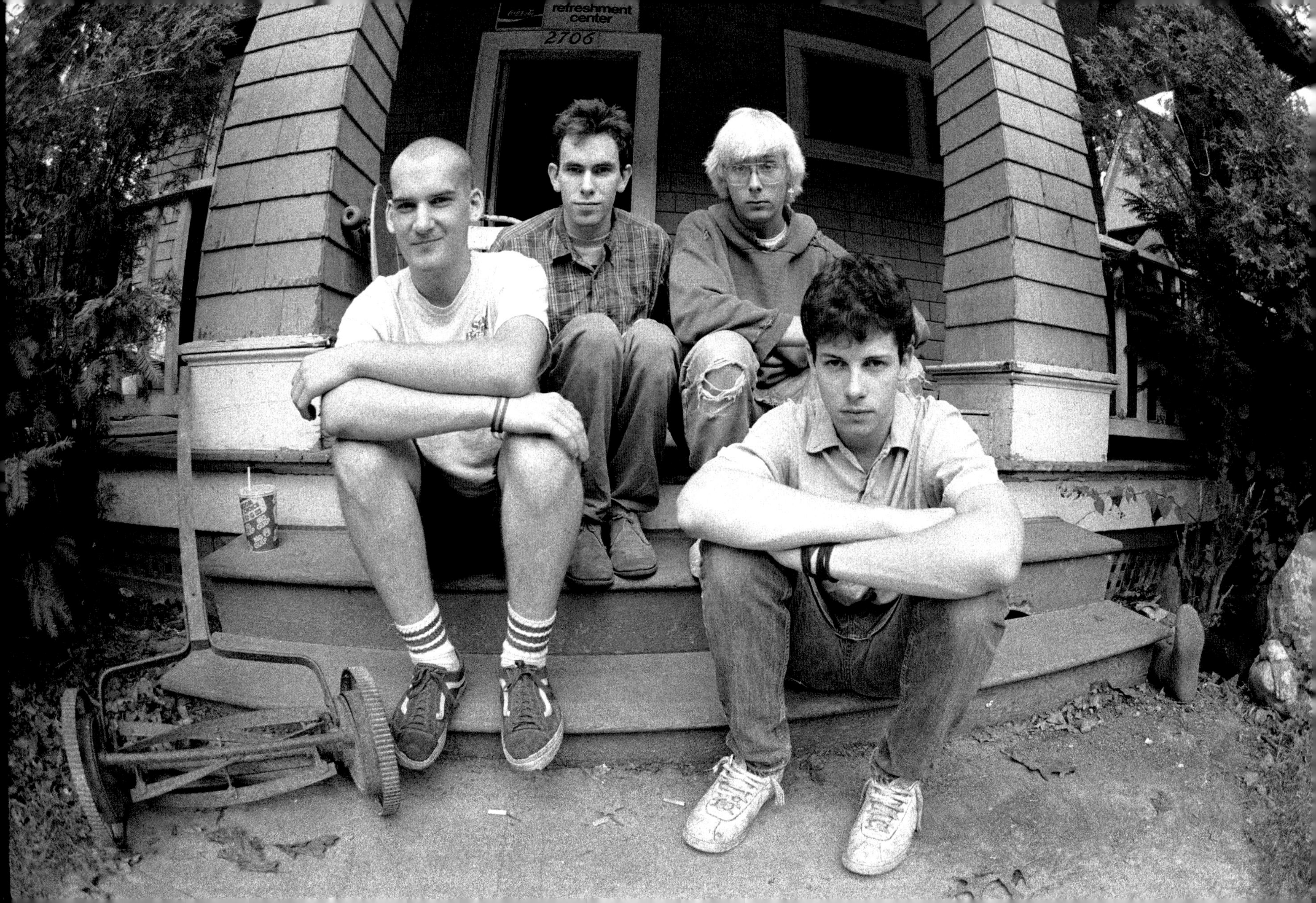
refreshment
center
2706

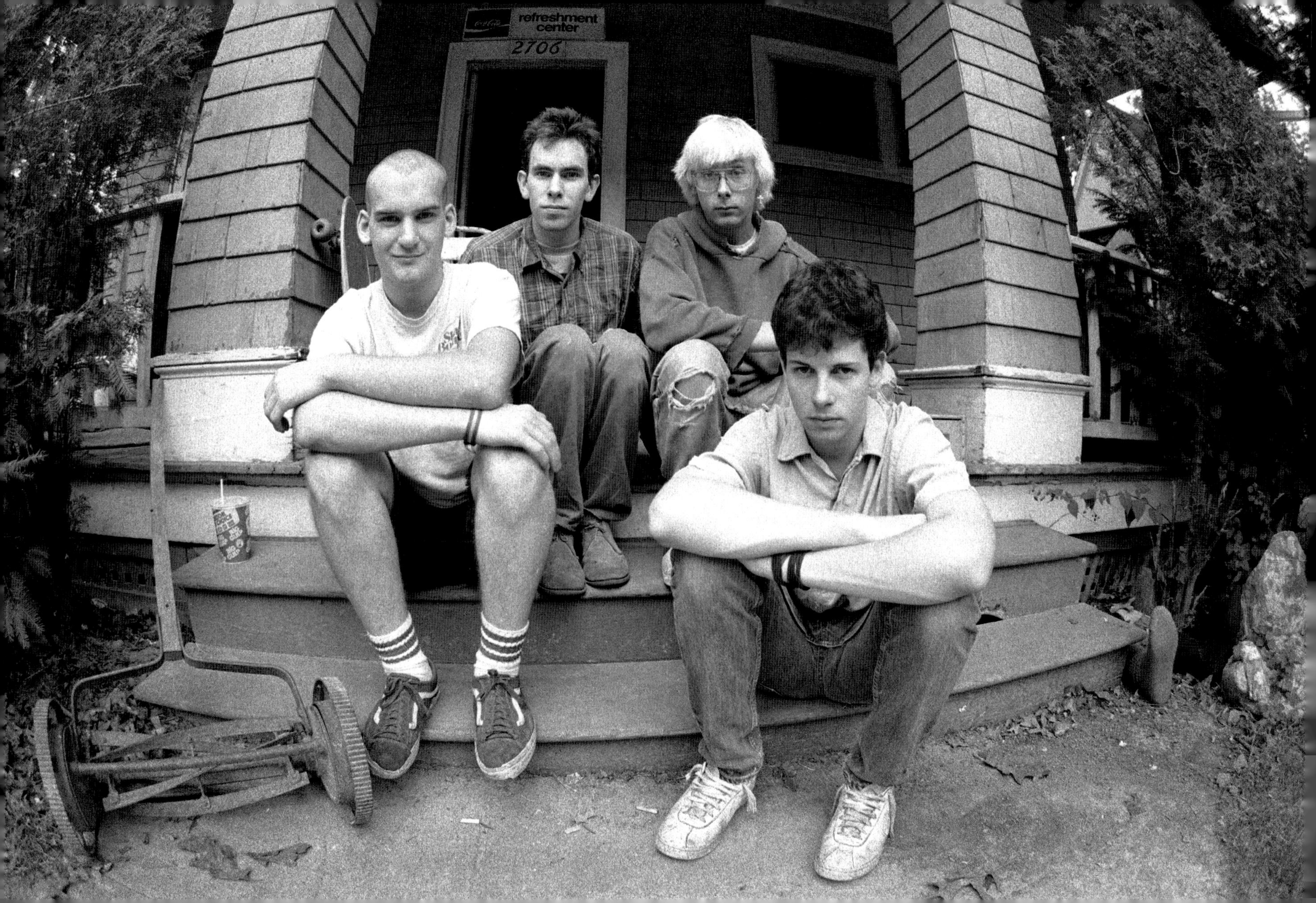
refreshment center
2706

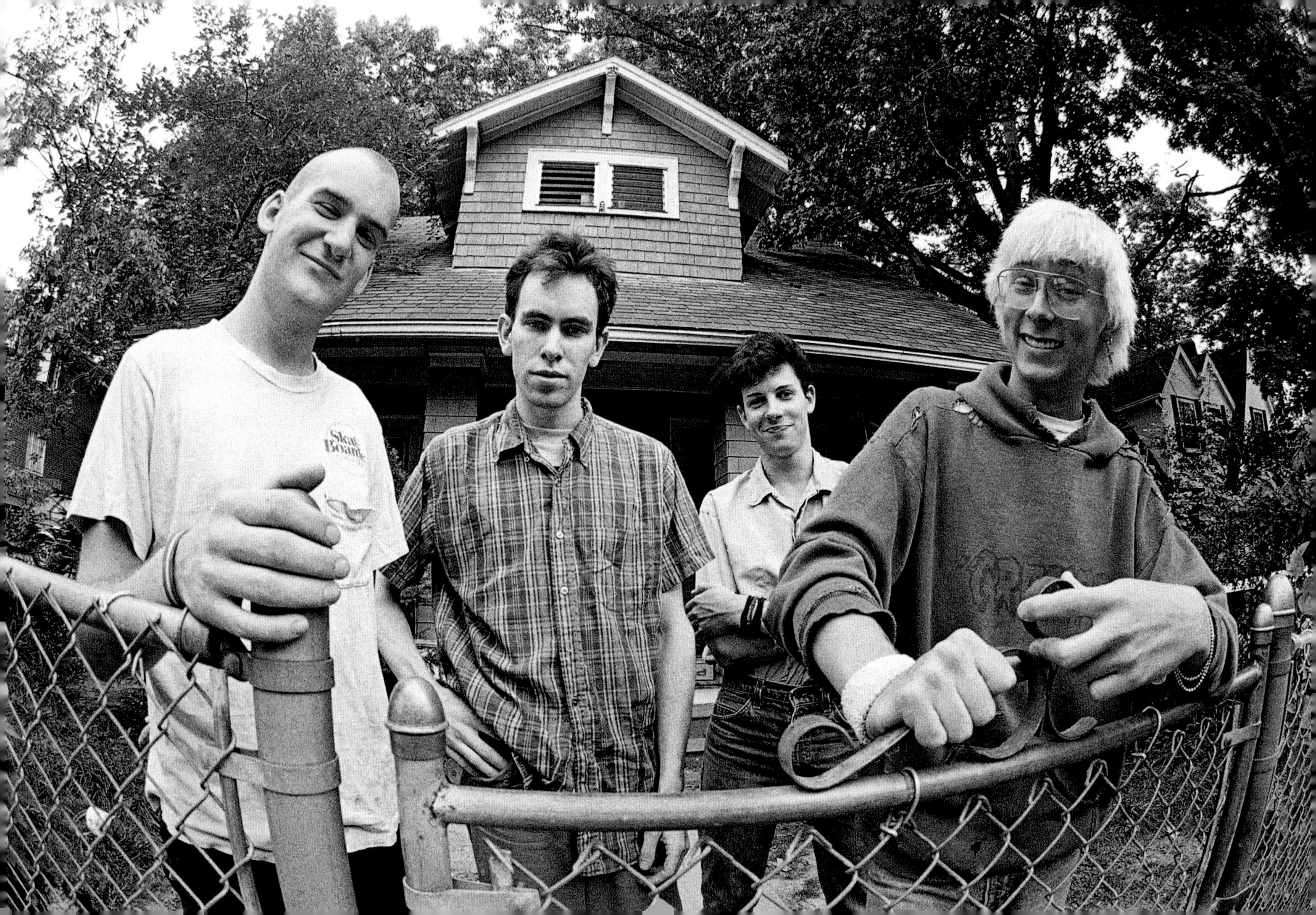

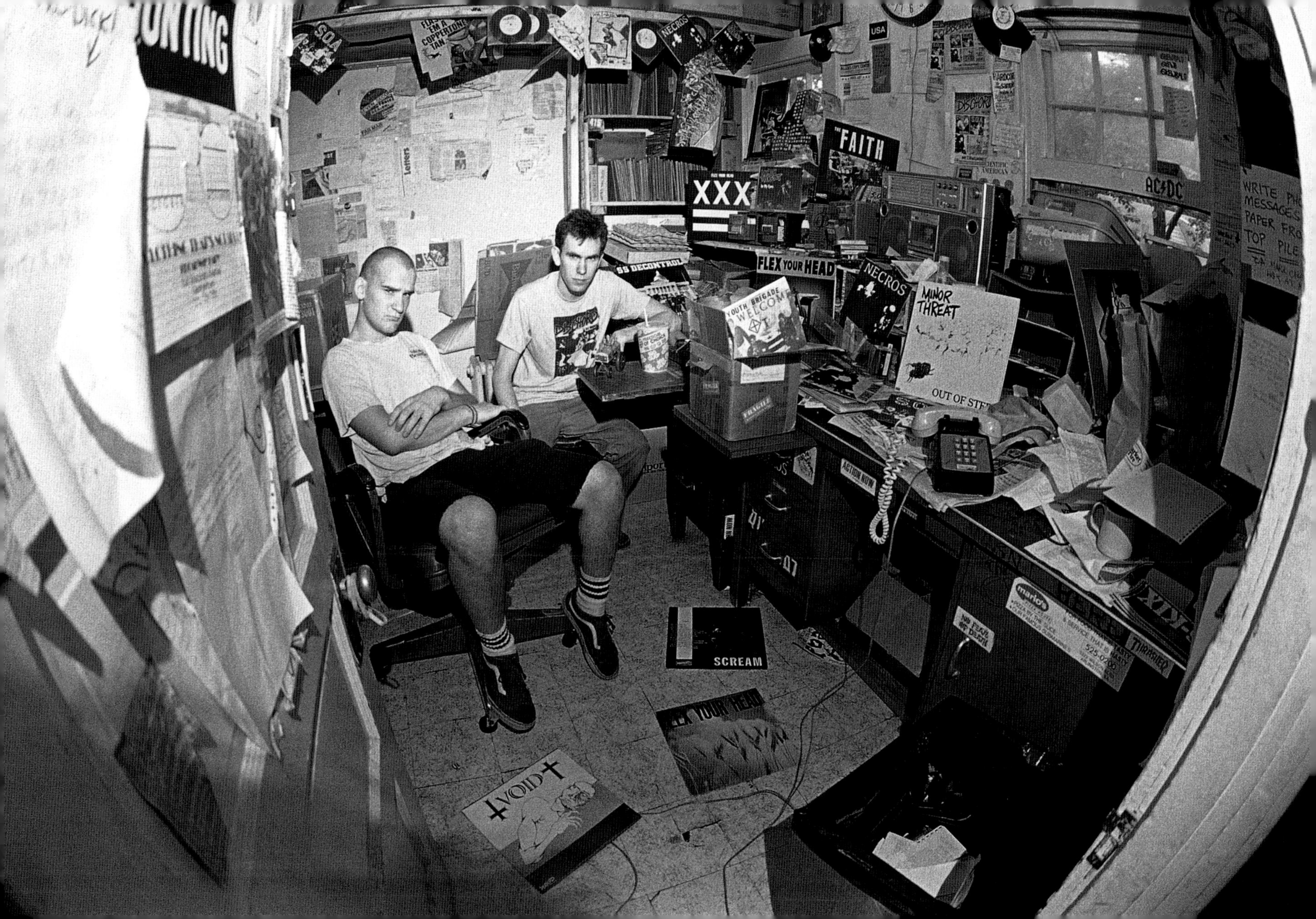

SOA
NECROS
USA
DISCHORD
Letters
THE FAITH
XXX
AC/DC
SS DECONTROL
FLEX YOUR HEAD
NECROS
YOUTH BRIGADE
MINOR THREAT
ACTION NOW
SCREAM
VOID
marlo's

In My Eyes

by Zack de la Rocha

It's hard to measure the impact of Glen E. Friedman's work. It's like if a meteor were to travel hundreds of thousands of miles at great speed, burning through the atmosphere to strike a spot miles off the Pacific Coast. From the point of collision, it would be very difficult to know where the swells generated would eventually land, or precisely how the waves would crash. What wouldn't be hard to see, if you were standing on the sand, is that the contours of the coast, wherever it was hit, would be permanently altered. What might have started as spontaneous documentation of radical intersections between punk rock, skateboarding, and hip hop, grew in size and significance over time to become historical portals of social and cultural movement. I was very fortunate to have seen one of those waves break at a very critical time in my life.

In 1971, a year after I was born, my parents separated following eleven years of marriage. Leaving our Long Beach neighborhood was a priority for both of them, given the roughness of the area and also their now-separate trajectories. My father, a Chicano artist, returned to his original home in the Los Angeles barrio of Lincoln Heights, and my mom was accepted into a doctorate program at the University of California Irvine. For the next twelve years, I would move back and forth between these dramatically different worlds, from the city that capital was abandoning to the suburb where it was being redistributed; and thus, from where white folks were fleeing to where they were headed and being unjustly prioritized. Where their upper-middle-class comforts were maintained by cooks, nannies, farmworkers, landscapers, car washers, nurses, and gas station attendants—all of whom looked like me.

Much later, while working some of those jobs, I began to notice the colonial relationships that were hiding in plain sight. Just behind the idyllic subterfuge of pristine green space and the police-protected tract-home tranquility was that air of untouchable arrogance seeping from everywhere. The only way I could cut through it was on a skateboard. The whole place had an aura of tennis-club exclusivity, and in most exchanges I was left to contend with either contempt or my own invisibility. This was a rancid atmosphere, and there I was, a Chicano transplant. The brown fly in the white ointment. Which is why skateboarding for me was more than a thrill or stylish expression—it was a tool for building feelings of self-worth, at a time when I experienced very little of that.

In the environment I was immersed in, a person's value was implicitly determined by two things I was not: rich and white. I had very little contact with people who shared my experience. So seeing Glen's photos of other Chicano/Latino skaters in the hallowed pages of *SkateBoarder Magazine* in that period was beyond inspiring; it was healing in a way that words can't capture. *Gente* like me. Reflections of me, with names like Ray "Bones" Rodriguez, Eddie "El Gato" Elguera, and Steve Caballero. And, of course, the greatest skater of all time, Tony "Mad Dog" Alva, a young man who moved through the world with his head up, brash and confident; a one-man mobile exhibition of style and fearlessness, taking flight, defying gravity, charging, cocky, irreverent, moving with blinding speed through Glen's confrontational frame, exposures burning trails of light, surreal like an apparition; or through a dagger-sharp image staring directly into the lens, calm like a matador brushing off the laws of physics, past vert, one centimeter of urethane clutching the edge of the coping, casually making the seemingly impossible possible.

What was tacit in those photos spoke in high volume, as if to say, *Catch up, hermano! Get over here, this is where the energy is, your energy. This will define you, not that place, and not those people.* This *will define you.*

It became an obsessive drive—to renew a fractured confidence with each new trick landed, with each new line I dangerously drew on a bank or in a pool. I was rewriting the story one downhill run or long grind at a time. From 1977 to 1982, I was skating vertically. I was competing, I was redefining. And that *otherness* once internalized as something foul or defective had begun to transform into a weapon of beauty and power like a skateboard. Like a camera, like a band. Like MINOR THREAT.

X X X

It begins. The first chord is struck, distorted to the point of atonality. It bleeds over a rumbling, barely discernible bass, increasing in volume, the strings crashing off the fretboard in perfect counter-rhythm to the sixteenth-note storm of snare hits approaching from nowhere. An almost unbearable tension rears and converges, with the weight of three trains headed toward the same spot on the sonic map. A fourth force, a voice of uncontainable melodic fury, smashes into them. The song "Filler" had started, but what I thought art could be, and what I thought it meant, had ended.

I'm staring at the beleaguered figure on the cover. Body folded over, his head driving its weight into crossed arms. A position not to be confused with simple exhaustion, but someone unable in that moment to mask despair, bathed in a sharp red tint. Stare at it long enough and there's suddenly a sense that you're sharing a moment not meant to be shared. A front-row seat to a painful reckoning or even a breakdown. An existential crossroads; about to face the business end of the barrel of adulthood; the figure's agency laid to waste. You're in the room now, gripped by the complexities of his predicament, the weight of his dread, the uncertainty and fear.

At fifteen years old, I stared at this image long enough to realize it was a mirror.

The record continues as a narrative begins to emerge. The figure is off the steps now, swinging, caught in a dialectic between fight and flight, and flight is on the ropes. Anger is his fuel but reason is his main weapon, carving away at the apathy that surrounds him. An eight-part reclamation of autonomy; each song erupting with a relentless catharsis. Songs like "Seeing Red" and "Screaming at a Wall" begin to reveal the internal conflict bleeding through every moment of the performance; each new screamed phrase delivered with searing efficiency, laying bare the urgent need to be heard, seen, and respected—or else. Songs like "Straight Edge" and "Bottled Violence" further illustrate the peril in his world, and it is a fearless intellect that steers him through the violent and self-destructive waters in which he refuses to drown.

This is not some polished coming-of-age story. This is a sober, unapologetic rendering, at times dark and hostile, devoid of cheap optimism. This is grounded truth warming its hands on a pile of burning Hallmark cards. And out of the ashes comes a sense of a new, formidable subjectivity. One of communal identity and power. A transformation that announces itself in what is now a timeless declaration: "*We're not the first, I hope we're not the last / 'Cause I know we're all headed for that adult crash / The time is so little, the time belongs to us / Why is everybody in such a fucking rush? / Make do with what you have, take what you can get / Pay no mind to us, we're just a Minor Threat."*

"We have a lost tooth up here . . . everybody check your mouths."
—Ian MacKaye, between songs, Minor Threat live show, 1983

In boxing terms, it was time for the smelling salts. Don't even bother with the count. Coming back to my senses, what was immediately clear was that the impression was indelible. From that point forward, Minor Threat became a sort of standard-bearer for heart and intensity. A model of intent. Part of my ambition for any art I was making from then on was to burn at that same temperature. Whatever was driving that sense of reckless abandon sounded as if it had been welling up for decades, before finally boiling over onto wax. Which is why at times it's difficult to write objectively about Minor Threat. Their records cut a little deeper into my psyche than others.

At that time, I couldn't see beyond the callous parameters of my own life, and Minor Threat's sound was the closest representation of the anxiety that circumstances had forced me to carry. A kind of energy that felt like they didn't have a choice in the matter in writing these songs. As it turned out, neither did I. When I began to write my own songs, the subtext was a kid who had been born with his back pressed against a wall. The distance from that troubled corner to dignified ground was going to be covered with sonically scorched earth. It was the kind of pain that could only be exorcised with feedback and thoughtful fury as its conduits.

Minor Threat possessed a subtle militancy, offset by a certain levity and irreverence. But that lightheartedness thinly masked what felt to me like a deadly serious approach to craft. They had established a truly rare balance where the weight of the lyrical subjects and the unique vocal inflections found equal strength through crushing bursts of energy, harnessed brilliantly by Preslar, Baker, and Nelson. Bursts of energy that could stop on a dime, as fast as light cut off by a switch, only to erupt again with a destructive intensity, creating a jarring but beautiful conversation between subject and sound. Because let's dispense with the old punk tropes about not needing to know how to play your instruments to make compelling art; if we're being honest, that's only part of the story. To be able to generate that unhinged, at-the-edge-of-a-cliff, seemingly-out-of-control-yet-in-command, swinging-for-the-fences-but-knowing-what-section-your-ball-is-gonna-land-in sound requires some ability. And these motherfuckers could play. I bet more than a few bands had second thoughts about coming onstage after this crew.

What is equally striking to me when listening to these songs, to this day, is the crystalline confidence with which Ian hurls his arguments at the world around him. There's fear there, but it's the kind of fear that's provoked when seeing cattle being prodded toward the blade. The kind of fear that emerges when watching supposedly rational people embrace institutions that he recognizes as useless or damaging. Because this is America after all, and here, to blindly accept conventional wisdom is a devil's bargain. Ian is having none of it. Zero. He sarcastically pokes holes in people's assumptions, then in an instant channel-switches to pure fury aimed at their irrationality. His frustration in the face of contradiction swells to the edge of violence. Then, on a tightrope of raw emotion, he returns to his jester persona, refusing the comfort of the palace, giving counsel to its prisoners in the basement. I don't think there's a band within the punk canon, or any other genre, that contends this seriously and this thoughtfully with the precarity and promise of youth. Minor Threat is a singular, timeless, and complex voice—one that eludes simple definition.

X X X

Glen E. Friedman's approach to image-making is also hard to define. Calling him a photographer or simply a documentarian doesn't encompass what's involved here. The line between witness and participant isn't just blurred, it's burned and left in ruins. Nothing makes that more clear than this collection of images of Minor Threat, some taken from a proximity most would cower under in live settings. Glen is hell-bent on matching the intensity of those he collaborates with; adhering to a minimalism where composition and movement take precedence, with an irreverence for gloss or high-tech commercialized aesthetics, which he considers undisciplined shortcuts, and for which he holds a deep disdain.

Glen's work reflects the punk ethos that for him requires hard work and careful consideration. I see these less as shots taken *of* the band, and more of a visceral conversation *between* he and Minor Threat. An additional instrument. A frontline visual communiqué revealing once-invisible histories that have now become fixtures in the ephemeral landscape of global subcultural resistance. This is why both Minor Threat and Glen E. Friedman have become, in my eyes, generational voices who continue to inspire with work that demonstrates the enduring outcomes of threat by example.

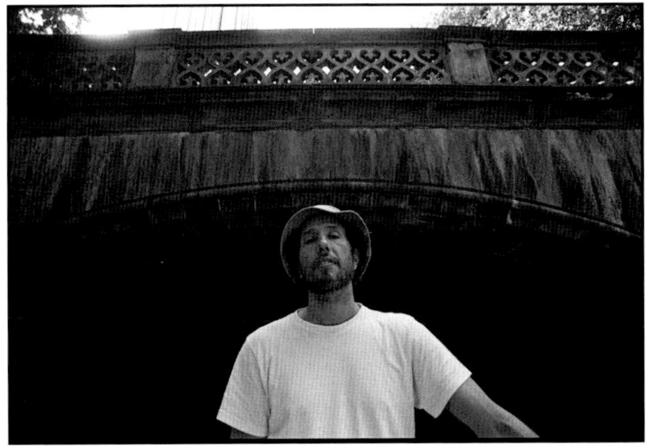

Zack, 2022.

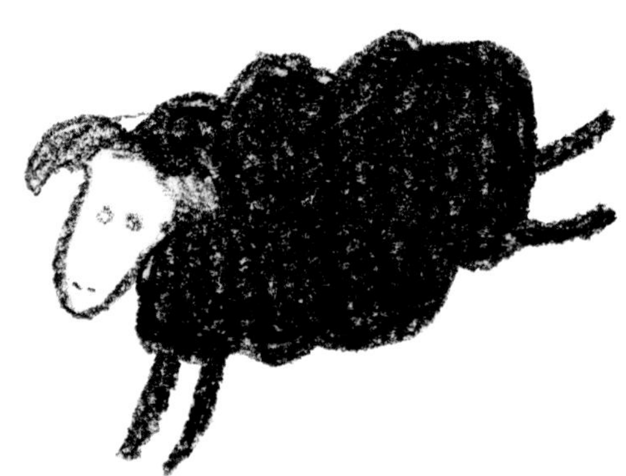

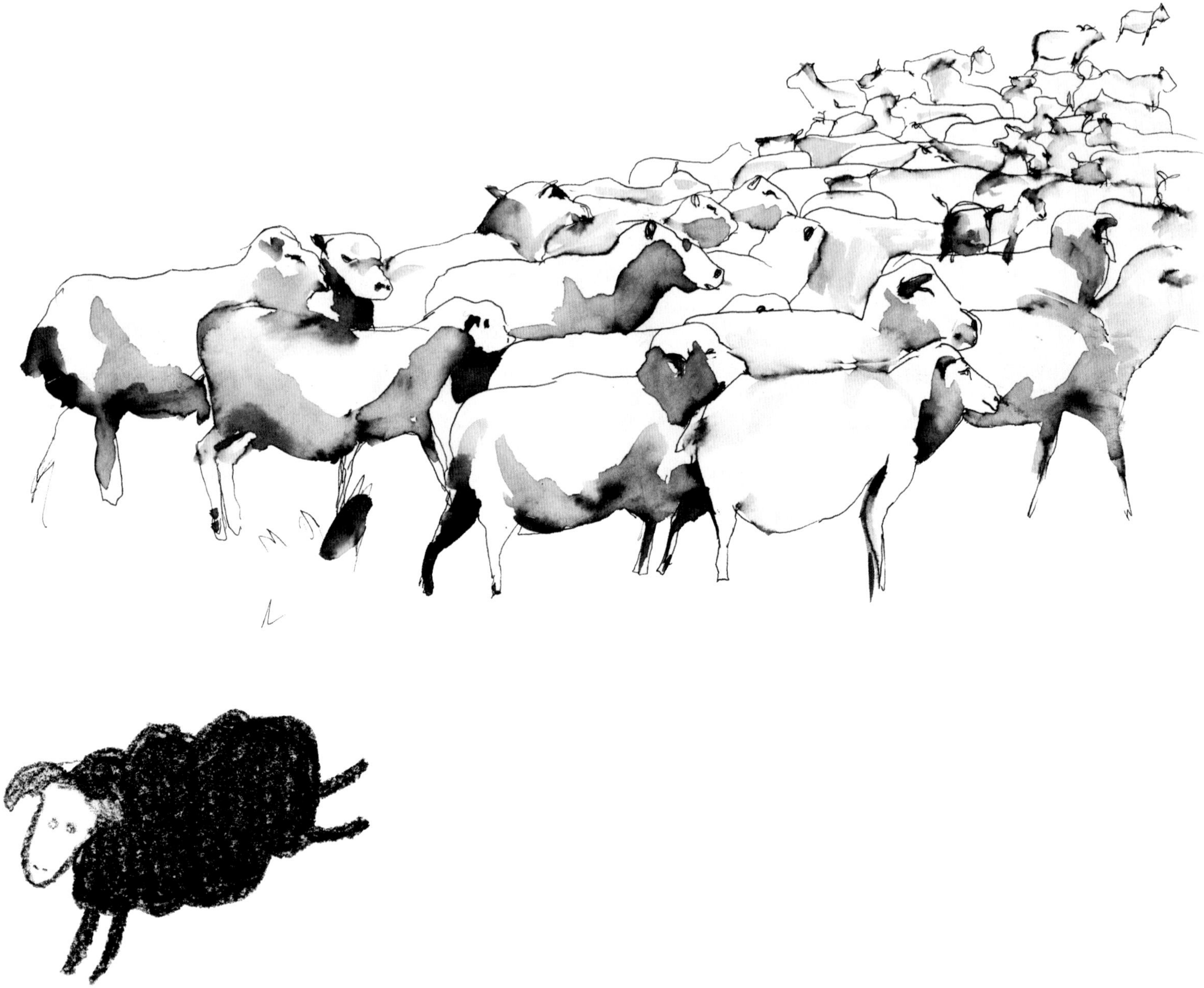

Illustration by Cynthia Connolly.

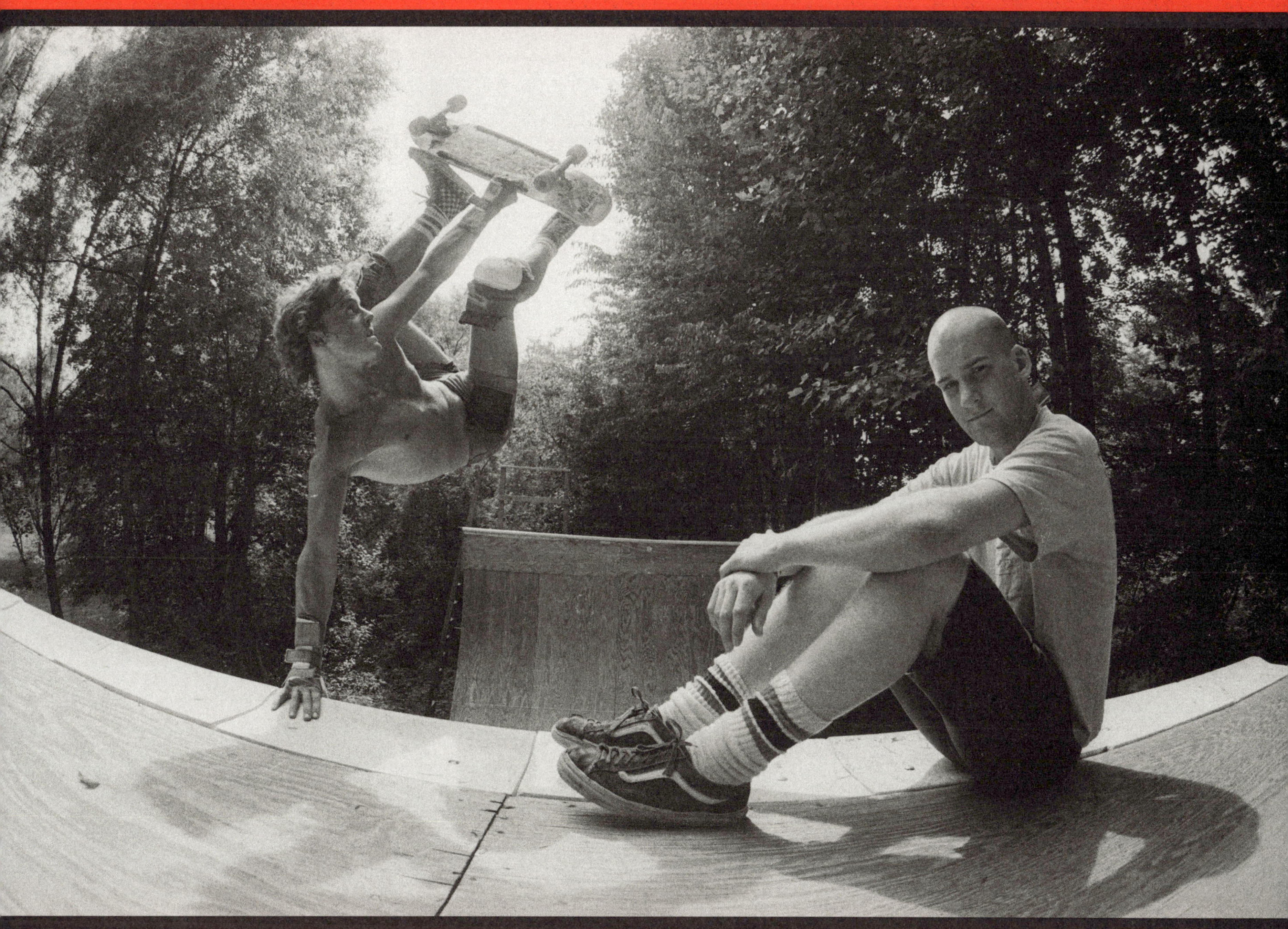

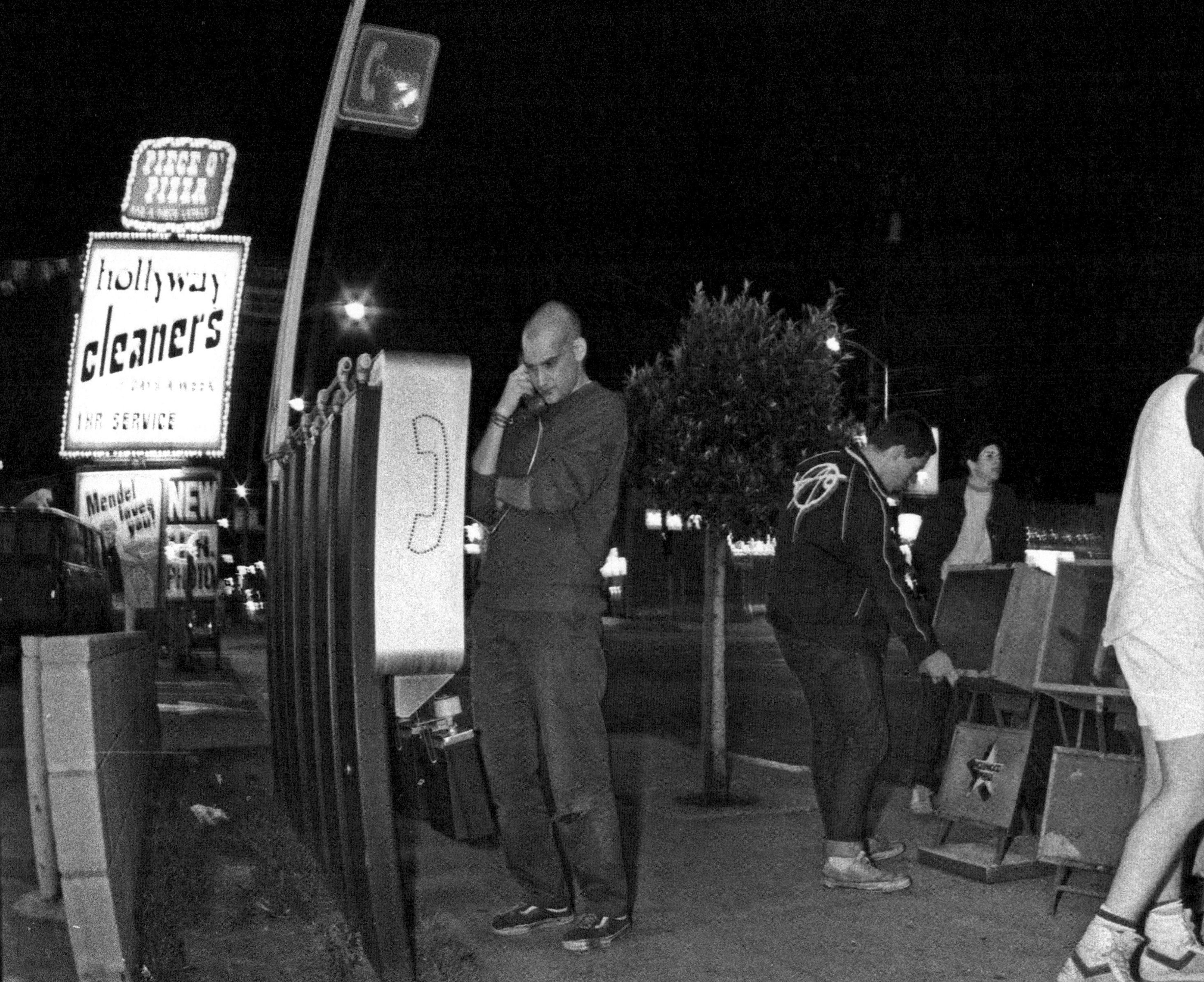

West Hollywood, April 1983.